A Landscape Photographer's Guide to
Joshua Tree National Park

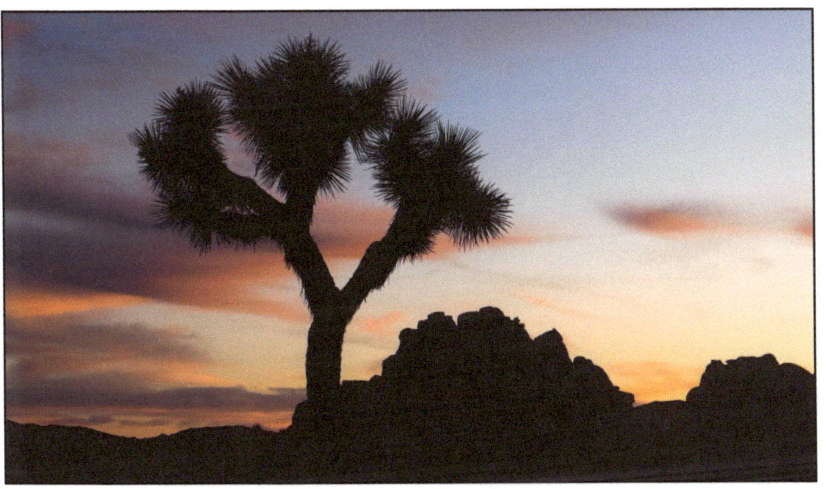

Anthony Jones

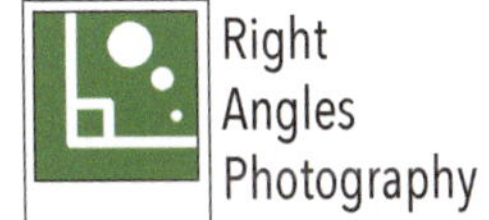

*To my mother and my stepfather, who showed
me how to teach from the heart.*

Right Angles Photography
P.O. Box 473
Ravensdale, WA 98051
www.rightanglesphotography.com

First edition

ISBN-13: 978-1-7321680-2-2

**MAPS PRINTED IN THIS BOOK ARE FOR ORIENTATION ONLY
AND SHOULD NOT BE USED FOR NAVIGATION.**

Media Sources:

Satellite Imagery, pp. 24, 46, 59, 68, 71, 77, 86, 94, 97, 102,
113, 115, Google Earth, Copyright © 2020 by Google.

Park Maps, pp. 4-8, 10, 12, 14, 50-51, National Park Service,
public domain.

All other images by the author.

Contents

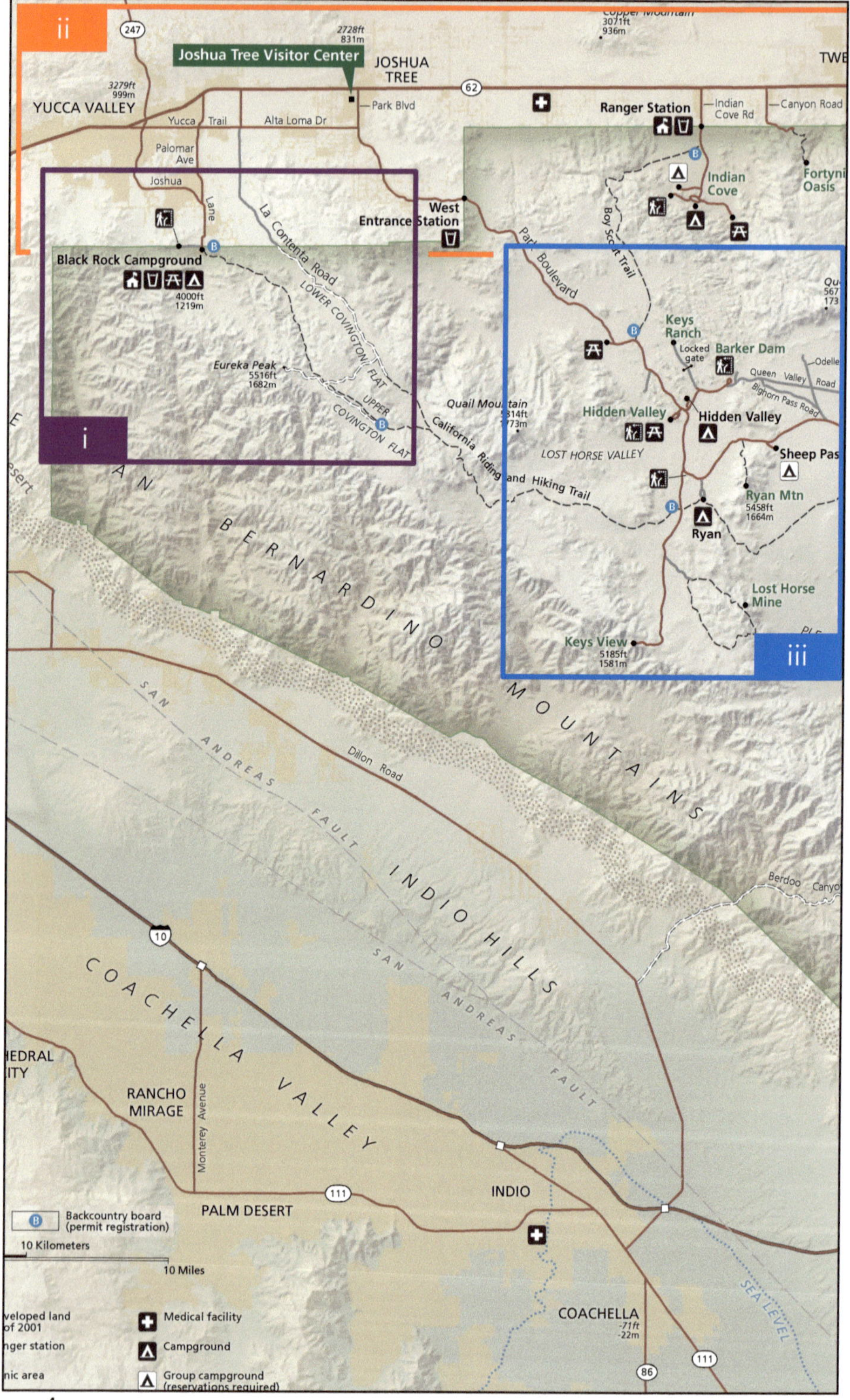
ii
247
Joshua Tree Visitor Center
JOSHUA TREE
2728ft
831m
Copper Mountain
3071ft
936m
TWE
62
YUCCA VALLEY
3279ft
999m
Yucca Trail
Alta Loma Dr
Park Blvd
Palomar Ave
Ranger Station
Indian Cove Rd
Canyon Road
Joshua Lane
Indian Cove
Fortyni Oasis
Black Rock Campground
4000ft
1219m
B
La Contenta Road
LOWER COVINGTON FLAT
West Entrance Station
Boy Scout Trail
B
Keys Ranch
Barker Dam
Qu
567
173
Eureka Peak
5516ft
1682m
UPPER COVINGTON FLAT
B
California Riding and Hiking Trail
Quail Mountain
5814ft
1773m
Locked gate
Queen Valley Road
Odelle
Bighorn Pass Road
SAN
BERNARDINO
MOUNTAINS
Hidden Valley
Hidden Valley
LOST HORSE VALLEY
Sheep Pas
Ryan Mtn
5458ft
1664m
B
Ryan
Lost Horse Mine
Keys View
5185ft
1581m
iii
PL
SAN
ANDREAS
FAULT
Dillon Road
INDIO HILLS
SAN
ANDREAS
FAULT
Berdoo Canyo
10
COACHELLA VALLEY
HEDRAL ITY
RANCHO MIRAGE
Monterey Avenue
PALM DESERT
111
INDIO
COACHELLA
-71ft
-22m
SEA LEVEL
86
111
B
Backcountry board
(permit registration)
10 Kilometers
10 Miles
veloped land of 2001
nger station
nic area
Medical facility
Campground
Group campground
(reservations required)

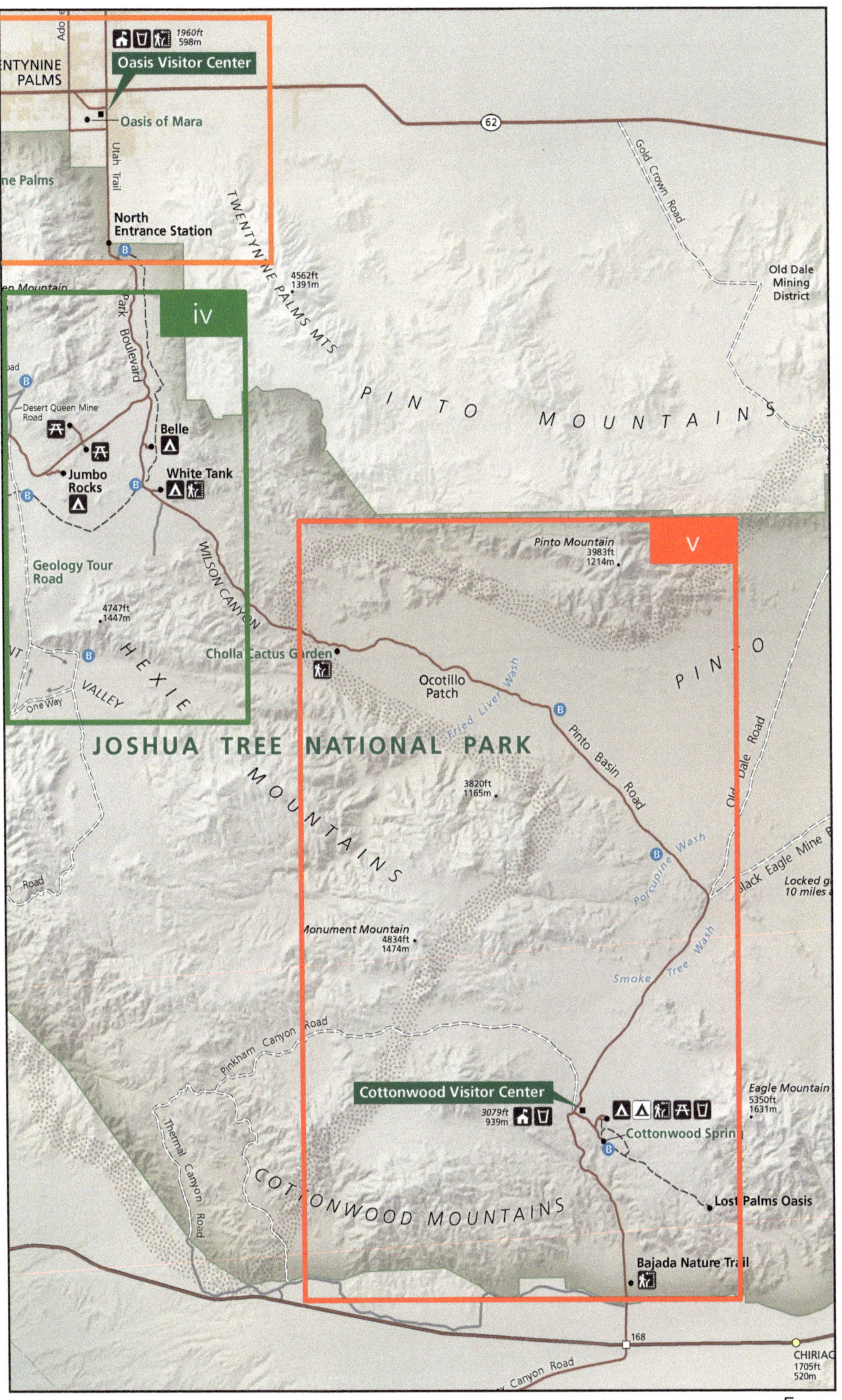

TWENTYNINE PALMS
ne Palms
Oasis Visitor Center
1960ft
598m
Oasis of Mara
Utah Trail
North Entrance Station
B
62
Gold Crown Road
Old Dale Mining District
en Mountain
iv
Park Boulevard
B
Desert Queen Mine Road
Belle
Jumbo Rocks
White Tank
B
WILSON CANYON
Geology Tour Road
4747ft
1447m
4562ft
1391m
TWENTYNINE PALMS MTS
PINTO MOUNTAINS
Pinto Mountain
3983ft
1214m
v
PINTO
HEXIE
One Way
VALLEY
Cholla Cactus Garden
Ocotillo Patch
Fried Liver Wash
B
Pinto Basin Road
Old Dale Road
JOSHUA TREE NATIONAL PARK
MOUNTAINS
3820ft
1165m
Porcupine Wash
B
Black Eagle Mine Rd
Locked g
10 miles
Monument Mountain
4834ft
1474m
Smoke Tree Wash
Road
Pinkham Canyon Road
Cottonwood Visitor Center
3079ft
939m
Eagle Mountain
5350ft
1631m
Cottonwood Spring
B
Thermal Canyon Road
COTTONWOOD MOUNTAINS
Lost Palms Oasis
Bajada Nature Trail
Canyon Road
168
CHIRIAC
1705ft
520m

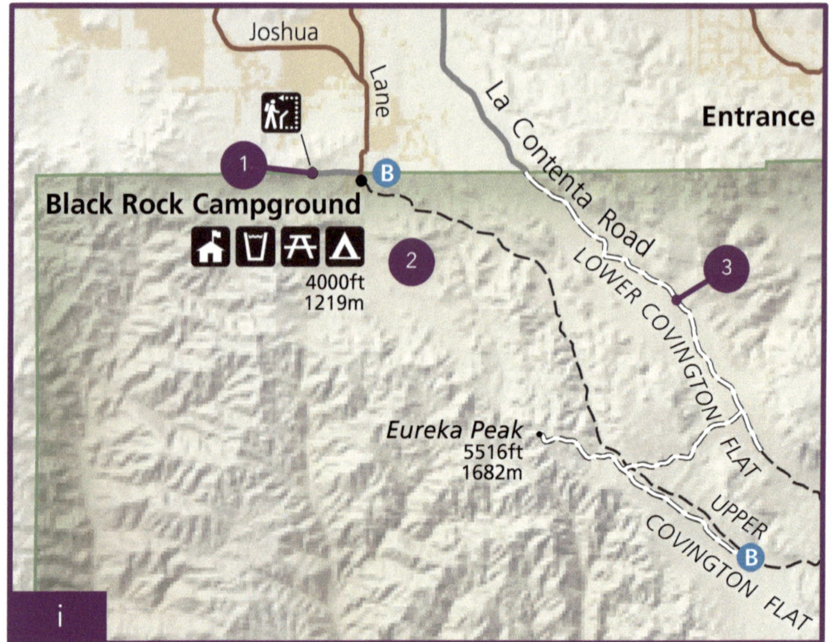

1.   High View   46

Superb vista for capturing early morning light on San Gorgonio Mountain. Close-proximity to adjacent Yucca Valley and Joshua Tree.

2.   Black Rock Area on Horse   48

An alternative and enjoyable way to experience the uniquely-beautiful terrain of the Black Rock area. Many routes are available through multiple outfitters, from 2 to 6 hours.

3.   Covington Flat Roads to Eureka Peak   53

Looking to venture off-pavement and give your legs a break? One of two behind-the-wheel excursions in this guide… Drive alongside some huge Joshua Trees near Eureka Peak, which provides a delightful 360° view of the surrounding areas. Bring a picnic lunch!

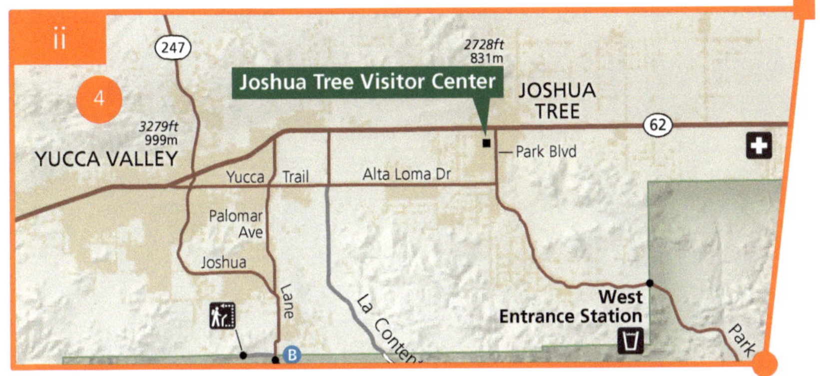

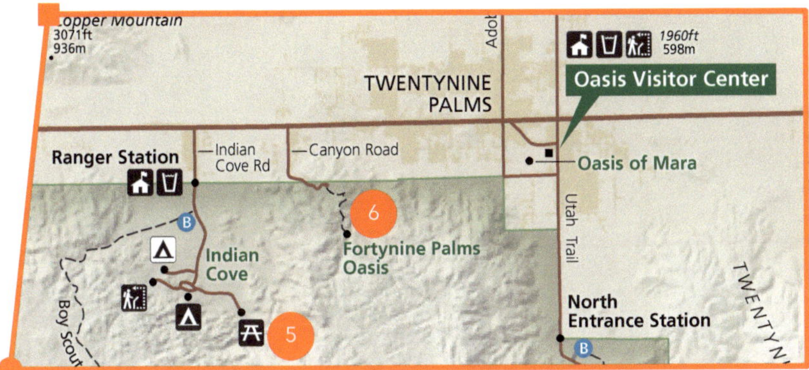

4. Pioneertown 56

An easy 4-mile drive north of Highway 62 from Yucca Valley, this 1880's themed town is popular, and for good reason! Choose morning for a quiet stroll down "Mane Street," photographing storefront details, or evening for wild west re-enactments.

5. Rattlesnake Canyon 58

A dramatic slot canyon, often with pools of water, carved through white granite. The hike is relatively short, but it is the most technical in this book.

6. Fortynine Palms Oasis 62

Hike up, then descend to a true desert oasis. A dense cluster of California Fan Palms provides pleasant shade to recharge. Multiple pools of water are also usually present, providing for interesting ground-level compositions.

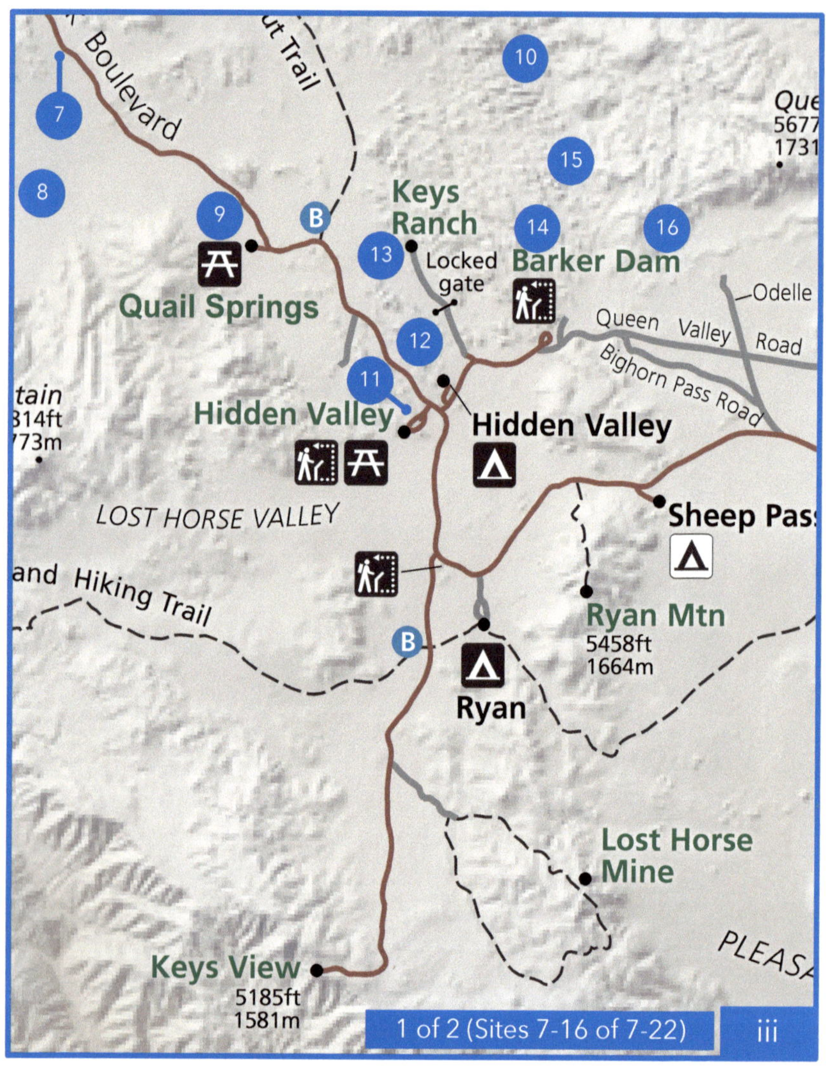

7.   Painting with Light   66

You can "paint with light" anywhere, but here is a particular tree that just begs for this attention. (Thanks in large part to its close proximity to the West Entrance for nighttime work.)

8.   Samuelson's Rocks   68

Cross the desert to find quizzical carvings on large rocks by an area resident, John Samuelson, from the 1920's. Eight thought-provoking inscriptions on 7 rocks. GPS highly recommended.

Another nighttime activity – capturing long exposures of passing cars' lights. The Rock formation at the Quail Springs Picnic Area provides easier bouldering, for elevated compositions along Park Boulevard.

Trek east over mostly-flat terrain through various landscapes to the transition into the Wonderland of Rocks where a small grove of Desert Willows thrive.

Explore this hidden "valley" where rustlers moved stolen cattle in the late 1800's. Popular today with beautiful rock formations, vibrant springtime wildflowers, and adventurous rock climbers.

Venture north from the Hidden Valley Campground on a desert scavenger hunt for this mysterious stone- and iron door-guarded enclosure. GPS recommended.

Join a ranger-guided, outdoor tour of Joshua Tree National Park's most famous homestead, Bill Keys' Desert Queen Ranch. Photogenic subjects are in abundance! Reservation required.

Sensational reflections in this seasonal body of water. Also along the hike find petroglyphs carved into a curvaceous rock formation.

Enter the Wonderland of Rocks… Trek north along the namesake wash to find the "Red Obelisk." GPS highly recommended.

My favorite "mill" site in Joshua Tree National Park. Complete with a fenced-in mill (of course, albeit quite photogenic), one very cool abandoned truck, a windmill, and more!

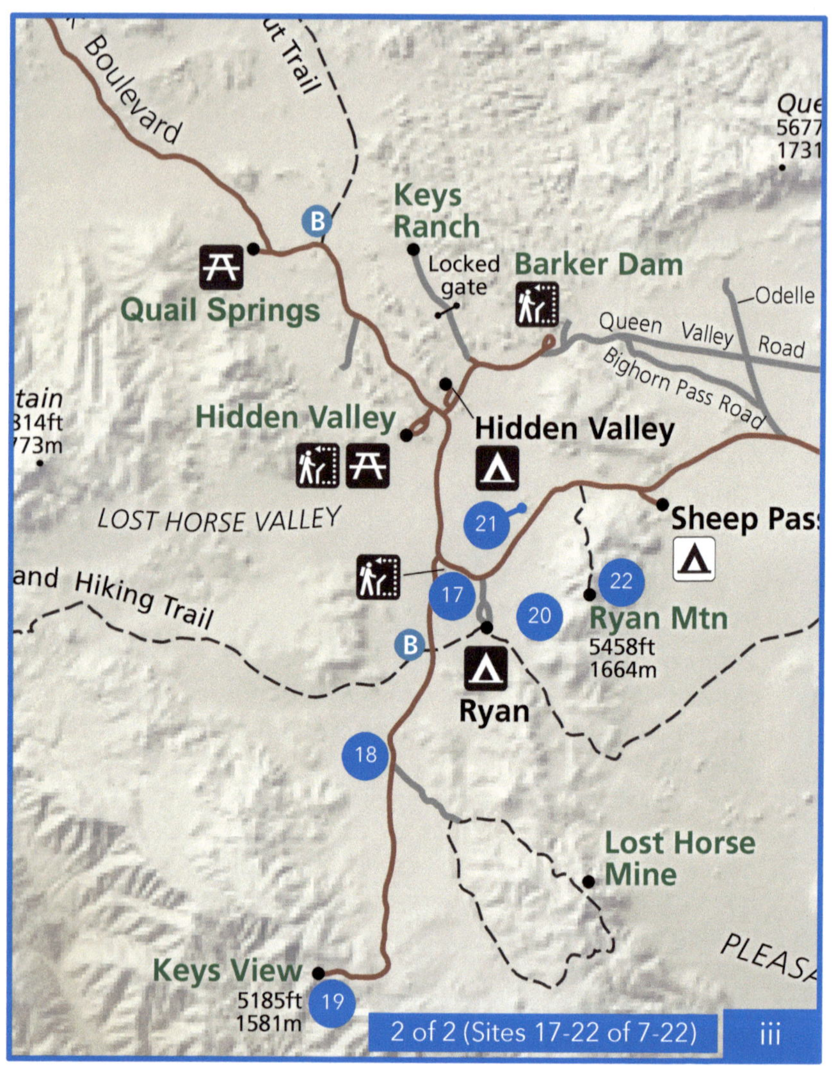

17. Cap Rock   90

Meander around this rock formation and find your favorite composition for this seemingly-cantilevered rock.

18. Johnny Lang Tombstone   91

Visit the resting place of Johnny Lang, cowboy turned gold miner and longtime area resident. (Roadside, but somewhat camouflaged.)

19. Keys View   92

Relax and enjoy the setting sun at this mile-high panoramic view of the Santa Rosa & San Jacinto Mountains along with the Coachella Valley to the southwest below.

20. Ryan Ranch   94

This ranch house ruin is a marvelous subject, with a feeling of heft, though with soft lines. Additional ranch structures and artifacts remain, making for a great area to thoroughly explore.

21. Hall of Horrors   97

An eerie, narrow passageway with a car-sized boulder perched ominously above. Some scrambling is required to access the entrance.

22. Ryan Mountain   100

For those who like to summit, Ryan Mountain provides airplane-like views of Ryan Ranch, Hidden Valley, Malapai Hill, and other adjacent Joshua Tree National Park landmarks.

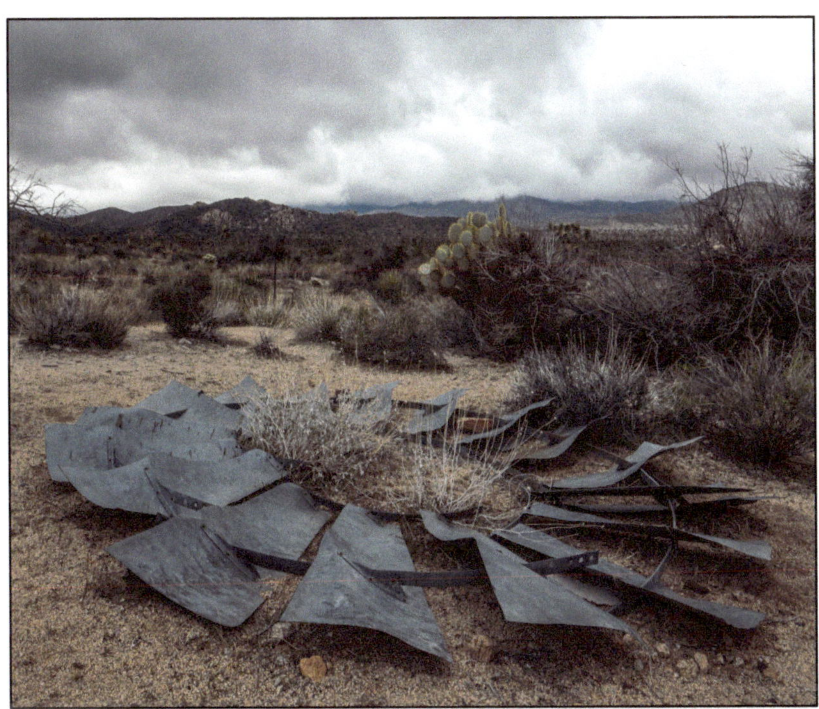

Metal Graveyard at Ryan Ranch   20mm f/11 1/80s ISO100

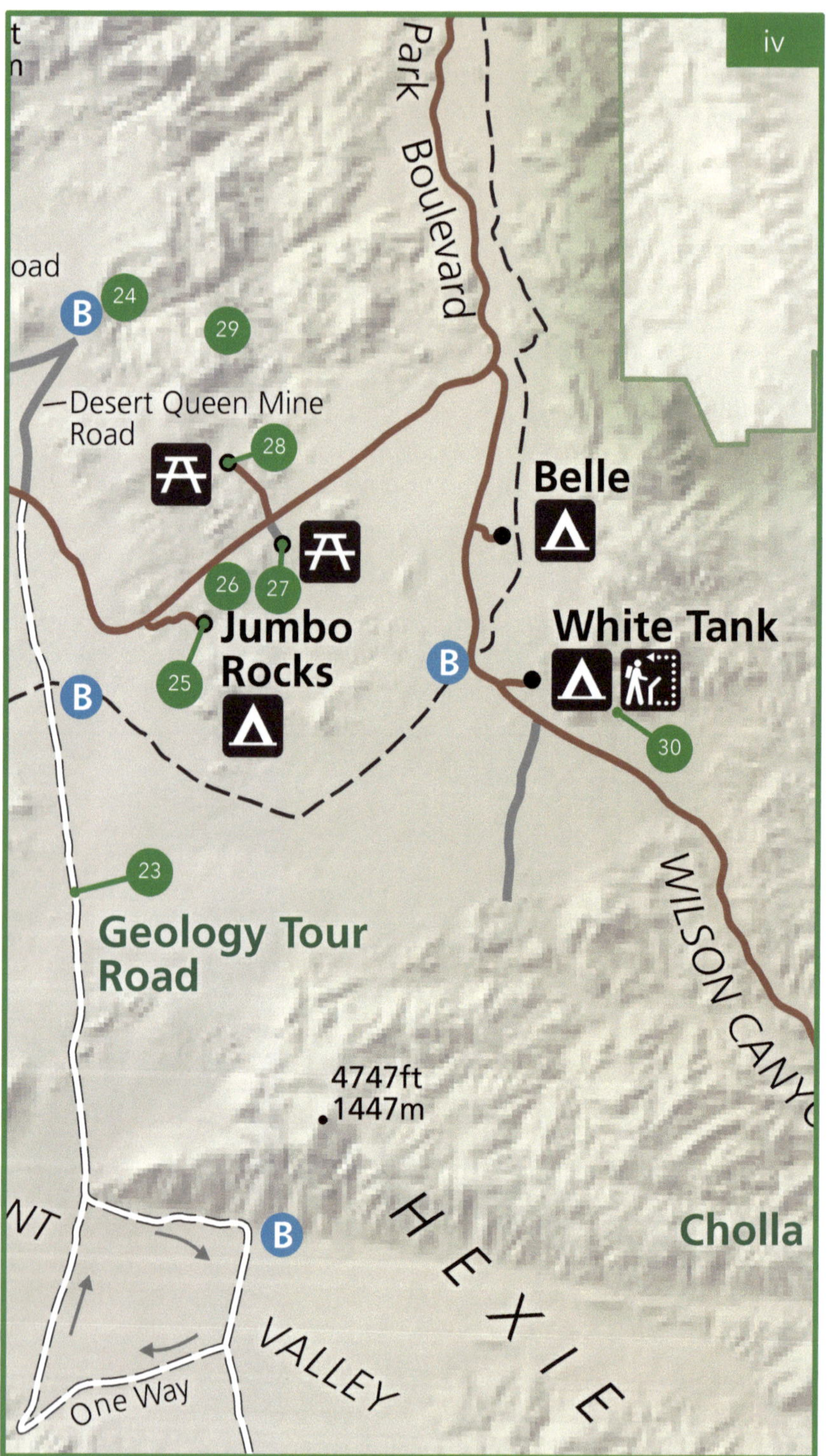

iv
t
n
oad
24
29
Desert Queen Mine
Road
28
Belle
26
27
Jumbo
Rocks
25
B
B
White Tank
30
23
Geology Tour
Road
WILSON CANYON
4747ft
1447m
Cholla
B
HEXIE
VALLEY
One Way
NT
Park Boulevard

23. Geology Tour Road   102

Grab a free map of this drive and find the waypoints for a fun off-pavement "tour" across varied terrain. No hill-topping vista, per se, but more variety than Covington Flat Roads (3).

24. Desert Queen Vista   104

See a well-crafted stone ruin and a hilltop cable winch. Peer down upon the scattered and vague remains of the Desert Queen Mine.

25. Jumbo Rocks   106

Are these rocks any more "jumbo" than the rest? No, not really. Regardless, a mandatory stop for the Joshua Tree photographer. Home of two famous compositions.

26. Skull Rock   108

Probably the most-visited site in the entire park, due to its roadside perch. Visit anytime, but its real personality pops during foggy weather and at night under stars & artificial light.

27. Live Oak   110

Photograph a large Live Oak tree, birds feeding on its acorns, and quartz "dikes" abundant in adjacent rock formations. Bonus – this area is often overlooked, so parking is usually a breeze.

28. Split Rock   112

Hike this enjoyable loop trail, beginning and ending at the large "Split Rock." Route is abundant with photogenic, lifelike rock formations.

29. Eagle Cliff Boulder House   115

Without question, the most fascinating, preserved dwelling within the park. Take no artifacts, only photos. Some of the route is steep. GPS required.

30. Arch & Heart Rocks   118

Arch Rock is a Joshua Tree must do, and Heart Rock is an easy "why not?" add-on. Unfortunately, parking at the trail-head is limited to 4 spots… Additional parking is nearby but adds mileage to the hike.

V
Pinto Mountain
3983ft
1214m
Cholla Cactus Garden
31
Ocotillo Patch
32
Fried Liver Wash
NATIONAL PARK
B
PINT
Pinto Basin Road
Old
3820ft
1165m
Porcupine Wash
B
NTAINS
Monument Mountain
4834ft
1474m
Smoke Tree Wash
33
Road
Cottonwood Visitor Center
3079ft
939m
Cottonwood Spring
B
34
Lost Palms Oasis
ONWOOD MOUNTAINS
35
Bajada Nature Tra

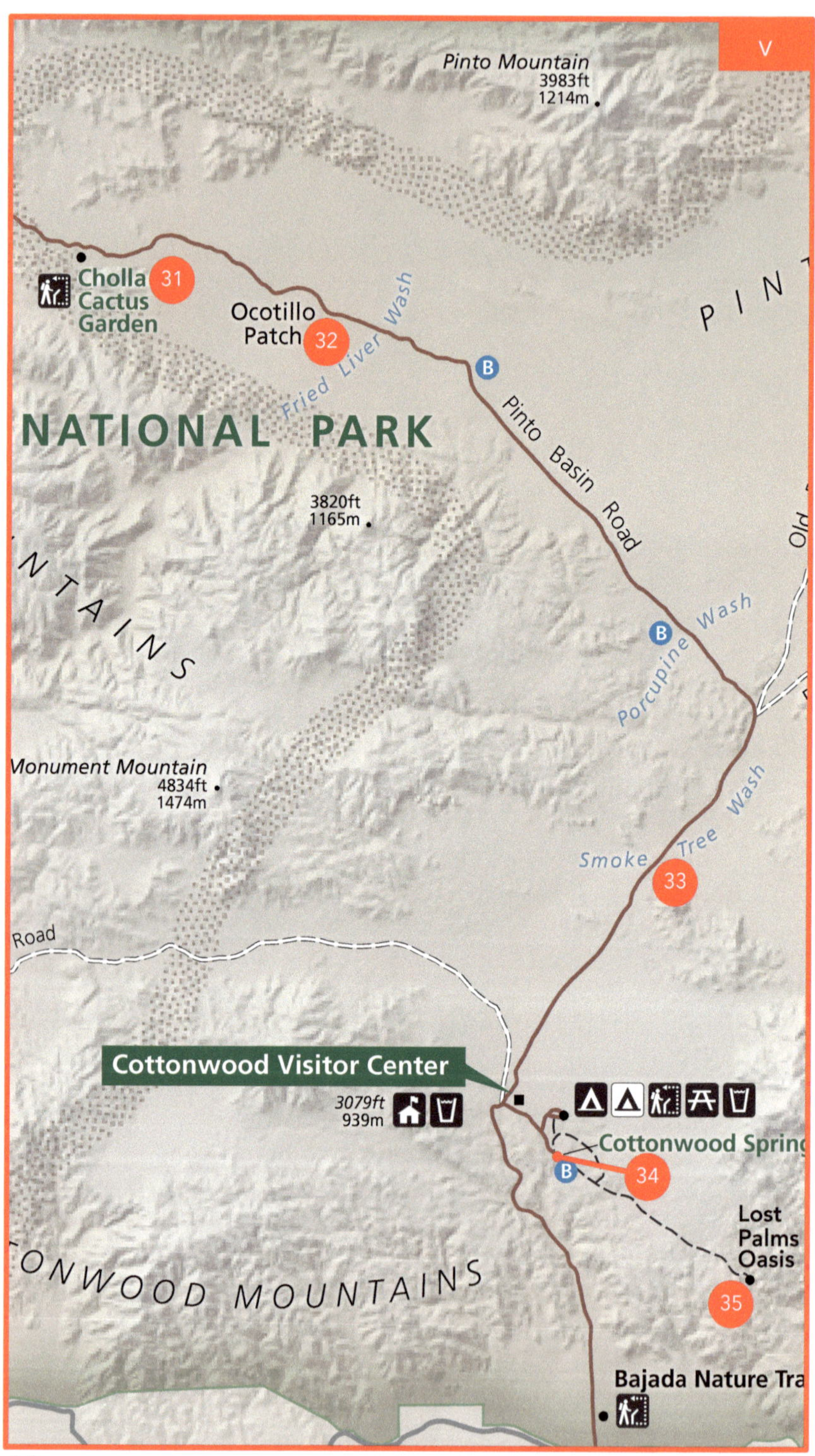

14

31. Cholla Cactus Garden   120

Plan for either a sunrise or a sunset at this hallmark Joshua Tree location, where these "Jumping" Chollas' needles appear translucent when backlit from the sun.

32. Ocotillo Patch   123

The striking Ocotillo plant flowers appear like paintbrushes, wet with red paint, at this easy roadside desert stroll. Its color is most vibrant following early spring rainfall.

33. Smoke Tree Wash   125

Wander a little or a lot through this patch of the golden Smoke Trees. Blue skies compliment their color and form.

34. Cottonwood Spring   126

Joshua Tree's most easily-accessible, dense oasis, Cottonwood Spring really pops with vibrant green colors and texture in April and May.

35. Lost Palms Oasis   127

Enjoy this hike (a favorite of trail runners) to a colonnade of California Fan Palms, providing cool shade from the bright sun above. Lost Palms Oasis tends to be a lot less trafficked than Fortynine Palms Oasis (6), and that's a good thing.

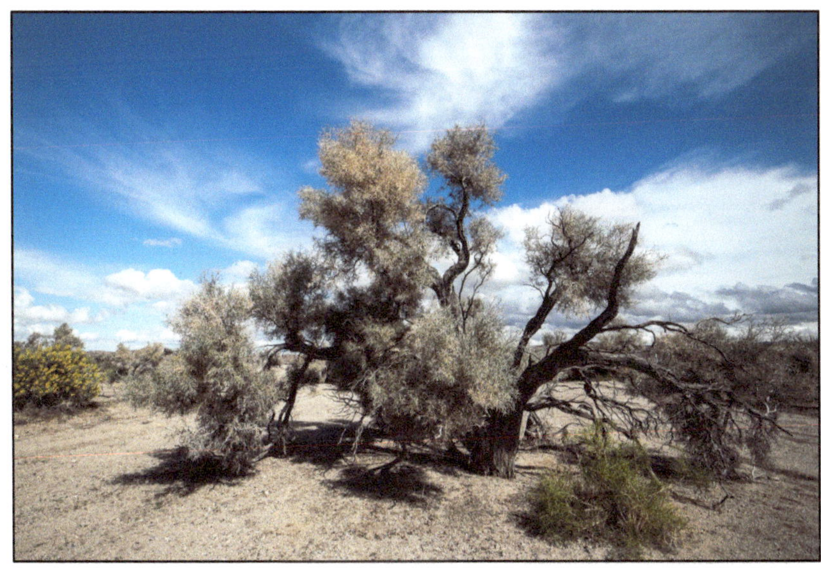

Smoke Tree Wash   16mm f/11 1/250s ISO200

Introduction

Welcome to Joshua Tree National Park, the very best of California's high desert. Rich with history (and ruins!), this intersection of the Mojave and Colorado Deserts boasts truly sensational geology, abundant wildlife, and unique plant life - including of course the whimsical Joshua Tree. Varieties of subject and composition are numerous. For the landscape photographer, capturing its essence via camera is straightforward and rewarding. *This park offers a lot.*

This park shines all day long *and at nighttime too.* I would venture to say while its very best hours encompass sunset, a close second is under the night sky. Sunrise produces great results (and midday as well). Alas, a park with little down time!

But I suspect that you already know a lot of this. And so, this guide isn't designed to persuade you to visit Joshua Tree National Park. Odds are that you have already made the decision to go. *Yes!*

Then what *is* this book's purpose?

Its core intent is to guide you **-the photographer-** throughout the park, to minimize "blind exploration" for sites, and to maximize the number of praiseworthy images you take home.

This book is especially catered towards those who I like to call "weekend photographers." Those who may visit the park only for 2-5 days – and for some people what may be their *only* visit to this national park. As such, the sites presented herein are more likely to be roadside or very short hikes, in order to maximize experiences, when time is limited. (There are some longer treks on the list, for those who do have the time.)

My style is also to provide honest information. Not every site is a "must see" / ★★★★. So sometimes the news is great; sometimes not so great. The idea is that you're armed with enough information to create a daily itinerary that meets or exceeds your goals as a landscape photographer on travel. My own philosophy as a traveling photographer, is that I seek destinations where the reward matches or exceeds the effort to get there. This is one of the governing philosophies of this book.

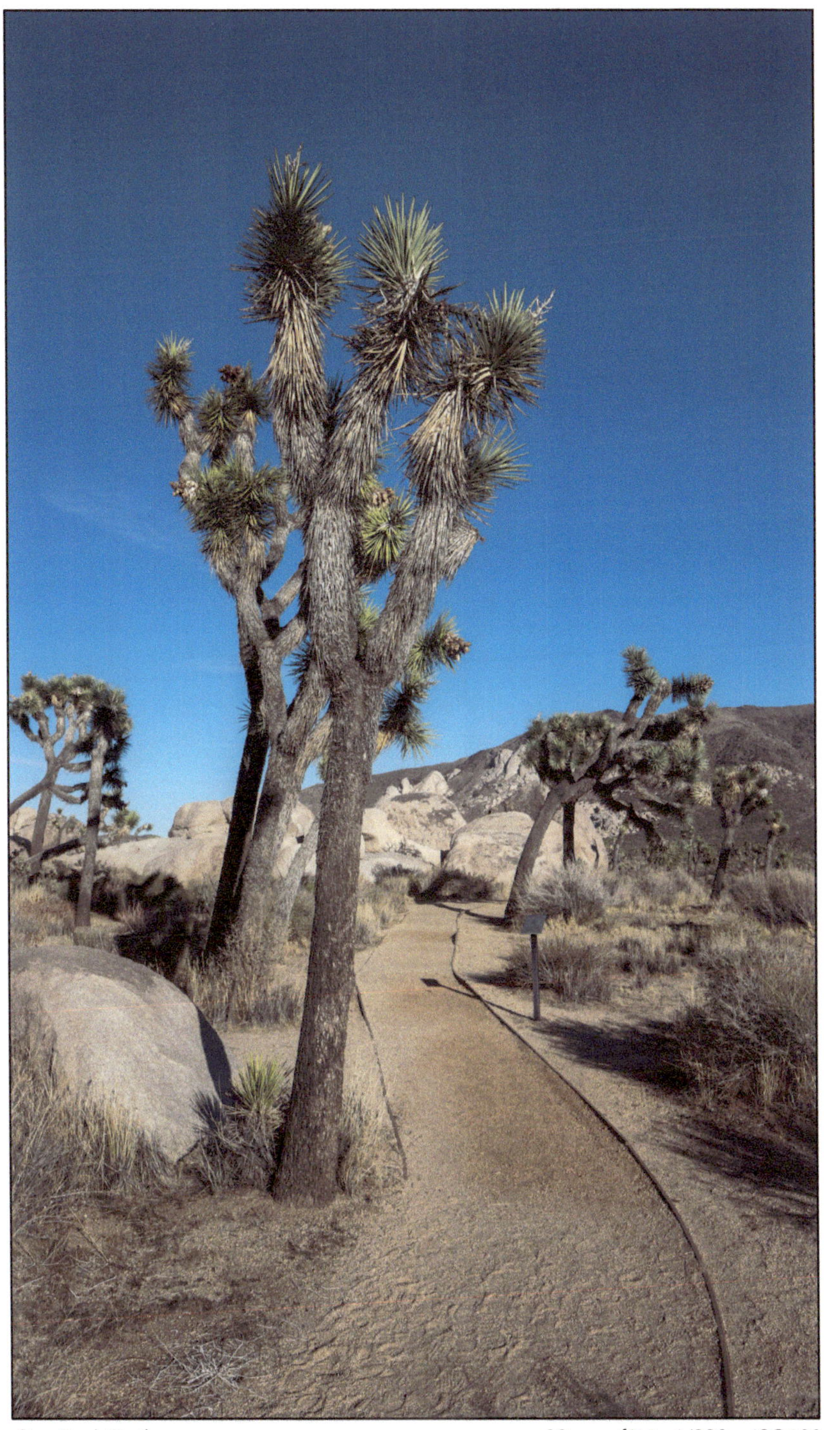

Cap Rock Trail

28mm   f/11   1/320s   ISO100

How to Use this Book

I have divided the park, for the photographer's needs, into 5 areas. For quick reference, please see that each area's color is consistent throughout the book. (This is for quickly finding maps, sections, etc.)

While a lot of literature you will come across may speak to the park's history, geology, flora, fauna, and so on, this book will focus mostly entirely on elements useful to the photographer. I'm no historian, geologist, or botanist, and it would be wasteful to reproduce a lot of that information in here, as it would only add to the volume's heft. I sincerely hope that you have room for this book in your camera bag, and that you take it along with you every step of the way.

I've also omitted the most basic "general" photography lessons in here as well. There are many excellent resources on that topic. I will, however, cover some intermediate-level topics that I think are relevant to making the most of your photography while at Joshua Tree National Park. The Tips & Techniques section is for exactly this.

So let's dissect the information presented for each of these sites. The following is a sample, taken from the Iron Door Cave (12):

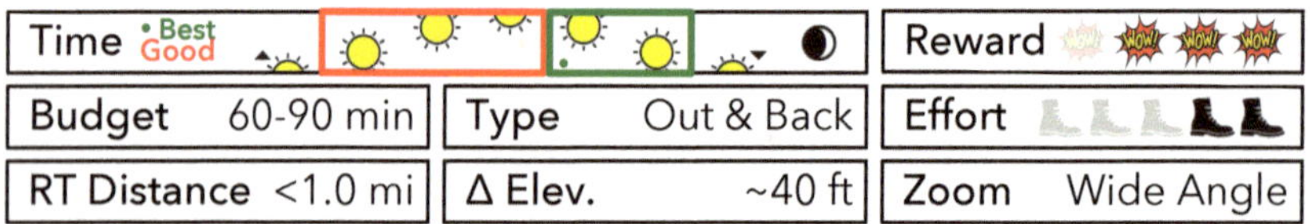

Time: The icons represent sunrise, early AM, late AM, midday, early PM, late PM, sunset, and nighttime. The green box(es) represent the best time(s) of day to be there. The red box(es) represent good time(s). Ideally you are visiting during the "best" times, but itineraries do not always allow this, hence providing multiple options. The above site is best in afternoon, and also good morning to midday. *One major caveat here: Clouds can change everything (and normally for the better!), offering softer, more accommodating light during other times of the day. Make impromptu adjustments, accordingly.*

Reward: One to 4 "Wow's." Now honestly, if it warrants printing in the book, then it's got merit, right? So a 1-Wow here isn't like a 1-star motel. It's just relative! The above site scores a 3.

Budget: Your time is valuable, and this is how much time you might expect to spend at this site (including getting there, if it is a hike). For the sample site, plan for between 60-90 minutes.

Type: This is the circuit that you will cover. "Roadside" involves some walking (but not hiking); you likely will work *near the side of the road*. "Meandering" means that there's not really a prescribed route, and so you should expect to explore the area via your own path. "Out & Back" is a route that you hike out one way, and then you turn around and hike back on the return. "Loop" begins and ends at the same place, though you mostly will not retrace your own steps. "Lollipop Loop" is an out & back with a loop at the far end.

Effort: This is the physical effort required while on the hike. Here, we are using the "Boots" scale. Zero Boots highlighted is typical for everyday walks, then 1-5 Boots reflect the effort, similar to using the Easy-Moderate-Strenuous scale, but here with a 2-Boot representing Easy-Moderate, and a 4-Boot representing Moderate-Strenuous. For the sample site, as you will read about on page 76, some minor scrambling may be required, hence its rating of 2 Boots.

RT Distance: "RT" is Round Trip. This is the total hiking distance. Our sample site's round trip distance is less than ("<") 1.0 mile.

Δ Elev.: Change in Elevation. I need to be careful here. There are many ways to talk elevation and how it is recorded on a hike. For this book and this purpose, what is presented is simply the difference between your lowest elevation and your highest elevation. Some trails go up-and-down, and up-and-down, and so on. This value does not capture the summation of all those ascents and descents; it is merely the difference between the highest and your lowest points, while on the trail. For the sample site, the change in elevation is approximately ("~") 40 feet. *If the hike warrants further explanation, it will be provided.*

Zoom: I'm a firm believer in "less is more." Taking every lens on every hike can be backbreaking. And being weighed-down is no fun. So, in this box, I'll suggest the key lens(es) you will want to take. Adding more, is up to you. Using 35mm (full frame-equivalent) focal lengths, please consider "Wide" = Wide Angle (15-35mm), "Norm" = Normal (24-70mm), and "Tele" = Telephoto (70-200mm+).

Finally, each section will have photos of *hopefully* what you can expect to see and photograph – or do better than I could! Below these pictures are the camera settings that I used for the shot. Ex:

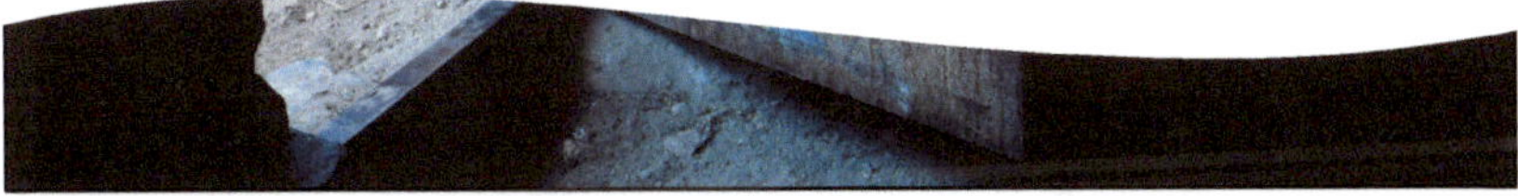

Inside the Iron Door Cave   24mm f/4 1/60s ISO800

The Five Park Areas

For your orientation and planning purposes, this book defines five geographic areas within the park – Black Rock, (along) Highway 62, "West" Park Central, "East" Park Central, and Pinto Basin Road.

Joshua Tree National Park is *large*, and because so its maps can be deceptive with their diminutive scale. For example, at a glance the Indian Cove Area does not look far away from Barker Dam, but it would take 45 minutes to drive between the two, not including any extra time at either one of the two entrance stations. These five sections' boundaries were defined to help primarily with this in mind. Think of your day(s) as efficiently portioned within these areas and across their boundaries. (See also the Driving Information section on page 31 for additional insight.)

Let's take a look at each area…

Black Rock

Whereabouts of an actual *canyon* in Black Rock Canyon is not widely agreed upon (nor even its presence in the formal name of the area), so here we are going to get our nomenclature in order and move forward simply with "Black Rock." The name does hold merit – the granite is noticeably different, with black veins running throughout.

The area is beautiful in a bit of an indescribable way, and vast. It is served by an abundance of hiking and horseback-riding trails. Curiously though, this maze of trails is not at all depicted on the main park map. See pages 50-51 for a representation of trails here.

In my opinion, **Black Rock is explored best on horseback.** The trails are longer here, and with the loose sand hiking can trend toward strenuous due to elevation changes and the frequently hot temperatures. Horseback, you can go farther and explore more. Black Rock Area on Horse (2) covers the planning aspects of this activity.

An Honorable Mention… If you cannot explore this area on horseback, the "Short Loop" trail may fulfill your appetite of this unique area. I recommend to hike it clockwise and include the short "Fault Line" trail on your route. It is 3.5 miles round trip. Parking is available near a Backcountry Registration Board on the east side of the road that exits the campground.

Highway 62

California Highway 62, aka "Twentynine Palms Highway," will be most visitor's conduit into Joshua Tree National Park. The communities of Yucca Valley, Joshua Tree, and Twentynine Palms offer accommodations, dining, supplies, and fuel. Each of these communities make for a great "home base" for your national park stay.

Yucca Valley

Yucca Valley tends to be the most economical of the three, providing many budget accommodations, multiple grocery stores, a broad variety of restaurants, and a Walmart (also with groceries). It is a 15-minute drive from Joshua Tree.

Two entrances into Joshua Tree National Park are accessed directly from Yucca Valley – one to Black Rock, and the other to Lower Covington Flat Road via La Contenta Road. Neither of these entrances have pay stations.

Though not inside the national park, Pioneertown (4) is a worthwhile visit while in the area. It is an easy 10-minute drive northwest of Yucca Valley. **Pappy and Harriet's** is a restaurant and bar in Pioneertown and a favorite of locals, with abundant outdoor seating out back. Live music is also regularly on tap.

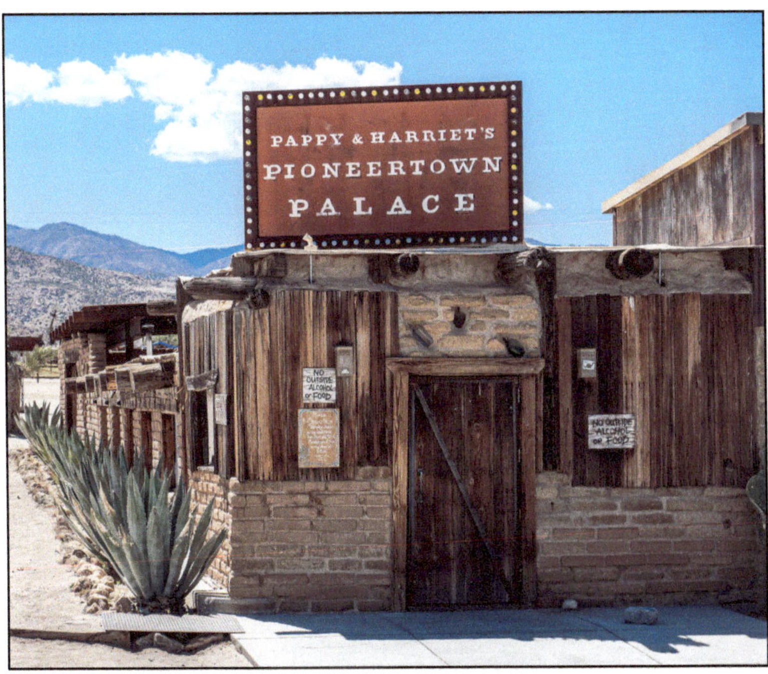

Business in the Front – Party in the Back   100mm   f/11   1/400s   ISO100

Joshua Tree

Joshua Tree is a funky and fun desert community, and *in spirit* the "main entrance" into the national park. Its amenities are the most limited of the three communities, with primarily boutique shops and restaurants, a few motels, and fuel.

The Joshua Tree Visitor Center is near the busy intersection of Highway 62 and Park Boulevard. It's worth a stop, at some point during your visit. (It can wait, if crowded. It is small.) Don't let the replica snake below the Joshua Tree inside the VC startle you!

The national park's "West" Entrance Station is 5 miles south of the VC, also on Park Boulevard (aka Quail Springs Road). This pay station entrance can get mighty backed-up. Use your judgment to gauge if you'll be making an attempt to enter through it during a busy day and/or time. Alternatively, the "North" Entrance Station outside of Twentynine Palms is rarely as busy, so you may save time and peace of mind by entering there.

About 200 feet before the entrance booth is a brick park entrance sign. I enjoy having one of these signs in the beginning of my photo album – it makes for a nice "introduction" to your portfolio of park photos. Unfortunately, this one is quite lacking in design, and the background is uninspiring in the daytime. The North Entrance Station one's daytime presence is at least better. This one, though, can make for a good nighttime composition:

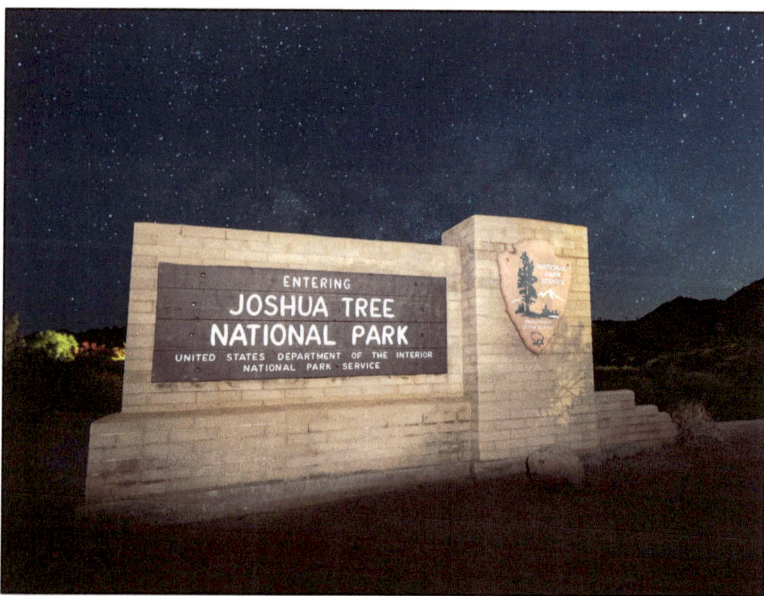

Joshua Tree National Park - West Entrance   24mm f/4 15s ISO3200

Twentynine Palms

The city of Twentynine Palms appears to be growing the most in this area, with new hotels and a truly grand entrance from Highway 62 to the Oasis Visitor Center along National Park Drive. Amenities are abundant, perhaps not as much so as in Yucca Valley, though I doubt you would be missing much except for fewer dining options.

Logistically speaking, while Twentynine Palms is a great place to stay during your visit, it is quite a bit further from the majority of the park's sites. While only a 20-minute drive to Joshua Tree, if you rely on its North Entrance Station, additional time is required inside the park for driving.

The Oasis Visitor Center is also worth a stop. Inside is an interesting 3D map of Joshua Tree National Park.

An Honorable Mention… the Oasis of Mara, behind the Oasis VC, has a 0.6-mile paved path that encircles the oasis with information boards describing the area's interesting human history. Peer high in the trees – many birds frequent the oasis.

Four miles south on Utah Trail, which becomes Park Boulevard, is the North Entrance Station.

Our "Highway 62" area contains two sites, in addition to the aforementioned Pioneertown – Rattlesnake Canyon (5) and Fortynine Palms Oasis (6). Both are between Joshua Tree and Twentynine Palms. (So many counting of palms!) Both are sensational. Due to their adjacent locations and time involved at each site my recommendation is to couple them for one morning's outing. Begin early, first with Fortynine Palms Oasis, due to the moderately-strenuous nature of this hike & direct sun exposure and follow with Rattlesnake Canyon. Have lunch afterwards and re-enter the park elsewhere.

West Park Central

From inside the West Entrance Station to Bighorn Pass Road, this area contains nearly half of this book's content – 16 of 35 sites. **If you only have one day in Joshua Tree National Park, spend it in Park Central (West & East).**

As you begin your drive, south into the park, you'll find Joshua Trees in abundance and "mountains" of rocks seemingly everywhere around you. So let's explore one topic that is confusing to most – just what is the "Wonderland of Rocks?" They're not visible… Yet.

The Wonderland of Rocks is particular section of rocks that run north-south between Indian Cove and Barker Dam. A satellite view helps, because the monzogranite is lighter here that found elsewhere in the park. This is due to a higher density of white quartz.

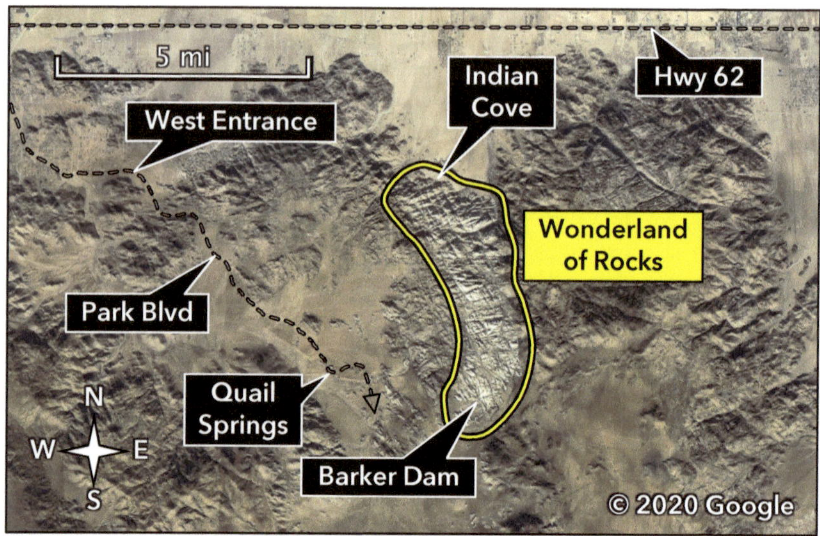

However, in the grand scheme of things, I do not think this has much bearing on what we are setting out to achieve while in the park! I have taken the time to point this out, simply because I want you to be informed on its whereabouts, because if your experience is like mine, you will hear about this area often. It is particularly popular with thru-hikers and rock climbers. Our best exploration beyond the boundary and into the Wonderland of Rocks is via the Wonderland Wash (15). Otherwise, Rattlesnake Canyon (5), Willow Hole (10), and Barker Dam (14) only barely breach its boundary. ...Honestly, it is not *that* different than other monzogranite areas. It is just that the rock formations are denser and lacking as much typical beige color.

OK, back to enjoying your drive in, find many visitors having pulled off the road taking ubiquitous "we have arrived" photos. It will take 6 miles before reaching the Quail Springs Picnic Area and another 3 miles before reaching the Hidden Valley Area.

The Hidden Valley area is a happening place. The actual "Hidden Valley" and accompanying nature trail is accessed via the picnic area and parking loop on the southwest side of Park Boulevard. Quite confusing – the Hidden Valley Campground is on the opposite side of the road (the northeast side) and is simply named after the somewhat-adjacent feature, although they are technically quite separate. Also on the northeast side is a large parking lot denoted by "Intersection Rock," the namesake rock formation at the intersection of Park Boulevard and Barker Dam Road. *This can be a congested area!* Some good news here – this greater Hidden Valley area works well with midday light, so consider a picnic lunch at a table in the Hidden Valley picnic area, and exploration on foot in the area before and after. Barker Dam is the one exception… It is quite underwhelming in midday light. It's at it best in the early morning.

Perhaps the greatest "lure" to this area is Keys View. It should be saved for sunset, but if you just have to go take a look during another time you might as well, as it's not a long drive. Joshua Trees and Parry's Nolina are in abundance along the way up.

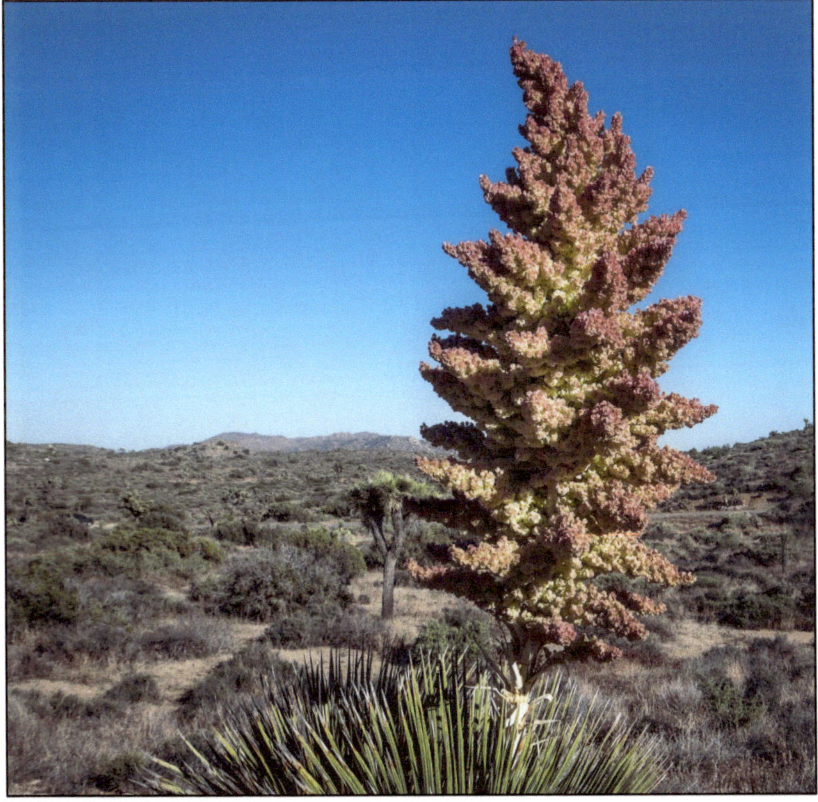

Rarely Red Parry's Nolina   40mm f/8 1/320s ISO100

Park Boulevard makes an eastbound change of direction near Cap Rock (17). The casual drive between here and just beyond the Sheep Pass Campground is rewarding. From inside the car, driving to and from sites, this is where I always feel most "at one" with the paved part of Joshua Tree National Park.

On the southside of Park Boulevard about 0.25-mile west of Bighorn Pass Road is one heckuva tall Joshua Tree. It is impossible to miss.

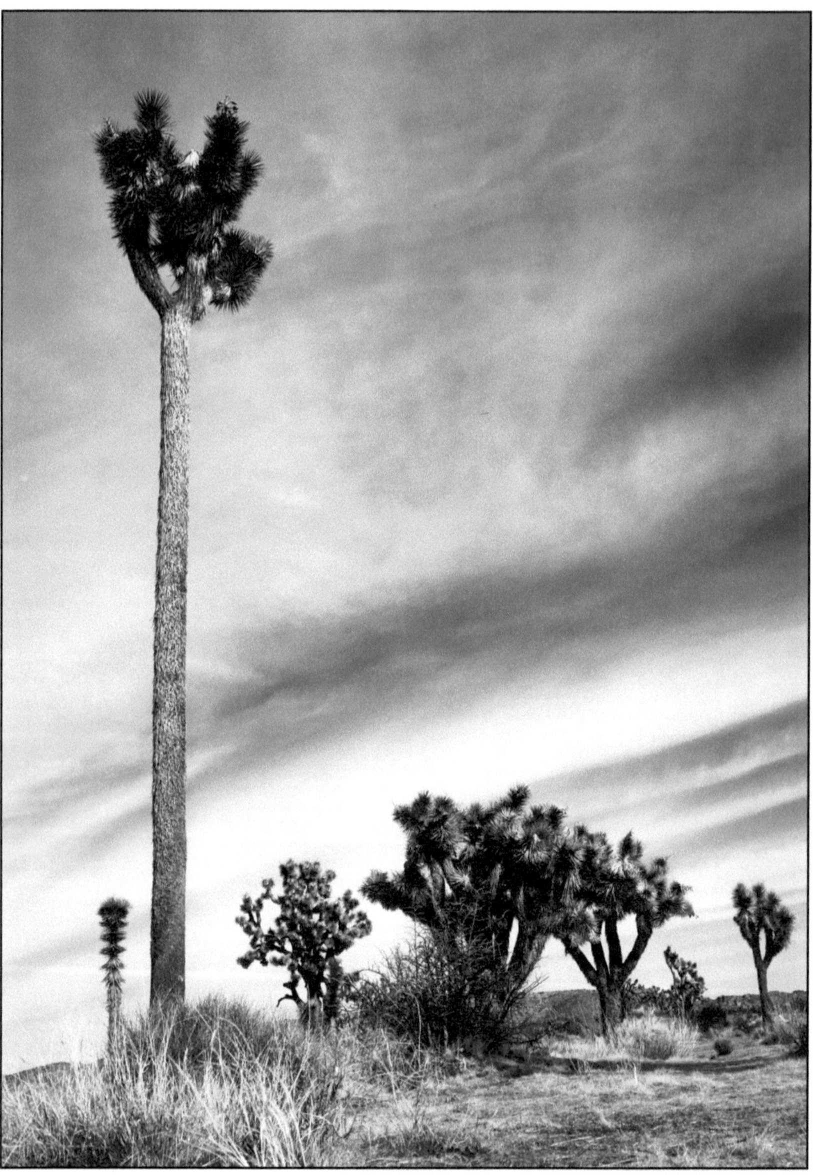

The Tall One   35mm f/16 1/100s ISO100

Bighorn Pass Road is an enjoyable drive, if ever traversing the park and looking for an alternate route. It is not paved and so usually does have a bit of a washboard surface. Note: The adjacent Queen Valley Road is less scenic and one way (westbound).

East Park Central

As we traverse west to east, Geology Tour Road and the opposite Desert Queen Mine Road mark our transition into this area that quietly compliments the more crowded west side. Many ill-informed day trippers quickly buzz through this stretch, only stopping for Skull Rock (26). This is unfortunate, because there are great sites in this area, and many require little time. Eight sites, and half of these are 4 "Wow's." Two are 3 "Wow's." That's photo quality density!

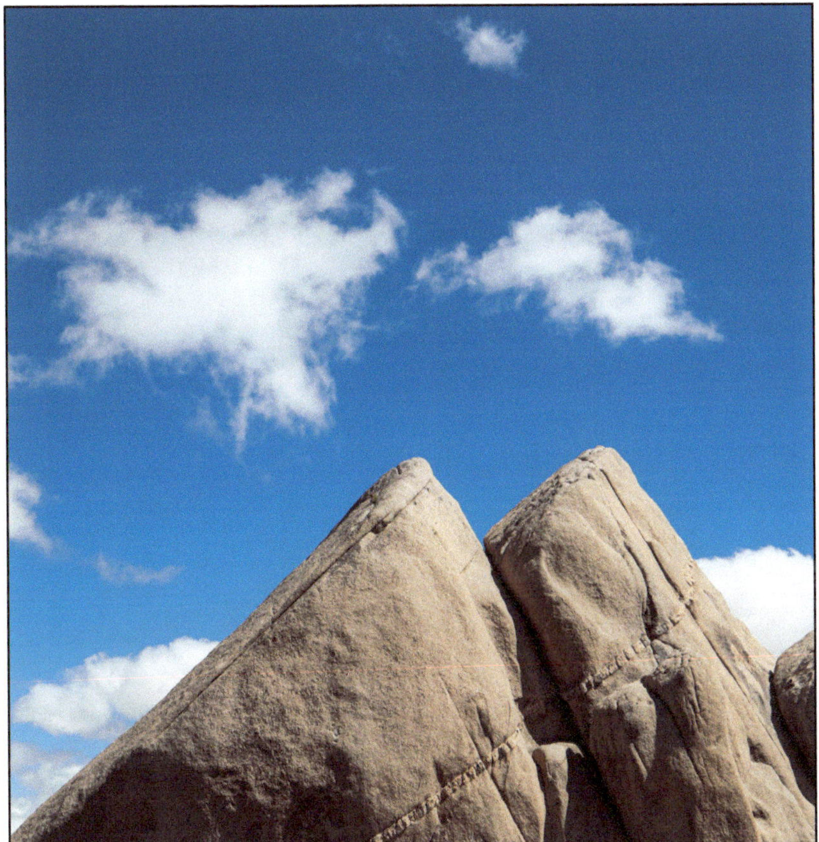

Dining Companions at Live Oak Picnic Area   35mm f/8 1/400s ISO100

I enjoy Live Oak (27). I believe that I rated it correctly with only 2 "Wows," but to me it's more. Perhaps because it doubles as a great place for a picnic lunch or afternoon snack.

Otherwise, this area is straightforward. There are not really any nuances to make you aware of outside the site narratives. Take a look through them, and do plan for stops in addition to Skull Rock.

Pinto Basin Road

Admittedly, I have blurred the line a bit between the east boundary of East Park Central and this final section, Pinto Basin Road. Arch & Heart Rocks (30) fall on Pinto Basin Road but are still within the Mojave Desert side of the park. That site's "spirit" is more in-line with its peers in East Park Central, hence its position there.

Our "Pinto Basin Road" area picks up southeast of Wilson Canyon and begins with Cholla Cactus Garden (31), in the Colorado Desert. The transition between these two ecosystems is mighty evident as you drive down the road.

Of utmost importance here, is an awareness of how long this section of road is. It cannot be traversed as quickly as you might think. Your daily itinerary will need to account for driving time while visiting this area of the park.

Cholla Cactus Garden is this area's most cherished location for land-scape photography. Lost Palms Oasis (35) is also extraordinary but is remote and requires a lengthy hike. On a short 1-2 day itinerary, I wholeheartedly recommend planning for a sunrise or sunset capture at Cholla Cactus Garden, but I would think twice about including Lost Palms Oasis. Consider saving the latter for when you have 3-4 days within the park.

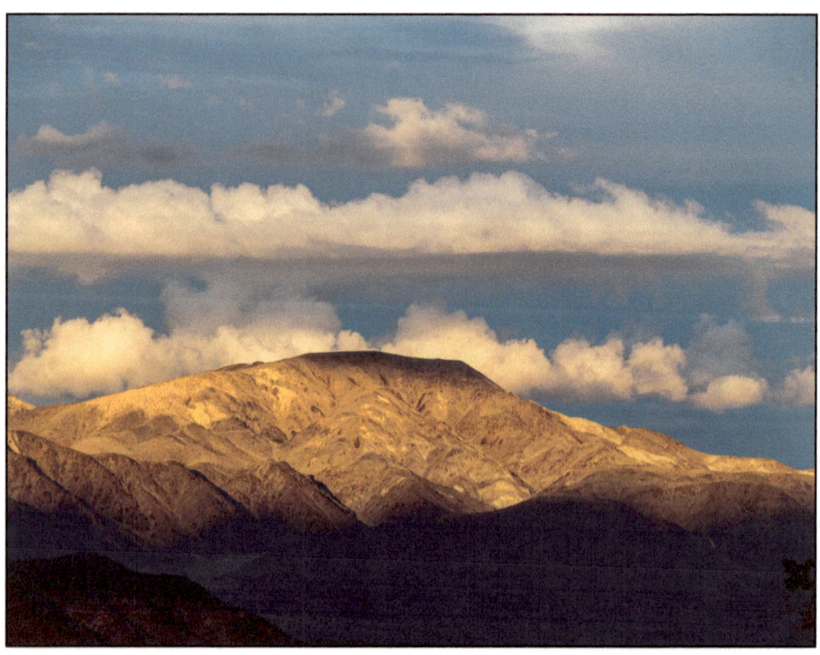

Sunset Light on Pinto Mountain   200mm   f/6.3   1/500s   ISO200

Tips & Techniques

As briefly mentioned in the "How to Use this Book" section, I want to share with you what I think are some of the more unique pieces of advice for your trip to Joshua Tree National Park. Some of this information is park-specific (logistics and planning, mostly), while other information is photography-related (i.e. techno-talk).

Let's get straight to it...

Additional Resources
Please do not skip this!

My goal, in writing this book, is to minimize the resources that you must seek-out, purchase or print, and ultimately rely on in order to enjoy *photography* at Joshua Tree National Park. So, along with the purchase of this book I recommend three additional resources:

1. The Joshua Tree National Park Website (www.nps.gov/jotr/index.htm),

2. A printed copy of the National Park Service map of Joshua Tree National Park, and

3. A purchased copy of National Geographic's "Trails Illustrated" Topographical Map of Joshua Tree National Park (map #226).

The Website...

I'm not going to guide you through the whole website – that would be silly. Though, it is in your best interest to make some time and explore it completely, or very close to. Also, a disclaimer – some of these subcategories listed here may change names over time, as the website evolves, so if you cannot find what you're looking for based on my guidance here, try finding it outside the website with your favorite search engine. Just be sure that when you follow the results, you're staying within the www.nps.gov domain. It is the most reliable.

Alerts

On the top banner there is a link to park alerts. This could be abnormal weather or road conditions, or any upcoming or emergency activities that visitors need to be aware of. Check this ahead of your trip, and as connectivity allows, check it regularly during your trip.

Weather

A direct link is available on the homepage. Weather conditions can change very rapidly in this region. Again, as connectivity allows, check this regularly during your trip.

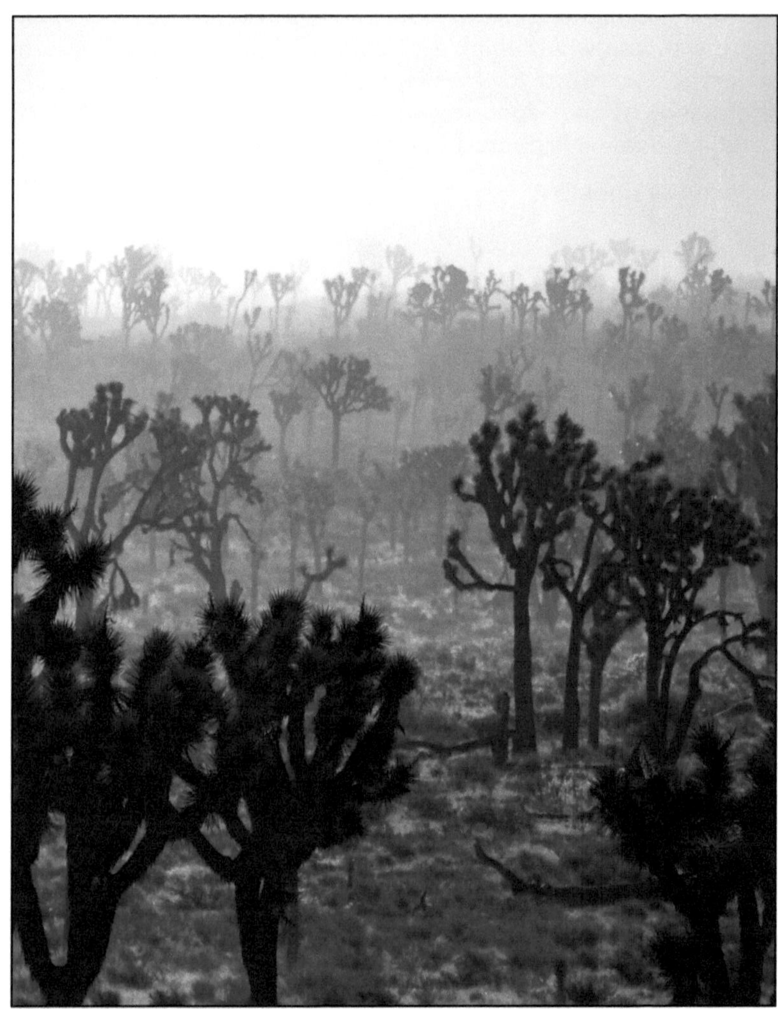

Intriguing Fog in West Park Central   400mm f/8 1/1000s ISO200

Maps

Again on the top banner, follow the maps link for an abundance of great information. Your first mission is to find and download the PDF of the park map that you will be provided once you arrive at a park entrance pay station. I advise to print in color your downloaded copy on the largest paper possible. The copy you will receive at the park, unfolded, is approximately 24 x 16 inches. This is the same map used on pages 4-14 of this book, and the same map that I listed as Item 2 above for you to carry during your visit.

Unfortunately, the aforementioned map lacks adequate detail in some places, especially for use while driving (and seeking topographic waypoints). Its scale is approximately 1 inch = 3.5 miles. Though not a "must," I strongly encourage purchase of the National Geographic map listed on page 29. It provides 2.7 times more resolution. This is a lot! (Its scale is 1 inch = 1.3 miles.) It is easy to find online and in many national stores.

The maps that I provide later in this book, for select sites, are mostly for planning purposes, and while on foot are for orientation only. These maps should not be used for navigation. (Orientation at sites without a provided map is either described in the site's text, adequately depicted on the free park map, or straightforward enough that the trailhead board suffices.) One exception for the Black Rock Area. I provide a National Park Service map on pages 50-51.

Driving Information

There are no fuel stations inside Joshua Tree National Park. Some national parks have fuel; some do not. This one doesn't. Plan accordingly.

When studying these maps, the driving distances do not seem that long, and therefore may surprise you. Here are some typical distances and driving times for your reference:

Yucca Valley to Joshua Tree	8 mi	15 min
Joshua Tree to Twentynine Palms	15 mi	20 min
Yucca Valley to Black Rock Campground	5 mi	10 min
Joshua Tree to Keys View Road	16 mi	35 min
Keys View Road to Pinto Basin Road	11 mi	20 min
Twentynine Palms to Pinto Basin Road	10 mi	20 min
Twentynine Palms to Cholla Cactus Gard.	20 mi	35 min
Cholla Cactus Garden to Cottonwood VC	20 mi	35 min

Seasons

Joshua Tree National Park is a true 4-season destination, though at anytime inclement weather (wind, fog, heavy rain, hail, or snow) may impede travel.

Spring

Early springtime in Joshua Tree is your best bet for comfortable temperatures, blooming wildflowers, and a higher water level at Barker Dam (14). Wildflowers activity varies by elevation… Lower elevations bloom first, and higher elevations bloom last. Wildflowers can bloom in Park Central as early as mid-March, but typically do not reach their full potential until mid-April. Some years this can be as late as mid-May. My recommendation is to plan for a middle-of-April visit. This provides for a bit more time for the wildflowers and also more water accumulation at Barker Dam. (Barker Dam is a must do when the conditions are favorable, so timing and good fortune here are desirable!)

Late springtime (mid-May through early June) allow for Milky Way photography, though the time of night for this event can be challenging. See page 39 for more information on this.

It is no secret that springtime visitation to Joshua Tree is widely recommended, so crowds are typically at their peak during this season. Weekday visitation helps immensely, especially Tuesday-Thursday, if your schedule will allow.

Summer

I hesitate to promote Joshua Tree in the summertime, because I want for you to be able to safely explore and photograph all day, each day. Extreme heat, though, will substantially limit your ability to do so.

In fairness, summer is not without its own "advantages…"

First, a guarantee of sensational Milky Way photography (so as long as there is not nighttime cloud cover).

Second, sudden and swift-moving thunderstorms can appear. While these can be dangerous (lightning, heavy rain, and flash flooding) if directly in one's path, if in the distance they can provide for wonderful skies and unique color casts.

Lastly, crowds will be more manageable than any other time of year.

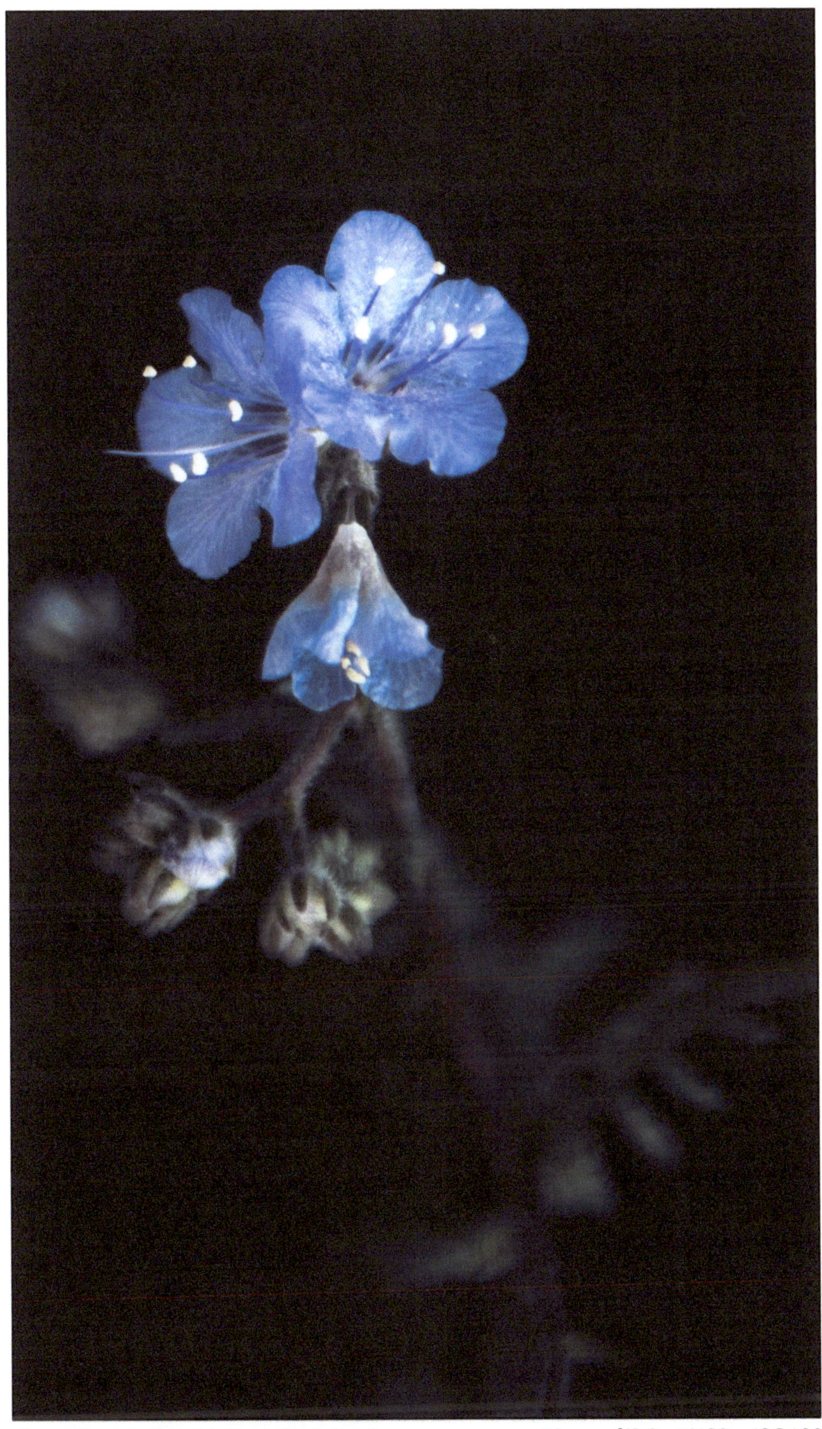

Canterbury Bells (with Black Backdrop)   50mm f/2.8 1/400s ISO100

Fall

Fall temperatures are much like those in spring, but there will be no wildflowers, and do not expect to find water to photograph. There is no "fall color" – no leaves changing from green to yellow, orange, and red.

Joshua Tree is a haven in the fall for rock climbers. Once other western U.S. rock climbing destinations become undesirable with cold fall weather, Joshua Tree provides an extension for the climbing year. Watching and photographing them is fun.

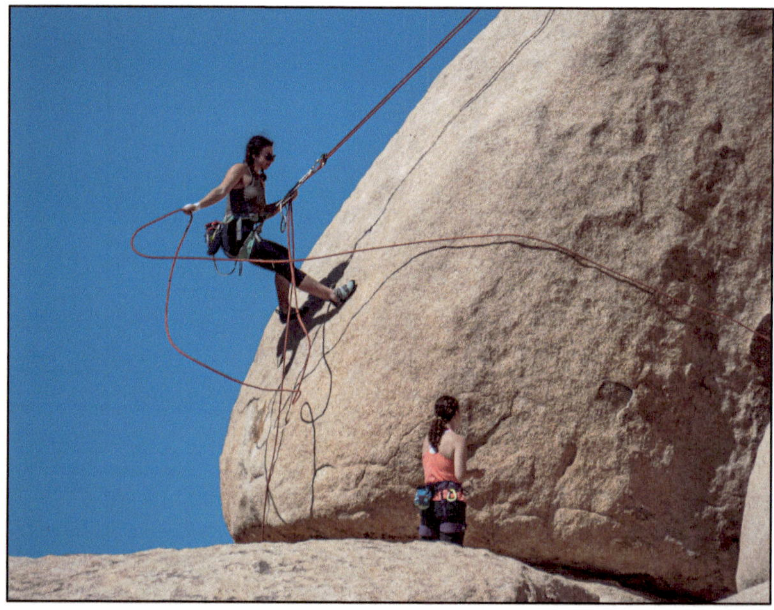

Coming Down...   600mm f/5.6 1/1600s ISO200

Fall's best months are November and December. Do you see the trend here? Summer heat comes early and stays long! These two months are too late in the year for Milky Way photography.

Crowds are common on Saturdays and Sundays.

Winter

Winters are cool but sometimes quite cold (more often at night). Crowds are manageable. Snow is possible but rare – typically only a few short-lived snow events occur each year.

Wildflowers arrive in the lowest elevations (Bajada Nature Trail to the Cottonwood area), usually in late February.

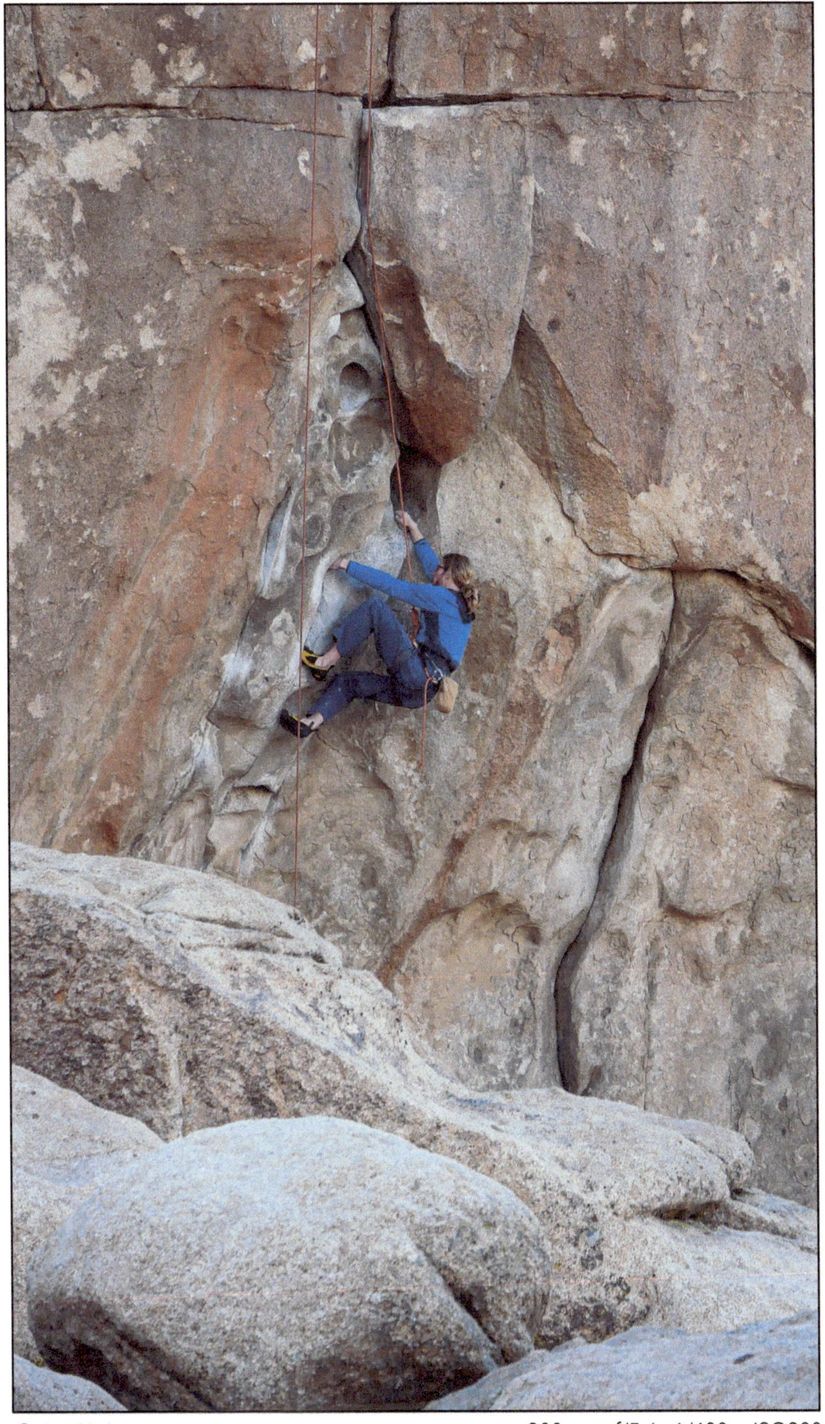

Going Up! 200mm f/5.6 1/400s ISO200

Sunrise, Sunset, and the Golden Hours

In the Introduction (page 16), I made two brief statements regarding lighting within the park, and which times are best. I would like to explore that a bit further, because "conventional" daytime landscape photography wisdom seems to work here only somewhat.

Sunrise

Sunrise within Joshua Tree National Park seems to come with little warning. Of course, we can find the precise time that the sun will rise for any day of the year, but most morning skies are clear and so the color is spread broadly across the eastern sky. Pre-sunrise light is also quite bright, so capturing its color essence along with any foreground still in the dark is problematic. Use of graduated neutral density filters helps little.

The very best place within the park to utilize sunrise (shooting easterly) is at Cholla Cactus Garden (31). I provide detail on this site within its writeup on page 120.

Otherwise, the rising sun elsewhere is used for illumination of subjects to your west. The most typical one being San Gorgonio Mountain, such as seen from High View (1).

Sunset

Sunset is my favorite time to work within the park, hands down. I might opt-out of sunrise work (especially if after a prior *night* within the park), but I never miss sunset.

The colors are often more sensational, usually with interesting clouds creating texture and depth. Its benefit is its predictability –

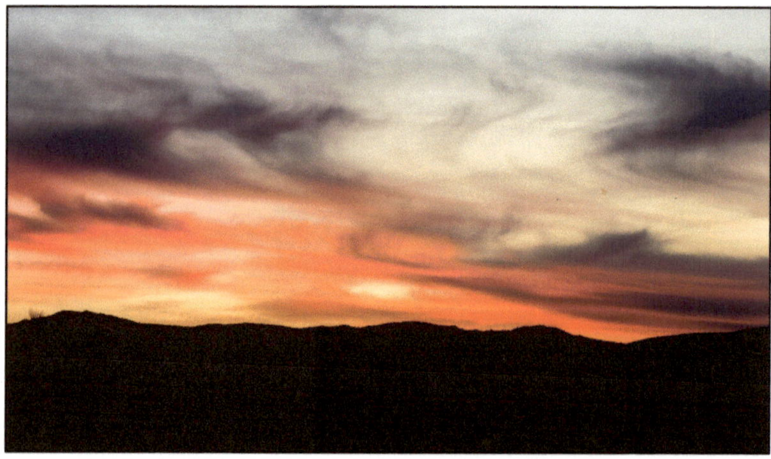

Western Sky (from the Hidden Valley Picnic Area)   135mm f/4 1/125s ISO200

as the sun makes its way towards the horizon, you can gauge its trajectory and exactly where it will slip away.

The western sky continues its show up to 30 minutes or more after the sun has disappeared. That's ample amount of time to walk around and try different compositions and camera settings.

Keys View (19), Ryan Mountain (22), and again at Cholla Cactus Garden are at the top of the list of the 35 "sites" to compose into the setting sun.

There is another option, that may be even more enjoyable, and that is what I call **Sunset Silhouettes**. The "trick" here is to rid your background of any profile that impedes direct view of the colorful sky. There are two places in the park that work especially well for this: 1) Just west of the entrance to Jumbo Rocks along Park Boulevard, and 2) in and around the parking loop at the Hidden Valley Picnic Area.

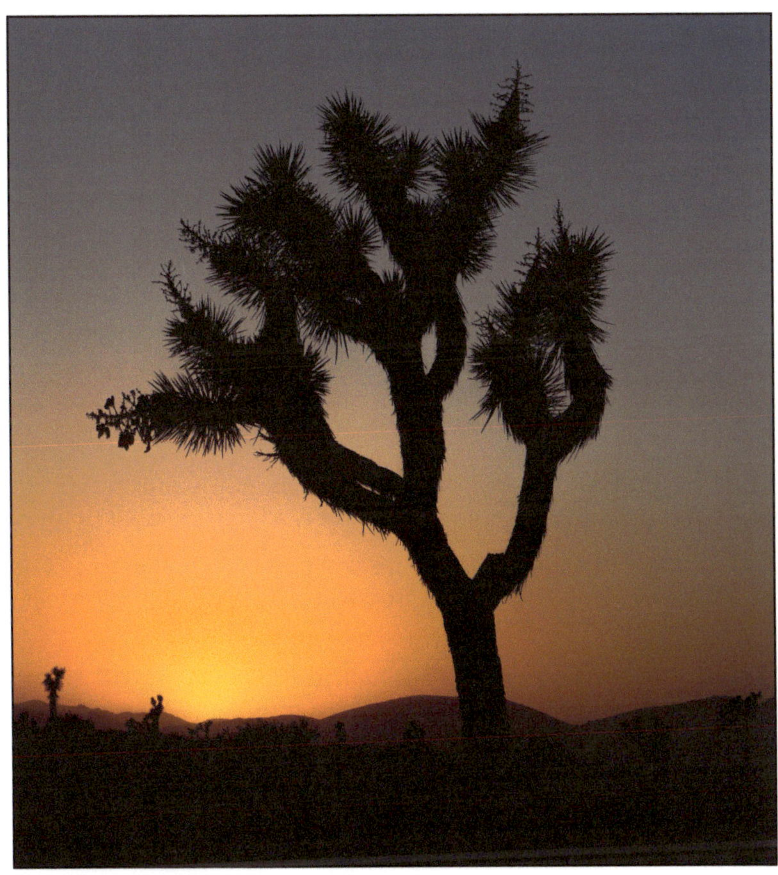

Sunset and Joshua Tree (near Jumbo Rocks)   100mm f/8 1/1000s ISO100

Golden Hours

The "Golden Hour" refers to the usual golden-hued, soft light that comes about an hour after sunrise and again about an hour before sunset. So really there are two "Golden Hours" in the day, yes? It's not only golden for its light hue, but generally also for the great results we landscape photographers achieve within this time.

Unfortunately, **the Golden Hour after sunrise in Joshua Tree is problematic**. I have seeked a scientific explanation for this but still am without one. The light during this time is extremely bright and tends to wash everything out within its path.

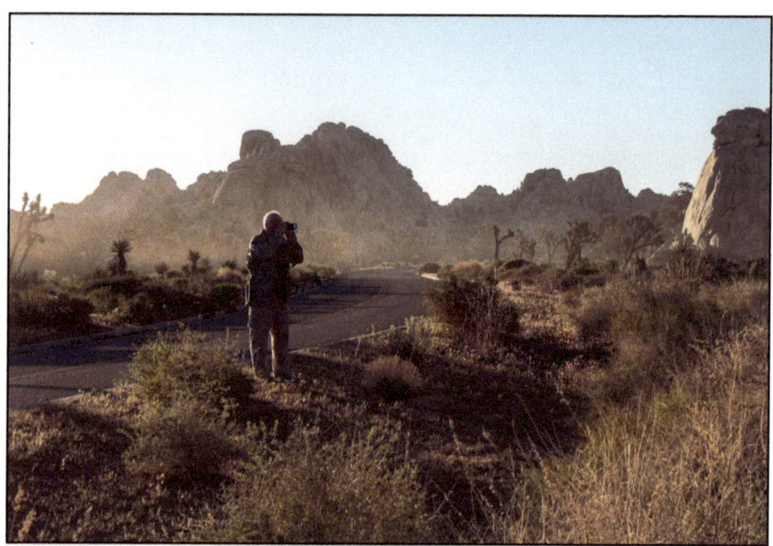

Morning Golden Hour (near Quail Springs)   50mm f/8 1/320s ISO200

You can see in the above how intensely-lit the rock face is on the right. It is not workable, unless this is a look you are going for.

Contrary, **the Golden Hour before sunset is marvelous**. Rejoice! It is as you would expect, producing desirable, soft light on rock surfaces.

Whether it be the challenging sunrises or the intense light at the morning Golden Hour, creativity trumps all "practical" advice provided here. If you have a photography vision or concept and see a need for these conditions, then pursue it wholeheartedly!

One final piece of advice for any sunrise or sunset, anywhere you are... Adjust your exposure compensation to -2 stops on your camera. This will help better capture the bold colors in the sky.

The Milky Way

Joshua Tree is a popular location for Milky Way photography, though all aspects of it can be a lengthy topic. If we covered this entirely, another 20 pages or so would be required. What I aim to do here is provide the core elements for you to pursue it with success, although some additional research will likely be required, perhaps especially on post-processing your photos in your "digital darkroom." (If shot properly, your camera is recording more detail and color information than your eye can perceive, but it does require some coaxing afterwards on your computer to achieve the results we typically see produced here and elsewhere.)

Let's get right to these key items…

Months & Time of Night

For the more "vertical" orientation of the Milky Way from within Joshua Tree, we can photograph it May, June, and July. These are the *approximate* times we can expect for it to be vertical in the sky:

May	June	July
2-4am	Midnight-2am	10pm-Midnight

We can infer why August didn't make the list. The sky is still bright between 8-10pm. It is not impossible, but it is more challenging.

The Moon & Clouds

The moon plays a key role in successful Milky Way photography. In short, you do **not** wish its brightness in the night sky. A new moon, or very close to new, is preferred. You can find its phase, rise, and set times for the dates you are interested in online.

Clouds… This one is obvious. They are undesirable.

Direction & Location

The Milky Way is on the south horizon. As it appears to "stand" to vertical due to Earth's rotation, it moves slightly southwest.

Seeking-out viable locations within the park for Milky Way photography is key. This is not just about location, but also composition. **Photographing only the night sky is boring. Some foreground is a must!** Search for locations with a foreground to artificially light or as a silhouette. But remember, you are looking for a composition generally facing south and one with a lower horizon so as minimize how much lower portion of the Milky Way is blocked.

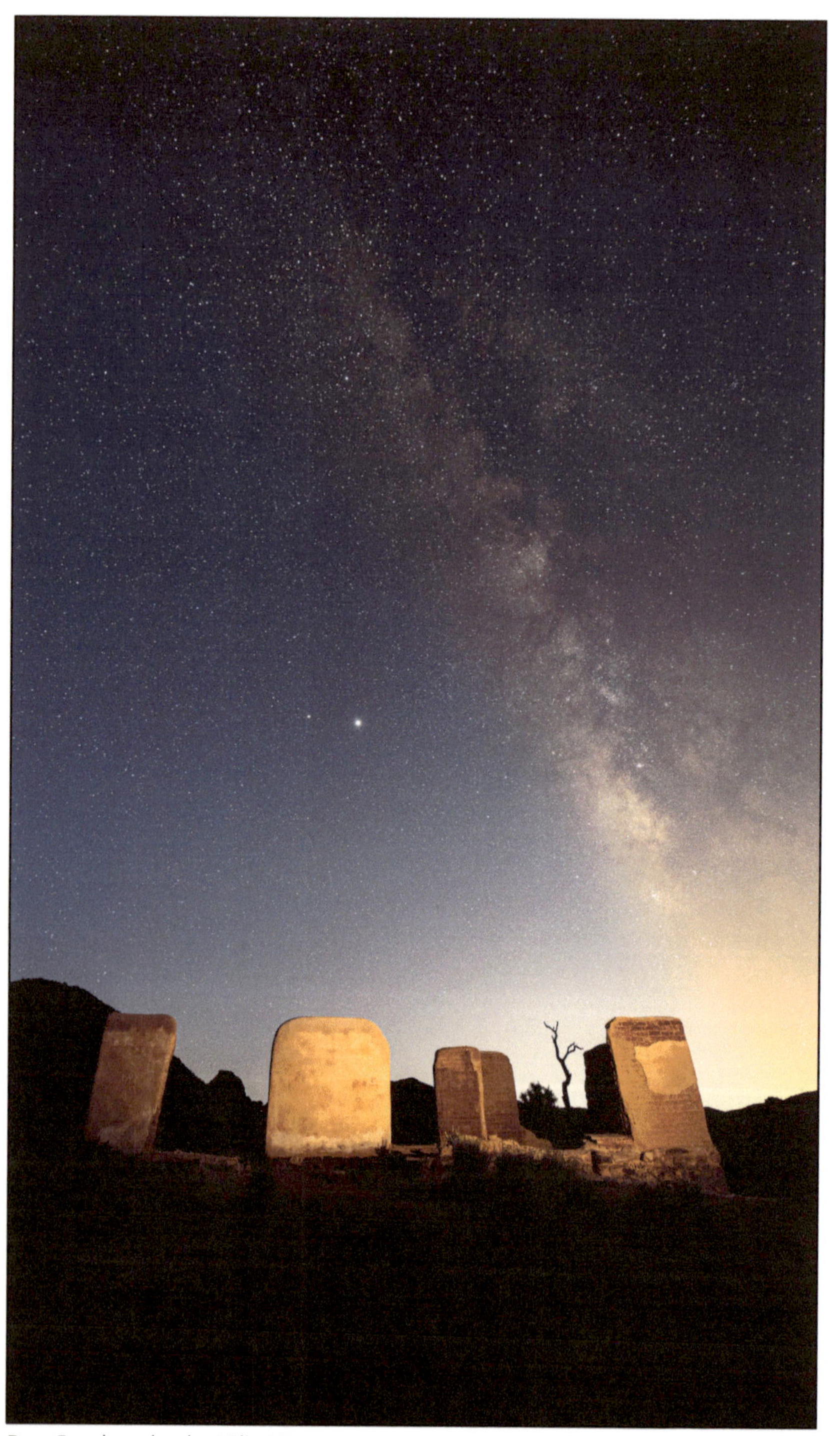

Ryan Ranch under the Milky Way

15mm f/2.8 20s ISO1600

Equipment & Settings

Some sort of rigid camera support is mandatory. I recommend a tripod. A headlamp or flashlight also helps immensely.

Lens selection... If you have the option, a fast wide angle is best. By "fast," I mean f/1.4-f/2.8. And by wide angle, 24mm or wider. You can use a slower lens; it just means there will be some compromises to ISO and shutter speed. This is all a bit subjective, so if you have multiple lens options, try each of them out, and learn their strengths and weaknesses for this work.

Here, perhaps, is the hardest part... You're going to need to manually focus your lens to infinity and leave it there. Leaving autofocus turned on is the best way to a very frustrating evening. It just won't work. So, illuminate something in the distance, lock-in focus, and leave it there. (Hopefully your lens has a focus window, and if it does check the lens' setting occasionally, to ensure it hasn't moved.) Warning!: If you are using a zoom lens for this, you cannot zoom in or out after you have set focus. Focus is only set for a particular focal length. So if you're using a zoom, be careful of this as well.

Alright, we're getting close... Compose your shot, as best you can. This can be difficult sometimes, depending on how dark it is. If after you take some shots, you can make some alignment and positioning adjustments.

Set your camera body to Manual mode, and now we need a starting point... The following table lists some near-equivalent options.

Aperture	f/1.4	f/1.8 or f/2	f/2.8	f/3.5 or f/4
ISO	1600	2000	3200	6400
Shutter Speed	15 sec	20 sec	30 sec	30 sec

Post-Processing

You're 2/3 of the way there – you found the right time & place and also have captured "the" photo. The remaining 1/3 happens on your computer. The mandatory corrections are as follow: Adjust white balance for desired night sky color. Fine tune exposure. Increase contrast and sharpness. Finally, add a decent amount of saturation to the Milky Way area of the sky alone.

– Trial & error required. This is a "learn by doing" activity. –

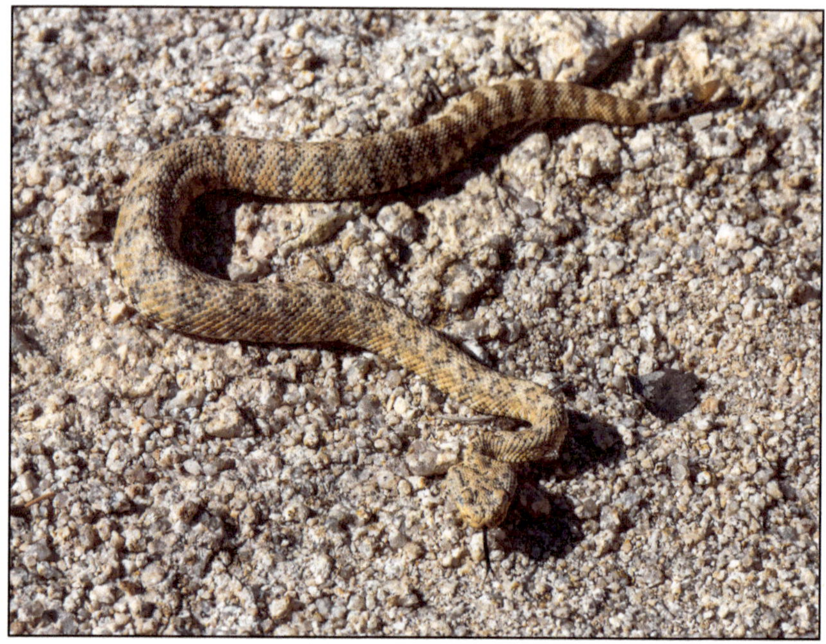

Juvenile Southwestern Speckled Rattlesnake   200mm f/11 1/2000s ISO400

If that's not an attention-getter, I don't know what is! I nearly stepped onto this snake while hiking Wonderland Wash (15). I slowly backed up to a safe distance, retrieved my camera, and made my best effort with "snake portraiture."

My "fortune" with wildlife encounters at Joshua Tree has been mixed. Having conversed with area locals and other visitors, it seems that this experience is typical. We all agree – luck plays the main role in what creatures you will come across during your visit.

Bighorn Sheep

There are three areas within the park where Bighorn Sheep are most prominent...

1. Along the hillside and in the wash adjacent to the West Entrance Station.

2. In the Wonderland of Rocks, especially at Barker Dam (14).

3. In the wash of Cottonwood Canyon, which is along Cottonwood Springs Road (the south stretch of Pinto Basin Road), between the Cottonwood Visitor Center and the Bajada Nature Trail.

Desert Tortoise

The Desert Tortoise excels at camouflage, for those of us casually scanning our surroundings. They are elusive while remaining in their natural habitat. Unfortunately, as they criss-cross these deserts, most Desert Tortoise encounters are on the road. Maintaining vehicle speed within the speed limit also helps ensure their safety when they are also on the road.

A higher probability area to spot one is again in the wash in Cottonwood Canyon adjacent to Cottonwood Springs Road. The Desert Tortoise also will trek and burrow uphill somewhat, under rocks.

Very many species of reptiles, amphibians, birds, mammals, insects, and spiders are found throughout Joshua Tree. Do keep an eye out. Also keep your camera ready while in the car, and have your telephoto lens mounted and other camera settings ready, so that if the opportunity presents itself, you're not wasting time getting your camera ready for the shot.

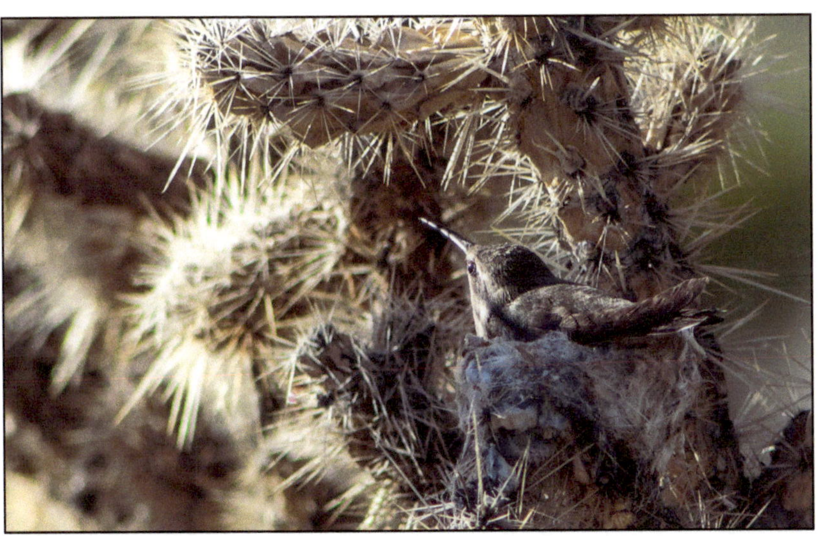

Hummingbird (near Barker Dam) 400mm f/6.3 1/1250s ISO400

Capture vs. Final

When capturing an image, I pay close attention to its histogram, and I encourage you to as well. (Go research this topic if necessary.) None of the photographs in this book are "straight from the camera." But then again, none have what some might call "voodoo" applied either. Just basic adjustments to shadows, highlights, saturation, contrast, etc. – to mimic, as best I can, what I remember seeing.

Wait, what's this? This wasn't in the Table of Contents!

I have a few of these throughout the book… Offbeat topics, usually that can apply anywhere – maybe even beyond Joshua Tree National Park. They're "just for fun."

Here we have a witty alternative to a traditional self-portrait. (I'm not wild about self-portraits, but I recognize that occasionally it's fitting to reflect that you were actually there!)

Joshua Tree has an abundance of "Exhibit Ahead" signs throughout the park. Why not make yourself and your entourage a park exhibit!

Here, my stepfather and I were on our way out of the park when inspiration struck. This was taken on Pinto Basin Road near the entrance to Stirrup Tank Road (just southeast of White Tank). His camera and tripod are in the foreground; mine was doing the work for the photo below. I had quite a 10-second run between starting the timer and standing in place!

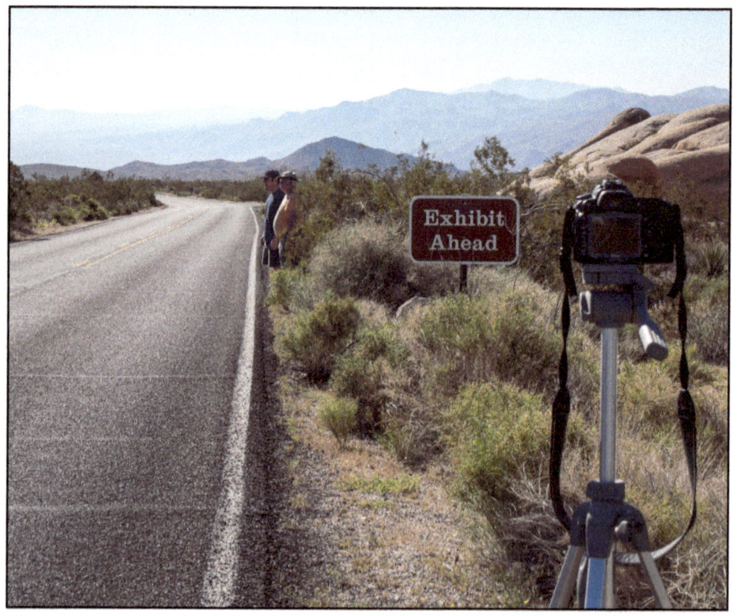

Photographers on Exhibit   50mm f/16 1/200s ISO200

It's nothing sensational, but it was fun and made for a good memory between us.

Do be careful with traffic!

Black Rock

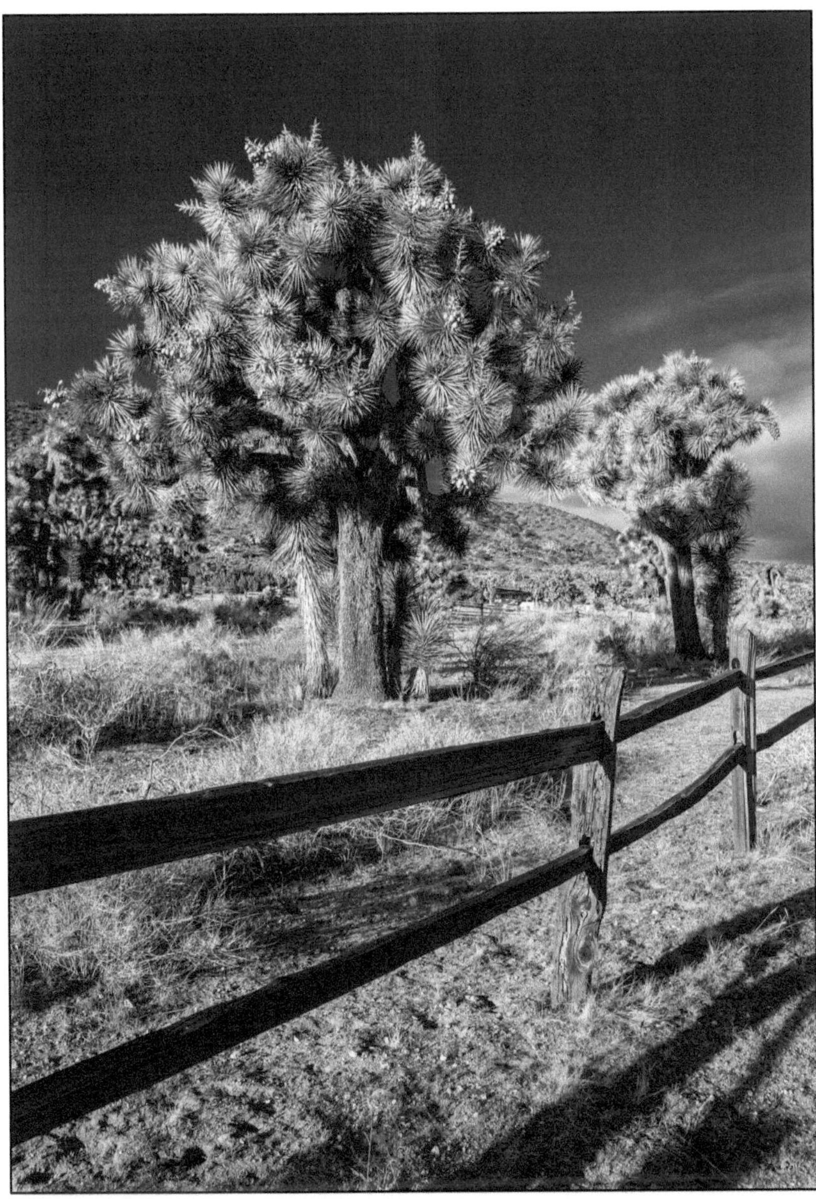

Black Rock Entrance   35mm f/11 1/80s ISO100

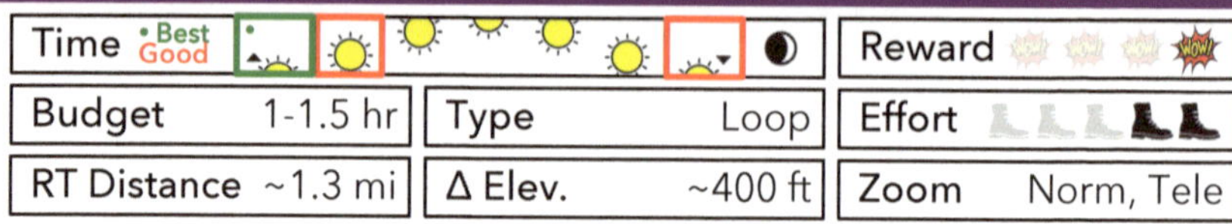

The High View Nature Trail is a great sunrise destination 1) if you're staying in nearby Yucca Valley or the town of Joshua Tree, or 2) if you want something a little different than what lies inside the central park area. I say this, because Joshua Tree National Park is as I see it primarily best-lit in the afternoon into the evening and beyond, so sleep becomes paramount at some point! High View requires a short drive and a short hike, so waking early for sunrise isn't "as early" as other sites may dictate (such as for Cholla Cactus Garden [31]).

South of Yucca Valley, follow signage/directions to the Black Rock Campground. Once facing the campground entrance, turn right (to head west) and follow an unpaved road to its end, the parking area for High View Nature Trail.

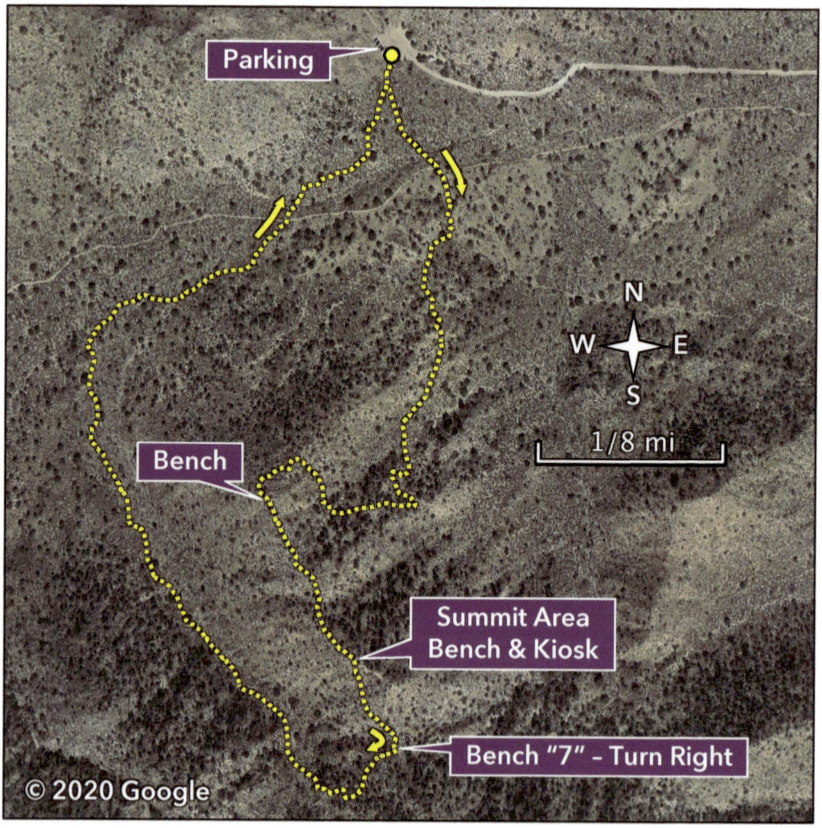

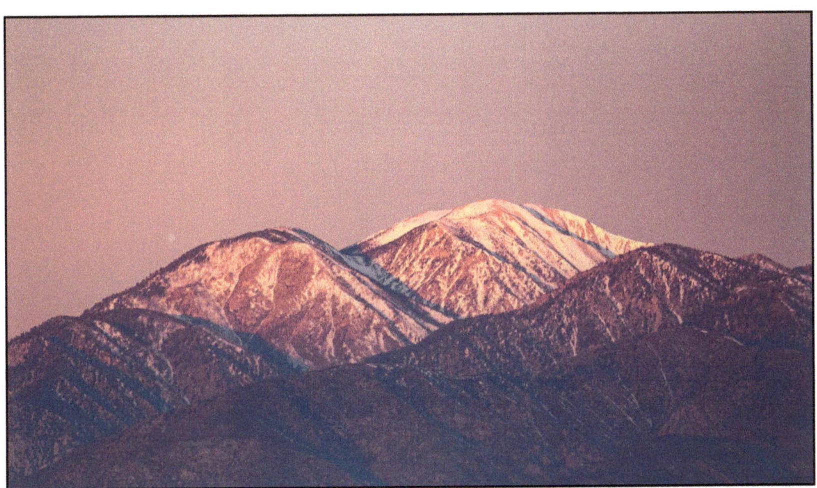

Alpenglow on San Gorgonio Mountain   300mm f/4.5 1/320s ISO400

Pace for first light on San Gorgonio Mountain at the route's summit, which may take between 20-40 minutes of hiking. Enjoy the sunrise and warming from the light. Once ready to continue on, descend to the backside of this hilltop and loop northerly back towards the beginning. Near the end, there are Joshua Trees (albeit sparse) fit for photography, especially with the now brighter-lit San Gorgonio in the distance.

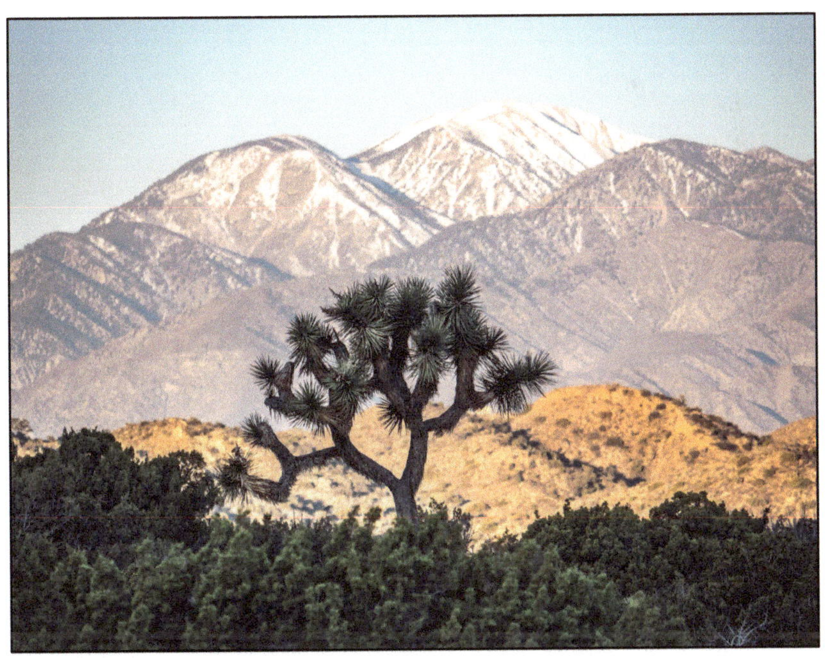

Joshua Tree & Mountain (near Trail Marker "19")   350mm f/8 1/400s ISO200

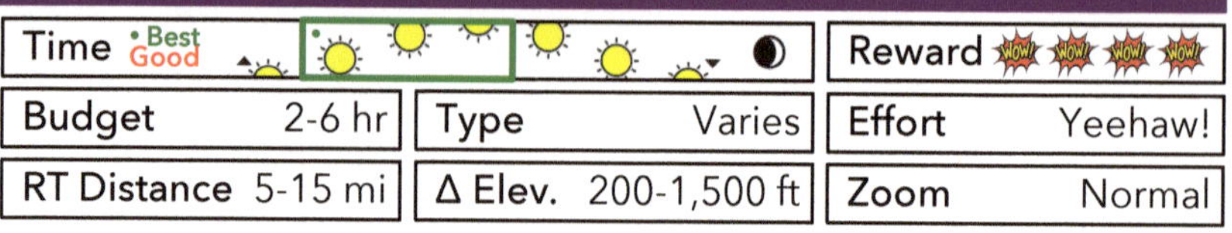

Time	Best / Good		Reward	WOW! WOW! WOW! WOW!
Budget	2-6 hr	Type	Varies	Effort Yeehaw!
RT Distance	5-15 mi	Δ Elev.	200-1,500 ft	Zoom Normal

I am very excited to share this horseback and photography experience with you. I wholeheartedly recommend it if you're looking to add some variety to your Joshua Tree visit. It is my favorite way to explore the unique Black Rock area.

Multiple outfitters (including guides) are in and around Yucca Valley. Perhaps the fastest way to find them on the Internet is to simply search for "Joshua Tree National Park Horseback Riding." While some outfitters present their options on routes and duration online, others you will have to email, call, or text. Short, 90-minute rides are available, all the way to full day excursions. Individual, small group, and large group options are offered.

A better understanding of the Black Rock area trails will help in your decision-making. A map created by the National Park Service is provided on pages 50-51.

Since there are so many options available, I believe my best advice is to provide some variables to consider, and therefore questions you may ask yourself or the outfitters whom you will be contacting…

- How long of a ride (in hours) are you interested in? *Do not forget that your body will be using muscles unaccustomed to this activity.*

- What is your skillset on horseback? *Consider the following:*

  ▸ Beginner – No riding experience to some riding experience on a horse or mule.

  ▸ Intermediate – Riding experience, likely having received instruction, and know how to attach a saddle to a horse.

  ▸ Advanced – Riding regularly and all five gaits on a horse.

- How focused on "photography" do you want to be on your ride? *While horseback, I prefer to leave the "big" cameras behind and enjoy the experience with either a point-and-shoot and/or phone camera. Communicate your photography desire (big equipment or small) with your guide beforehand.*

- Do you prefer a private and customizable experience, or would riding with others be acceptable (or even preferred!)?

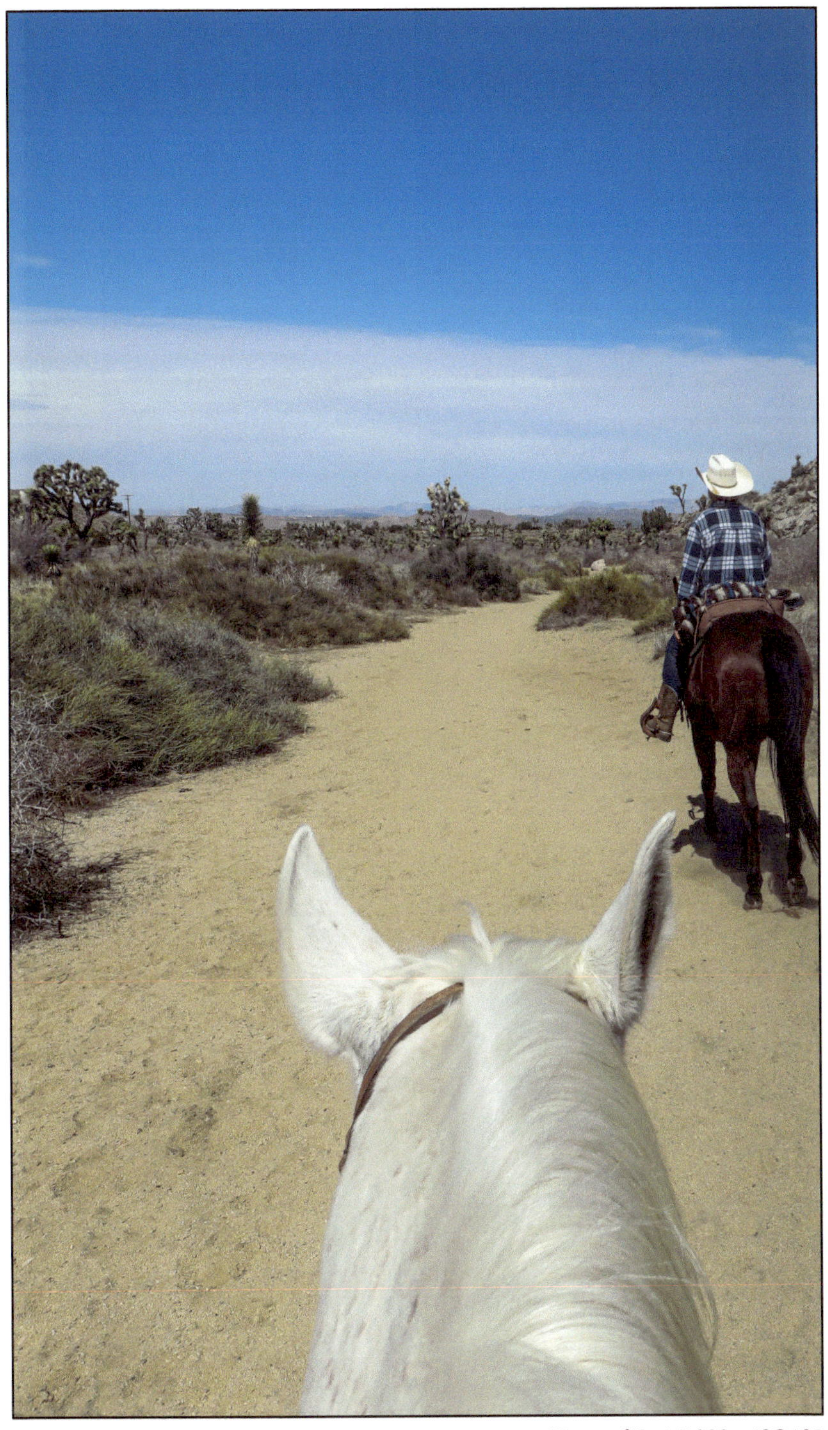

In the Saddle   28mm f/8 1/1000s ISO125

Eureka Peak Hike

(9.6 miles roundtrip) Leave from the backcountry registration board and hike along the California Riding and Hiking Trail. Head south on Fault Trail to the Eureka Peak Trail. Return via the Burnt Hill Trail. (moderately strenuous)

Burnt Hill Trail Hike

(7.3 miles roundtrip) Leave from the backcountry registration board and hike south on Black Rock Canyon Trail. Turn left at the Burnt Hill Trail sign. Return via Eureka Peak Trail, Fault Trail, and California Riding & Hiking Trail. Alternately, depart from site #30 via Black Rock Canyon Trail. (modernately strenuous)

Short Loop Hike

(3.9 miles roundtrip) Leave from the backcountry registration board and hike along the California Riding and Hiking Trail. Head south on the Fault Trail and join up with the Short Loop Trail. Short Loop connects to Black Rock Canyon Trail, which will lead you back to the backcountry registration board.

California Riding and Hiking Trail

(37 miles one-way) From the backcountry registration board, the trail runs across the park to Covington Flats, Ryan Campground, Twin Tanks backcountry board, and on to the entrance station at Twentynine Palms.

Trail Regulations

- Bicycles are not allowed on trails.

- Dogs are not allowed on trails or in the backcountry.

- Horses are not allowed on the Hi-View Nature Trail and may not travel crosscountry except in open active washes.

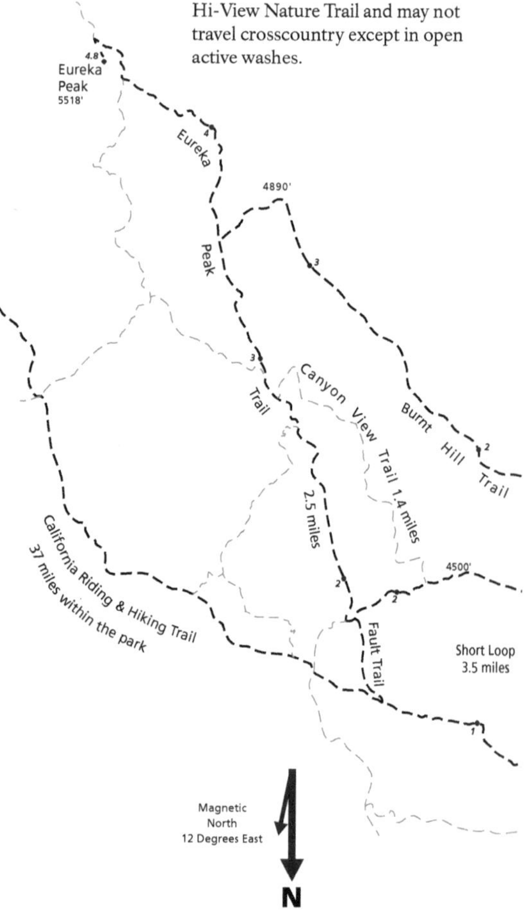

Please note: this map is depicted "upside down."

Trails

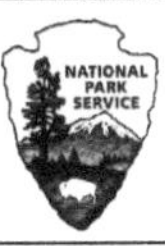

Trail Markers
BH – Burnt Hill
BR – Black Rock Canyon
CRH – California Riding & Hiking
EP – Eureka Peak
FT – Fault Trail
PL – Panorama Loop
SL – Short Loop
WP – Warren Peak
WV – Warren View
WS – West Side Loop

Panorama Loop Hike
(6.6 miles roundtrip) Leave from the backcountry registration board and hike south on Black Rock Canyon Trail. The first turn will take you up the steepest part of the loop. Alternately, begin at site #30 and follow the trail markers to Black Rock Canyon Trail. Turn right into the wash, heading south. (moderately strenuous)

Warren Peak and Warren View
(6.3 miles roundtrip) Leave from the backcountry registration board and hike south in Black Rock Canyon Trail. The trail will fork left to Warren View and right to Warren Peak. (moderately strenuous)

West Side Loop Hike
(5 miles roundtrip) Leave from the High View Nature Trail connector, west of the nature center between sites 20 and 21. At the junction follow signs for West Side Loop, or start from the High View Nature Trail parking area. (moderate)

Hi-View Nature Trail
(1.3 miles roundtrip) Take the road west from the entrance of the campground, past the horse camp and the water tank, to the parking area at the end of the road. (moderate)

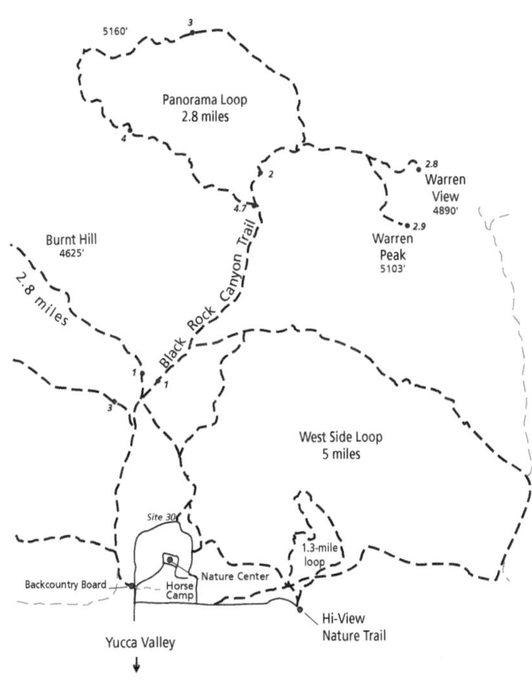

At time of writing, this map available online at:
www.nps.gov/jotr/planyourvisit/upload/BlackRockTrails.pdf

As I mentioned before, my advice is to take along either a point-and-shoot or simply use your phone's camera. Either should be tethered to your body. I prefer a point-and-shoot coupled to a shoulder strap, but hung over my head and one shoulder for a secure fit.

Shoulder bags & backpacks and horseback riding normally do not mix, for weight distribution (center of gravity) and rider safety. If carrying larger equipment is desired, stowage in a saddle bag will likely be required. Inquire with your guide if this remains of interest.

Your guide's priorities are safety, your enjoyment riding & sightseeing, and pace. Be competent and efficient in your handling of your camera. Practice with one hand how you will use your camera before you arrive for your horseback ride.

The photography along the way is straightforward. Listen to your guide for the area's interesting features and information. When appropriate, ask for time to stop and take photos.

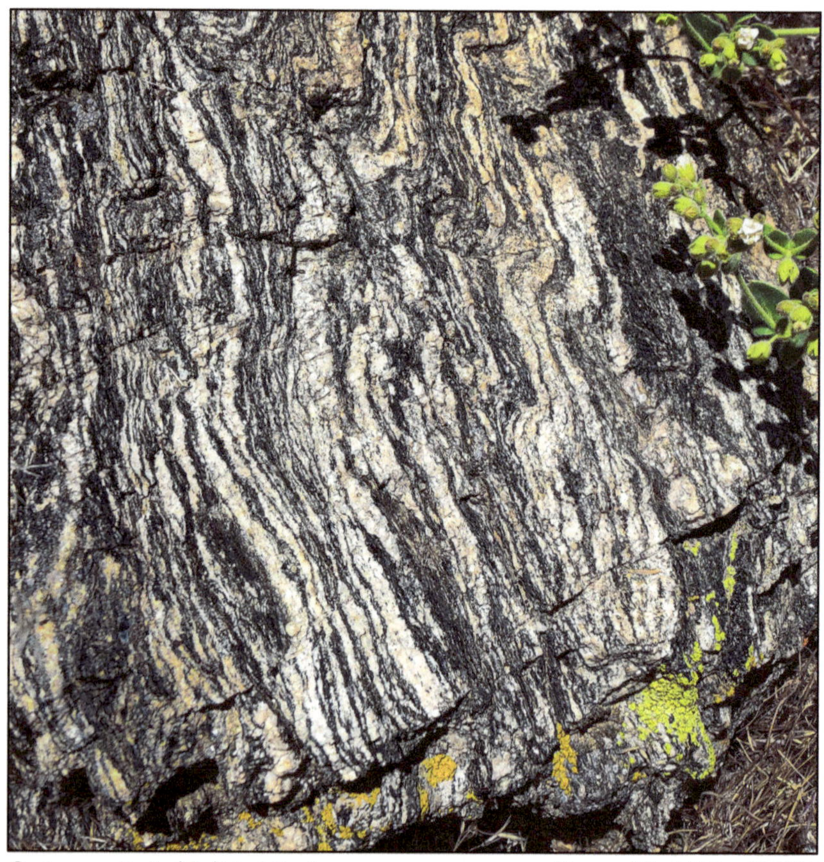

Cretaceous Period Foliated Gneiss

50mm f/8 1/640s ISO100

Time	Best Good ☀☀☀☀☀ ●	Reward 💥💥 **WOW! WOW!**
Budget 2-2.5 hr	**Type** Out & Back	**Effort** 🛻 + 🥾
RT Distance ~18 mi	**Δ Elev.** ~1,700 ft	**Zoom** Wide, Tele

Right on the footsteps (or maybe the hoofprints!) of the prior narrative, here is another "non-hiking" opportunity, now in the far southeastern section of the greater Black Rock area.

This route is 98% behind the wheel, and only 2% hiking (1,500 ft round trip, ~70 ft elevation gain) from the parking area to the vista at Eureka Peak. While I have not *yet* needed 4WD on these roads, I recommend a vehicle with additional ground clearance and capable of traction in loose sand. A sedan or sports car would not fare well.

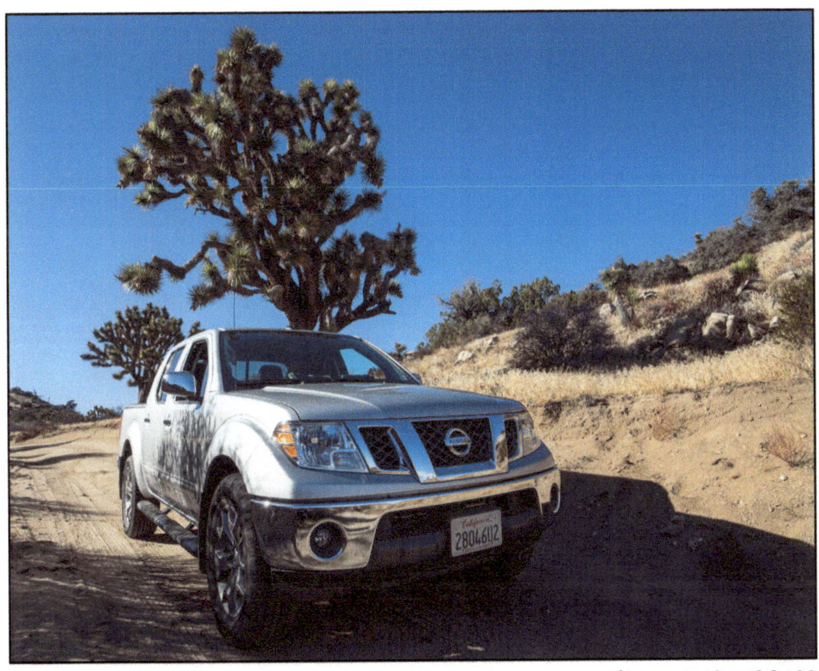

Coming Back Down (on Upper Covington Flat Road)   17mm f/11 1/160s ISO100

For safety's sake, I also would discourage a sunset or nighttime trip. This area is remote, and any vehicle problems late in the day could result in being stranded overnight. Daytime travel is wise.

With either your National Park Service map or your National Geographic "Trails Unlimited" map of Joshua Tree in tow, head south from Yucca Valley on La Contenta Road, to a brown sign directing you to veer left for the "Covington Flats Area." Zero your trip odometer here. Lower Covington Flat Road (aka Vermiculate Mine Road) begins its way southeast, to the national park boundary (1.6-mile). Continue straight, to the right of the national park sign. At 3.0-mile the main road bends hard right at a smaller, gated road straight ahead. *You know you chose correctly when at 3.2-mile the road bends hard left.*

At 5.9-mile reach a fork in the road. Take Covington Flats Crossover Road, the road to your right. Enjoy the slightly steeper grade, as you now head southwest.

Continue to 7.8-mile where you turn right onto Upper Covington Flat Road. The road becomes more challenging… It is time to slow your vehicle's speed substantially. The Joshua Trees also suddenly become quite large! At 9.1-mile you reach the parking area at the end. The hiking trail to Eureka Peak heads north.

Either the parking area or the vista make for a splendid location for a picnic lunch. From the vista, spin around and around to take in the 360° panorama. Photography here is typically not remarkable, but the whole Covington Flats "driving" experience is enjoyable. Let your photos capture the memory.

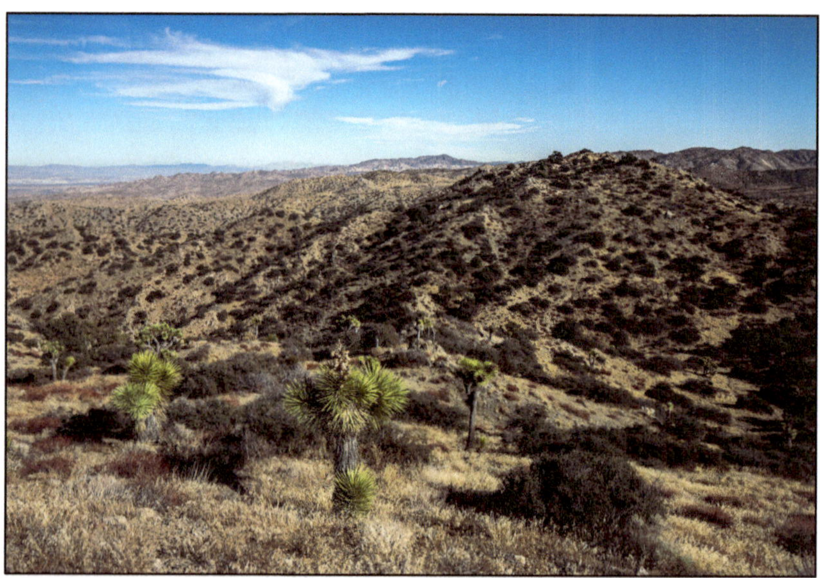

East towards the Wonderland of Rocks   28mm f/11 1/200s ISO100

Once satisfied with the views from this high-up perch, backtrack your steps to your vehicle and follow the same roads in return to Yucca Valley.

Highway 62

Yucca Valley to Twentynine Palms

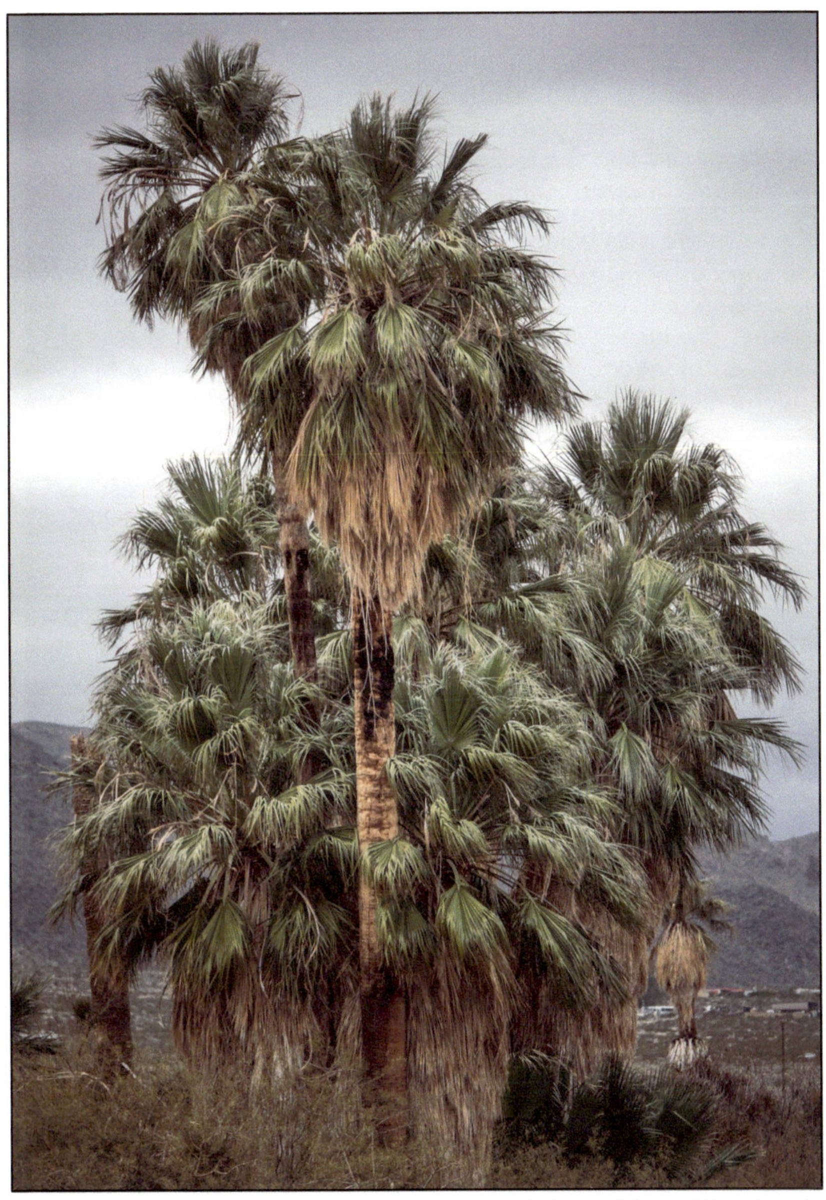

Oasis of Mara   200mm f/5.6 1/800s ISO400

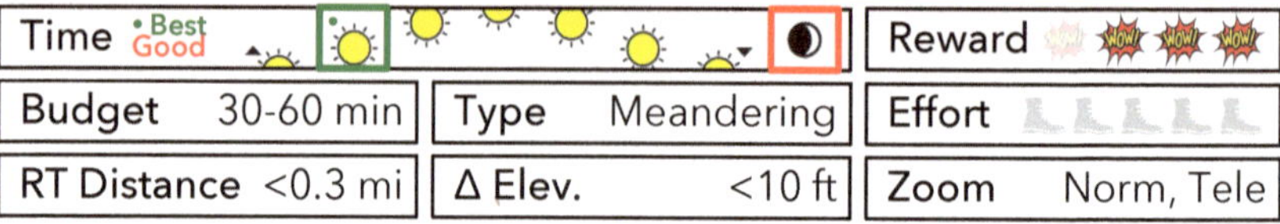

Time	Best Good		Reward	
Budget	30-60 min	**Type**	Meandering	**Effort**
RT Distance <0.3 mi		**Δ Elev.** <10 ft	**Zoom**	Norm, Tele

Pioneertown, an 1880's themed town, was constructed during the latter half of the 1940's as a *permanent* set for western films and television shows. Its main thoroughfare, known as "Mane Street" hosts an abundance of era structures, such as a saloon, jail, wash house, bank, post office, and many other interesting façades. Residents live and work in this area – this is no ghost town! Its "living" design was what made the concept unique at its inception.

The town site is an unincorporated community. Its land and buildings are owned by many private owners. An abundance of remarkable historic information, including the long list of films, shows, and videos produced in Pioneertown is available on the website **www.visitpioneertown.com**. The Mane Street Stampede, a wild west show, is performed regularly (when temperatures allow). More information on it may be found at **www.manestreetstampede.com**.

Pioneertown is a short side trip from Yucca Valley. If after visiting the national park for a few days and you're looking for an alternative side trip, this is a great one the area – definitely recommended.

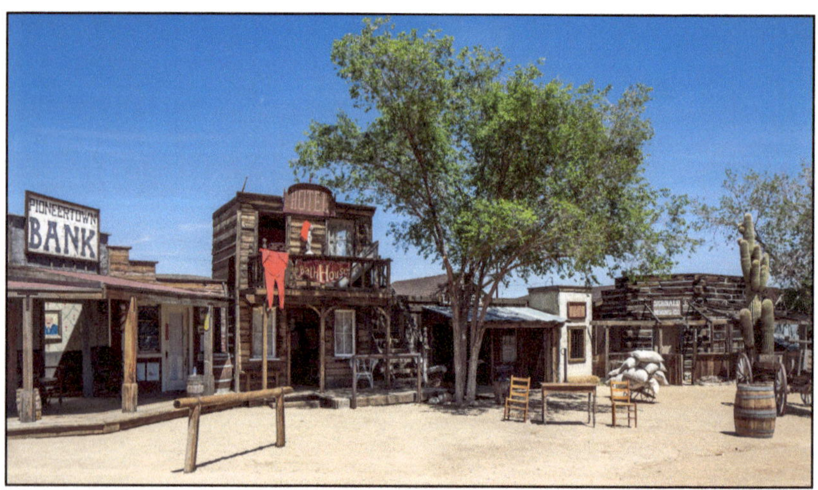

Pioneertown   28mm f/8 1/320s ISO100

From Highway 62 in Yucca Valley, turn north onto Pioneertown Road at an easily-identified, traffic signal intersection. The 4.4-mile drive heads north then west directly to Pioneertown. Find the beloved

Pappy and Harriet's restaurant and bar on your right and continue driving ~500 ft further to a large parking lot (also on your right).

I prefer morning visits to circumvent the crowds and also for softer lighting over the buildings and western details. I'll also usually follow a morning visit with a subsequent drive into the national park. Nighttime can be interesting too, with lighting on Mane Street. Consider refreshments and/or dinner at Pappy and Harriet's, followed by an evening stroll around the area.

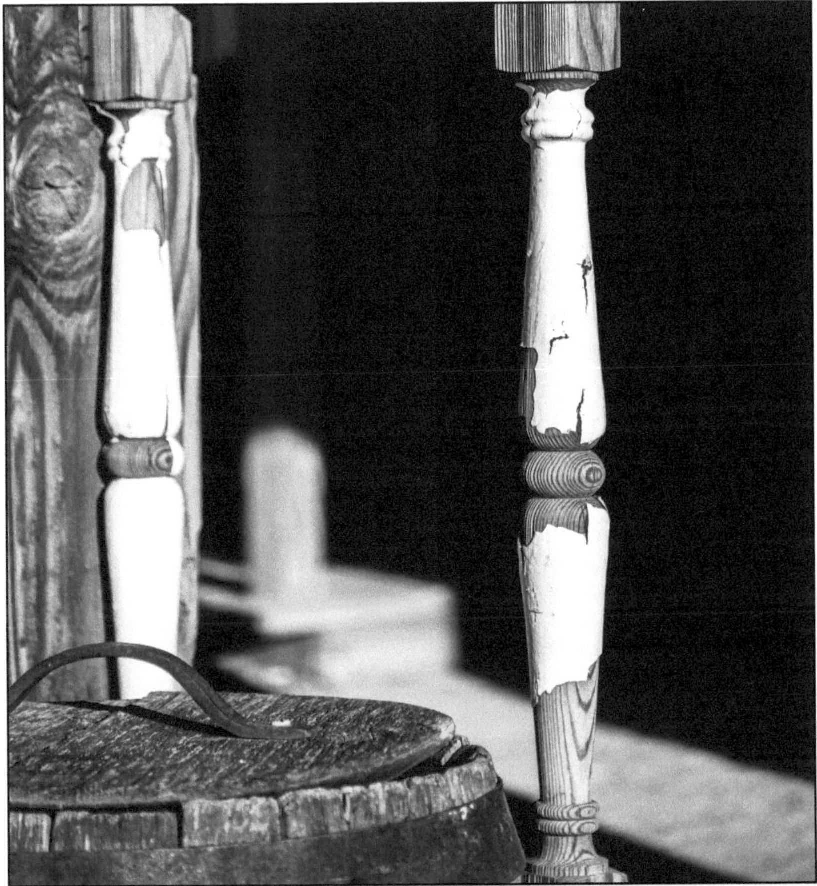

Front Porch Patina   200mm f/4 1/1250s ISO100

For photography, it is easy to compose the larger scene (as on the prior page) and also focus on the finer details. There are some power lines visible behind the northside buildings and some other "modern" era elements, so try to mask or camouflage these undesirable components for best results.

Want to take a group or self-portrait? Pioneertown is great for this too.

Time	Best · Good ☀☀☀☀☀☀ 🌑	Reward	WOW! WOW! WOW! WOW!
Budget	2-3 hr	Type	Out & Back	Effort	👢👢👢👢👢
RT Distance	~1.2 mi	Δ Elev.	~270 ft	Zoom	Wide, Tele

Rattlesnake Canyon is arguably as unique and rewarding as Barker Dam for your Joshua Tree National Park portfolio, but it is more difficult to access and with no formal trail. Albeit a short distance, route-finding and rock scrambling are required.

The prize? Small, eroded bowls of pooled water as it migrates down and out of the Wonderland of Rocks. This is a particularly light-shaded section of monzogranite rock, so its contrast with the colorful shades of water is delightful to see and photograph.

Regarding the technical effort on this hike… The granite here does not provide as much grip as elsewhere in the park, and when wet

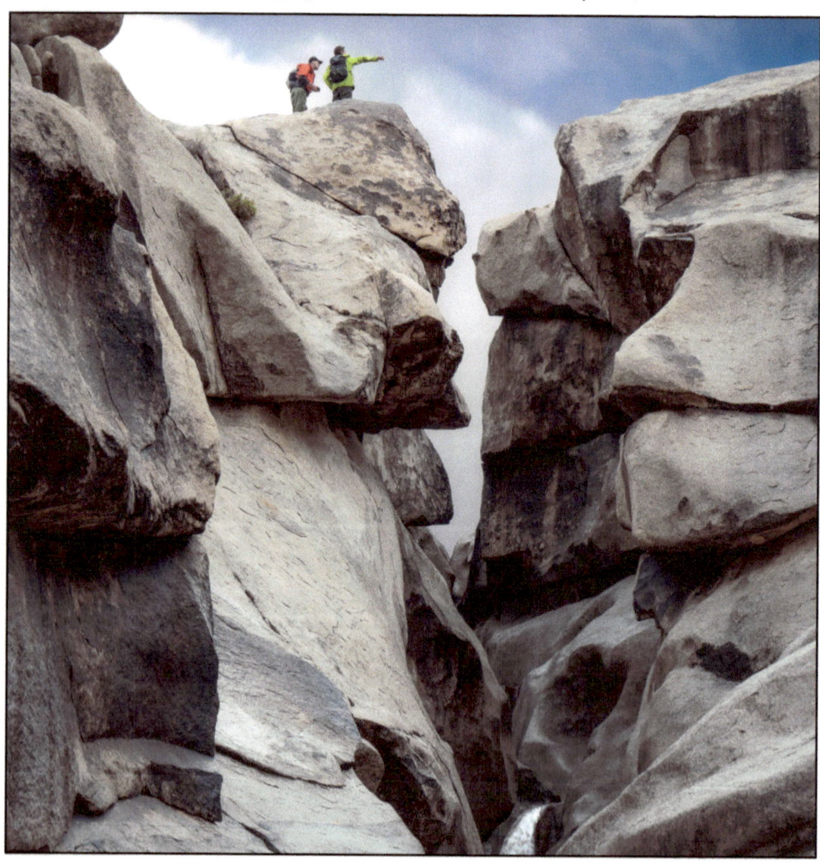

Low Clouds Approach Rattlesnake Canyon   100mm f/11 1/80s ISO400

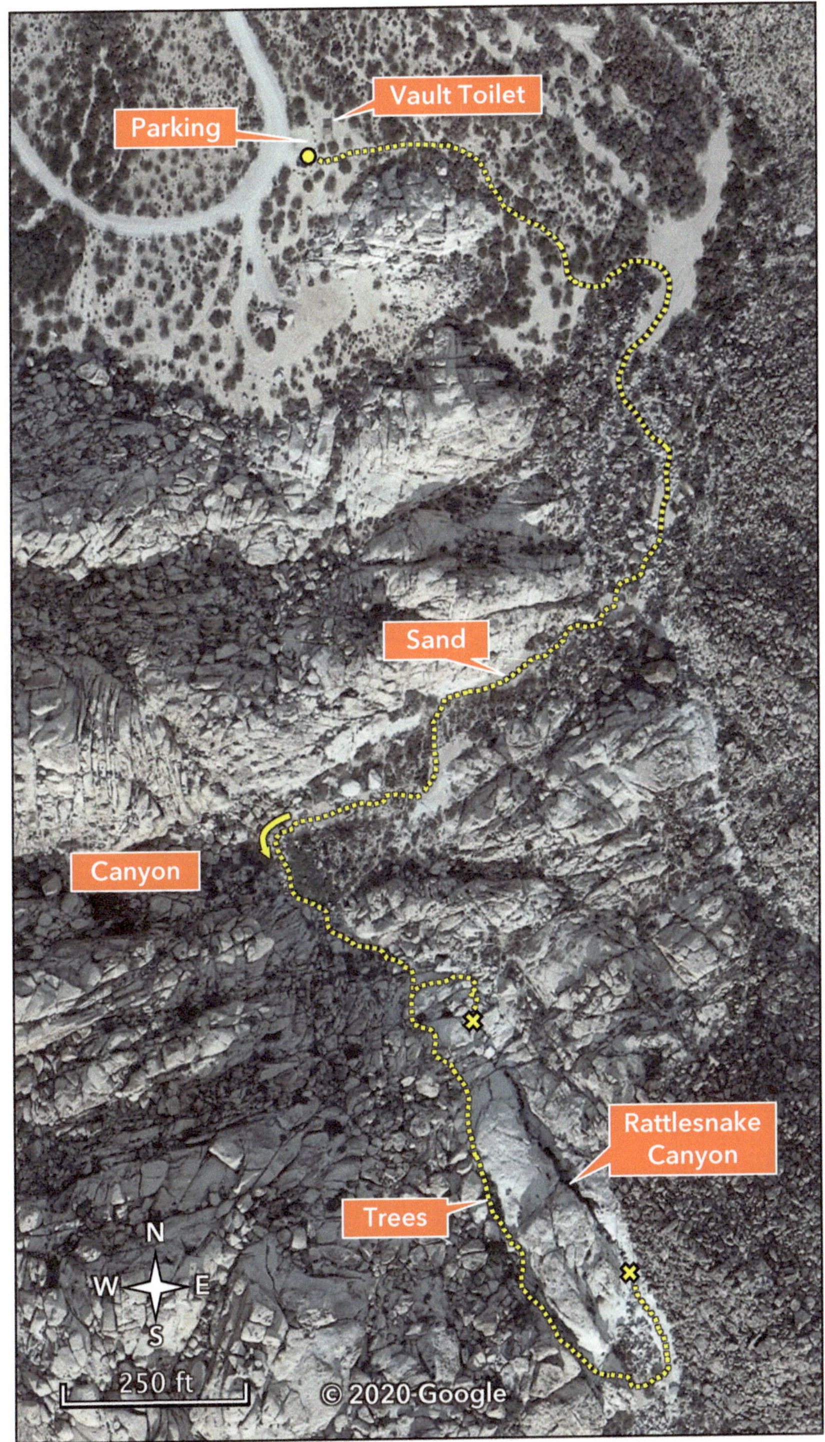
Parking
Vault Toilet
Sand
Canyon
Rattlesnake
Canyon
Trees
N
W
E
S
250 ft
© 2020 Google

can be dangerously slick when climbing. **Avoid this hike during wet conditions.** Climbing on "all fours" is at times required, once closer to the canyon. This route requires more technical competency and agility than all other sites in this book. Know your limit. It is never too late to turn around.

Rattlesnake Canyon is accessed from a picnic area east of the Indian Cove Campground. Signage to it is poor. Basically, once you arrive at the campground, bear left multiple times to exit the campground en route to this isolated picnic area. The "trail" begins adjacent to a vault toilet. Park here or nearby.

The route along the wash is straightforward. Head east towards the wash and begin following it south. As you do so, take note of the rock formation near where you started, to help later recognize your exit. Almost immediately you are confronted with rocks to scramble up, over, and around. At about 0.2-mile a wide, sandy opening welcomes you. At about 0.3-mile a duplicative canyon greets you... This is not your route. Here you bear left and continue to follow the wash. After another ~300 ft the route finally becomes less obvious.

Rattlesnake Canyon, pictured on page 58, should become evident. The best advice I have received and the best advice that I can provide to continue upward is along the far right side atop large, white boulders. Once over these boulders, there is a cluster of trees to walk through. Stay straight, and when possible curve left toward the accessible, weathered reliefs with pools of water.

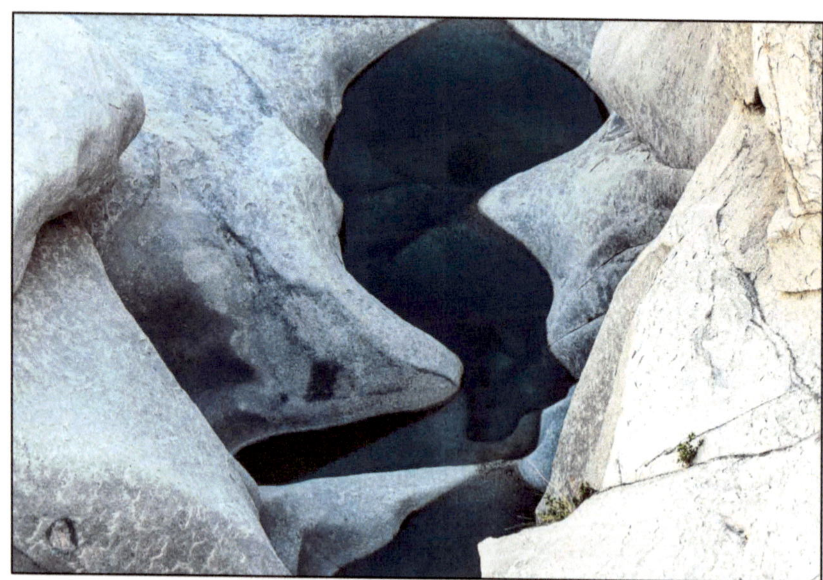

Colorful Pools and Wonderland Monzogranite   28mm f/16 1/80s ISO200

Explore this area but be careful! One time I was confronted by a Search & Rescue Team urging me not to work downcanyon, as hikers too regularly descend but cannot climb back out. Yikes!

Experiment with different angles, focal lengths, and various degrees of polarization (with your polarizing filter). One of my favorite features, not pictured here, are the black lines running through the white granite.

Once ready to head back, retrace your path back around, through the trees, and carefully down the same boulders you ascended. Now make your way over to the large boulders adjacent to pools of water at the bottom (exit) of the canyon and find multiple, short cascades of water. A telephoto focal length will be required to frame them, as they're still too distant to approach further. For best results, longer shutter speeds are required to smooth the water's flow.

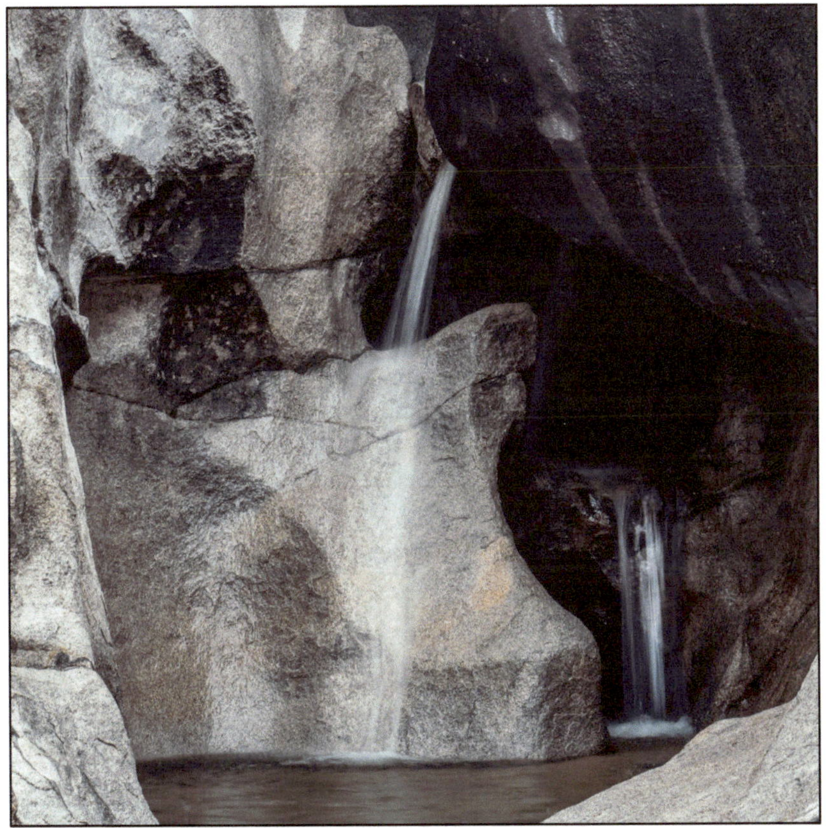

Final Plunge   135mm f/8 1/4s ISO200

That's it! Hike back and be on the lookout for that rock formation near the beginning to cue your exit.

Time	Best / Good		Reward	WOW! WOW! WOW! WOW!
Budget	2-3 hr	Type	Out & Back	Effort
RT Distance	~3.0 mi	Δ Elev.	~310 ft *	Zoom	Wide, Tele

* Significant elevation gain and loss. See elevation profile, page 129.

Tucked away in the desert not far from the city of Twentynine Palms, the Fortynine Palms Oasis is beautiful, with a dense cluster of California Fan Palms and pools of water. This is a popular hike, which means that it can be crowded. It also requires *in total* about 560 ft of climbing (round trip) under direct sun light. Arriving early is the best strategy to beat the crowd and the heat.

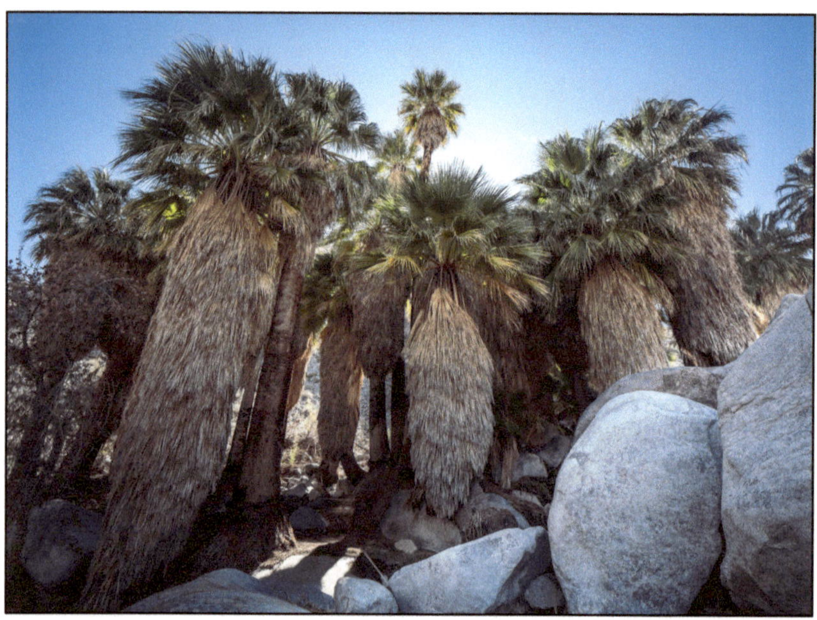

Fortynine Palms Oasis

18mm f/8 1/60s ISO100

The trail is clearly marked and easy to follow. Its steady ascent begins immediately. At 0.4-mile the trail makes a hard right turn. Here, to the left is a vista of Twentynine Palms and the Marine Corps Air Ground Combat Center. (No view here of our oasis destination.)

Continuing up, at 0.6-mile find another hard right on the main trail and another vista to your left. From this vista you can now see the Fortynine Palms Oasis. The composition is not extraordinary, and a telephoto lens is required, but it is worth a look and a picture to capture your approach. If you are hiking in the early morning, then

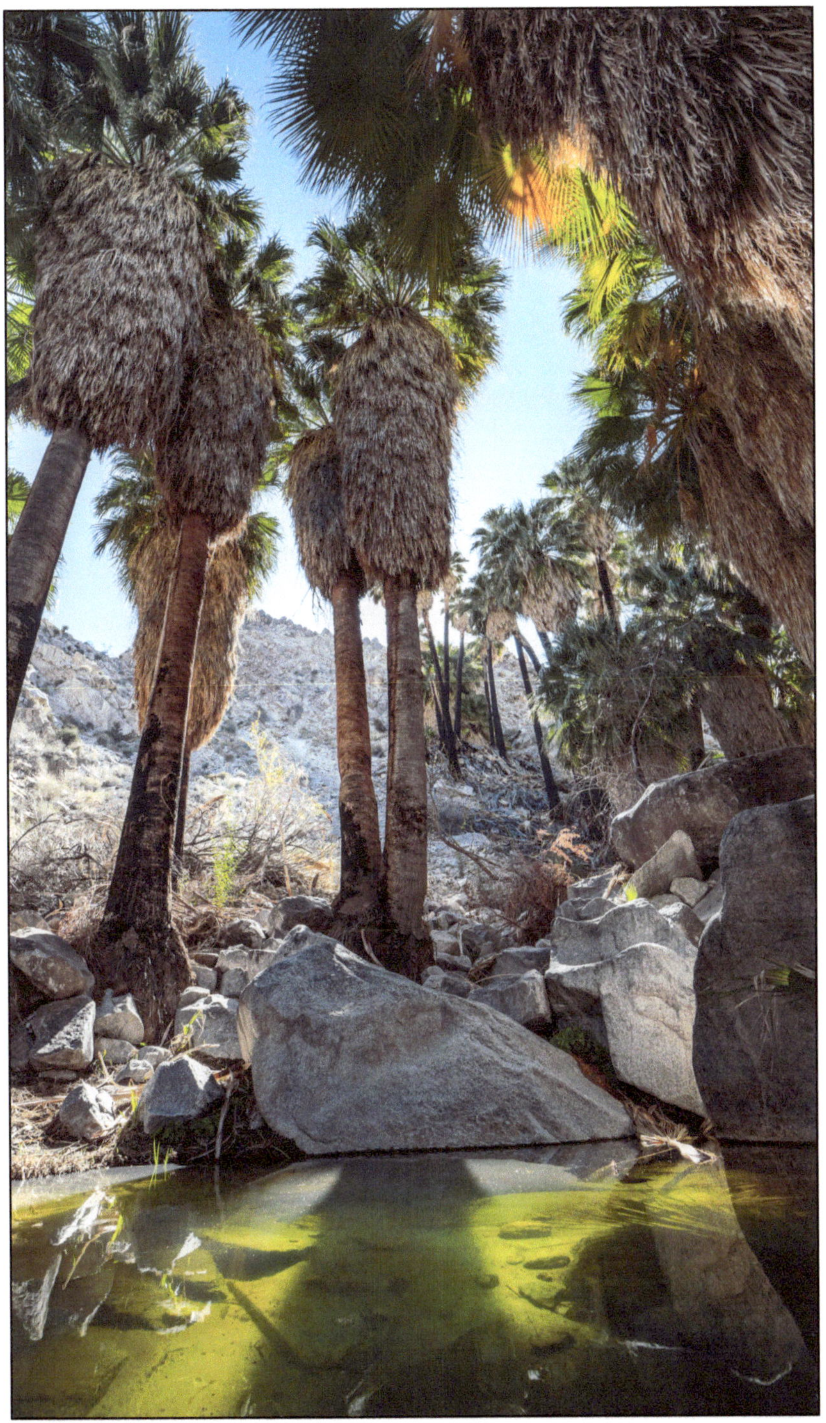

Respite from the Desert Sun   15mm f/11 1/30s ISO400

do stop on your way to the oasis and take your vista picture. If you wait on your return, the lighting usually becomes too harsh. I learned this the hard way during my first visit. Live and learn!

Back on the main trail, your steady descent soon begins. There are additional views of the oasis on your approach. The same holds true as before – if these compositions are of interest, be sure to capture them on the way there and not on the way out.

Once at the oasis, watch your footing and meander around. You will find that very many shots are possible. If the direct sunlight becomes challenging, use one of the trees to block it from your camera and lens.

I typically work with wider focal lengths here. There is a lot to frame in a relatively small space - perhaps especially the trees' remarkable heights. For the water photo, it will be necessary to work very low to the ground. A circular polarizer helps to refine the degree of what is reflected on the water and what is seen below its surface. A tripod makes the work easier but is not mandatory.

Birds frequent these desert oases, so here is where a telephoto lens can be utilized.

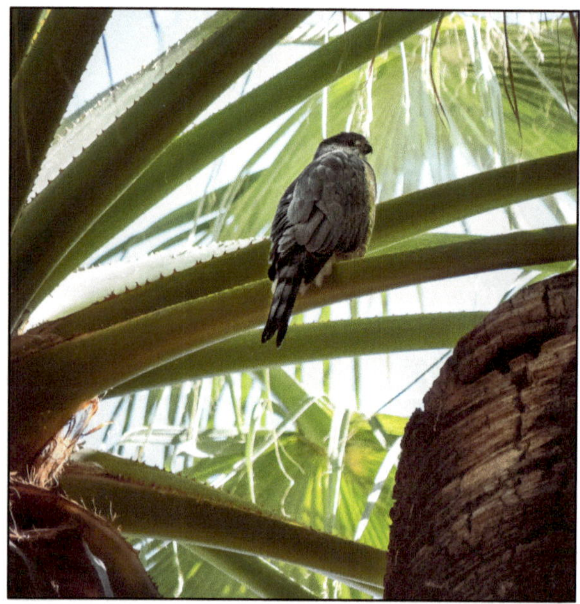

Cooper's Hawk   600mm f/5.6 1/500s ISO3200

Take a break, enjoy the shade, and when ready head on back. Check the temperature on the gauge at the trailhead and see how much the day warmed-up while you were away!

West Park Central

Inside the West Entrance to Bighorn Pass Road

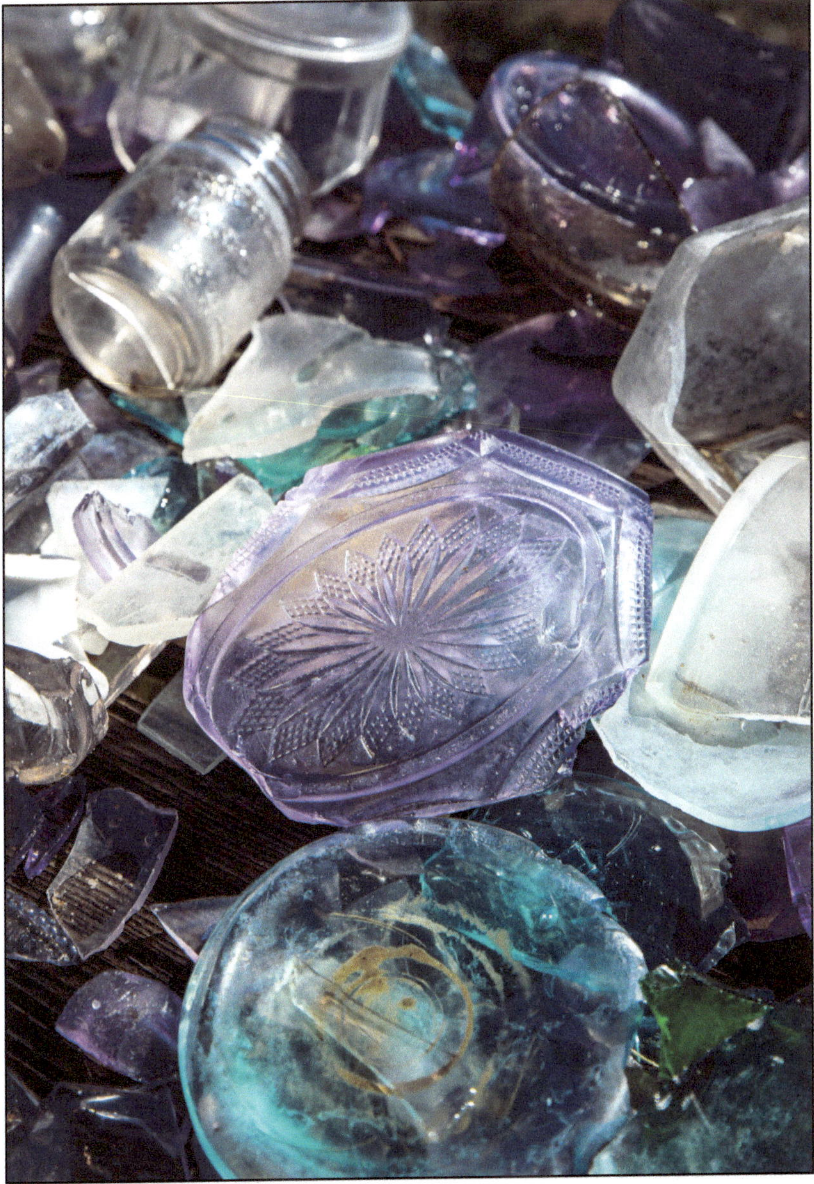

Keys Ranch Collectibles

35mm f/5.6 1/800s ISO100

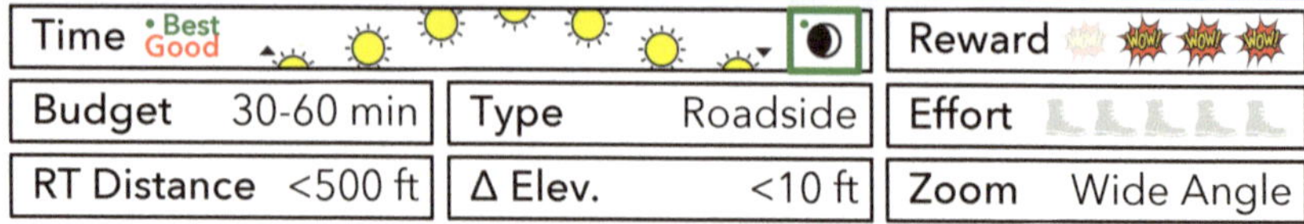

Pandora's box. That we are *not* opening here – the broad topic of lighting as it pertains to photography.

Rather, a concept for exploration after the sun has set and perhaps as you wait for the dark night skies to really set in. Or even for the sun to rise, you early birds!

Whether it be an off-camera flash (strobe), a headlamp, a flashlight, or passing car lights, here we have a fun and simple way to illuminate a subject that otherwise would be "in the dark."

At 2.3 miles in from the West Entrance, on the right is a paved pullout that serves a particularly handsome Joshua Tree. This tree is a wonderful subject for experimentation with artificial lighting under nighttime skies. At right, I preset my camera's settings (and focus) and waited for a passing car's taillights to illuminate it. The moon even helped with this tree's shadow. Fun!

Much of the advice provided on page 41 applies here. Check your in-camera results to see what adjustments could be made and iterate.

I've listed some light source ideas above. From my experience, softer light typically performs best. Car lights are soft. For something you can carry, look for a "medical pen light." I love these.

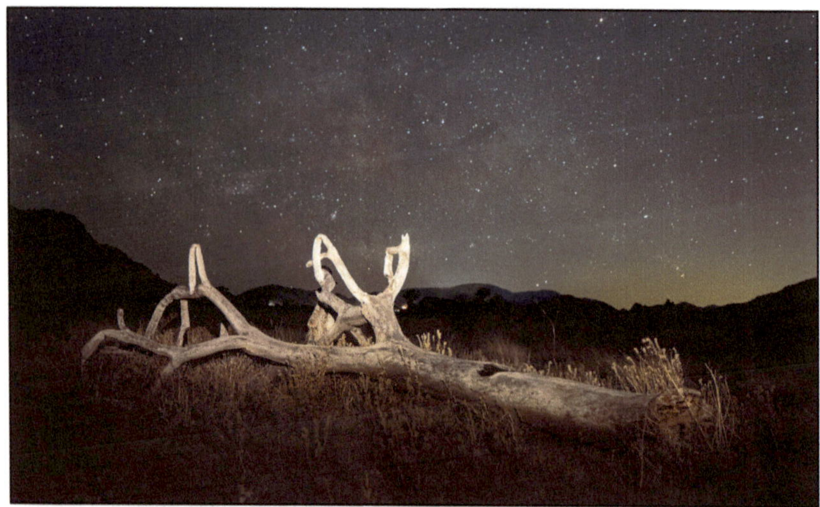

Fallen Knight (4.3 miles from the West Entrance)   35mm f/2.8 15s ISO6400

Strobes and headlamps work well with colored gels. See page 108 for Skull Rock (26) using one strobe (with a snoot) fired twice with two different gels. Short bursts of strong light go a long way here.

Pages 22 and 40 include more samples. This is really an exercise in creativity. Want to really spice things up? Blend this concept with Car Light Trails (9) for a lighting extravaganza!

Point is – there are no rules. Just have fun sampling different lights!

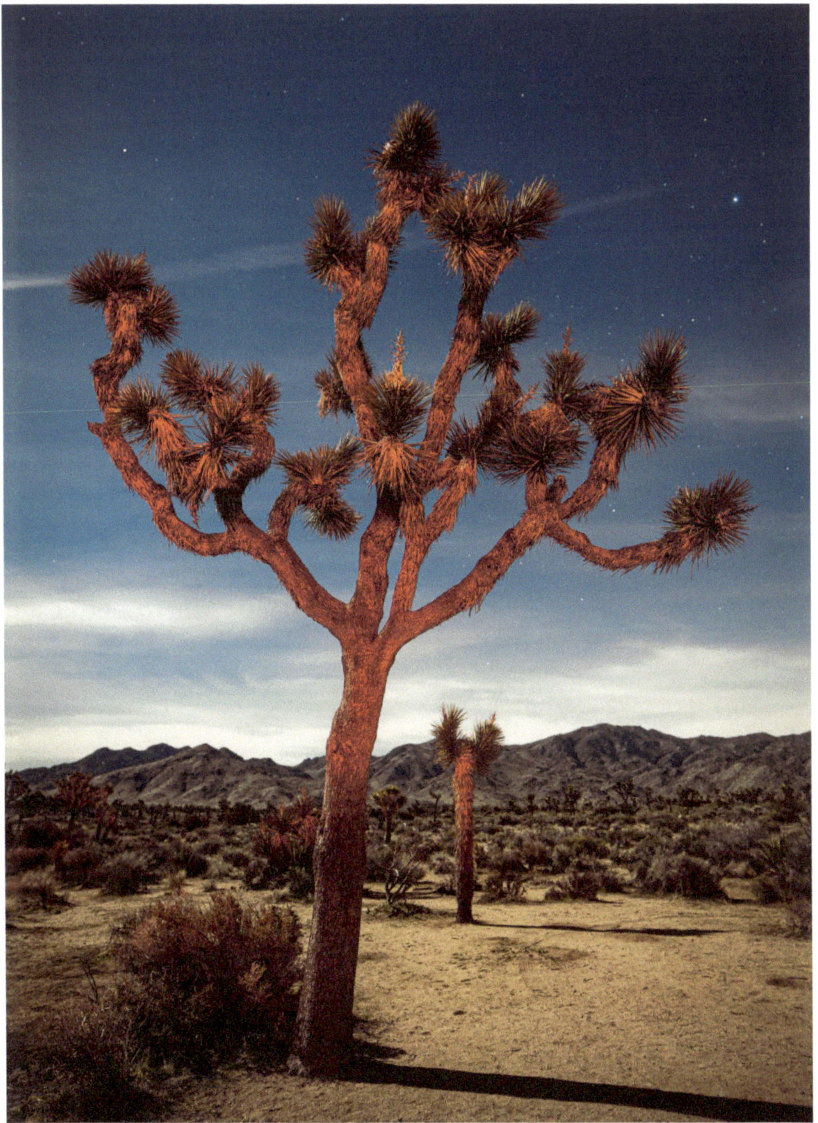

Primary Colors under a Full Moon   20mm f/2.8 15s ISO800

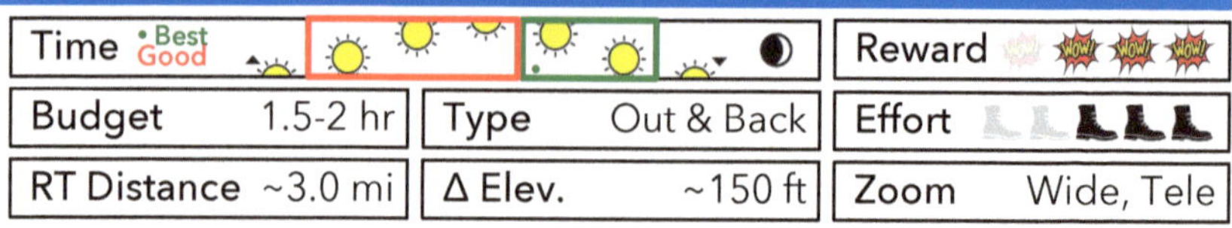

I love a good story, but I am already a bit behind pace here for this guide to remain portable, so I will have to leave it to you to find the marvelous story of John Samuelson's extraordinary travels before he landed in Joshua Tree as a ranch hand for Bill Keys in the 1920's.

Here at "Samuelson's Rock" (a short hill of *many rocks*), Mr. Samuelson etched philosophical, political, and theological musings on 8 faces of 7 large rocks.

There is no formal trail, and the hike is entirely in the open desert. While I think the lighting is a bit better in the afternoon, anytime is a good time for a visit, but because it is exposed be mindful of the heat and the direct sunlight. During the hotter months, a morning venture makes most sense. Rugged boots or shoes are a must.

The hill is visible from Park Boulevard, but until you know *where* to look (usually from already having visited it), it is difficult to pinpoint. For parking there is a long, paved pullout on the east side of the road, 3.9 miles from the West Entrance, or 1.8 miles from the Quail Springs Picnic Area. Via GPS: 34.05602°, -116.22060°.

The first waypoint (34.05097°, -116.22948°) leads you to a wash to follow. Once here, bear "right" into the wash and continue more westerly. At the second waypoint (34.04928°, -116.24162°) exit the wash and head towards the rocky hill (34.04810°, -116.24249°).

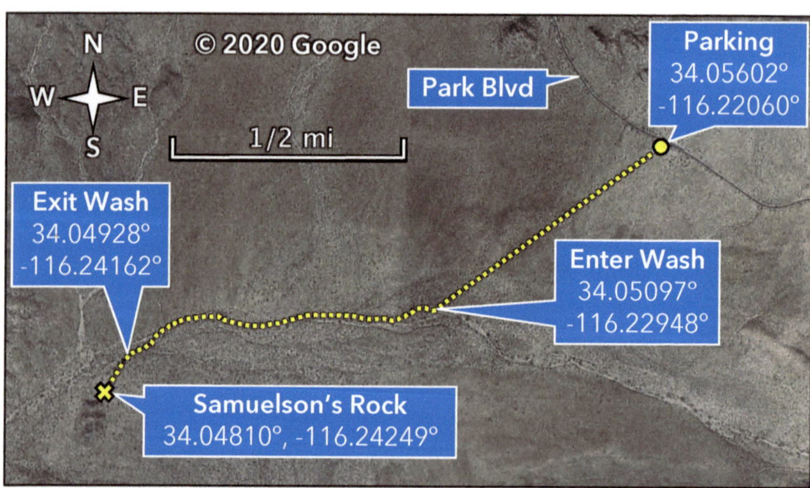

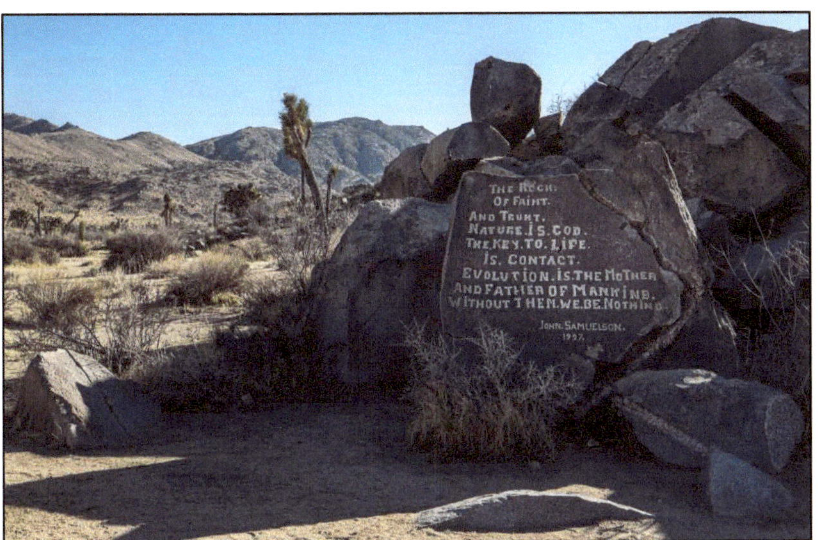

"The Rock of Faith"   35mm f/5.6 1/500s ISO100

Trails crisscross the hill, leading visitors to some of the carvings. Others are still challenging to spot. A desert scavenger hunt! The engraved boulders are fun to search for and of course also to read.

Be careful – there is some barbed wire around the area and some rusty artifacts strewn about. Do watch your step. This site can be fun but running around would be dangerous.

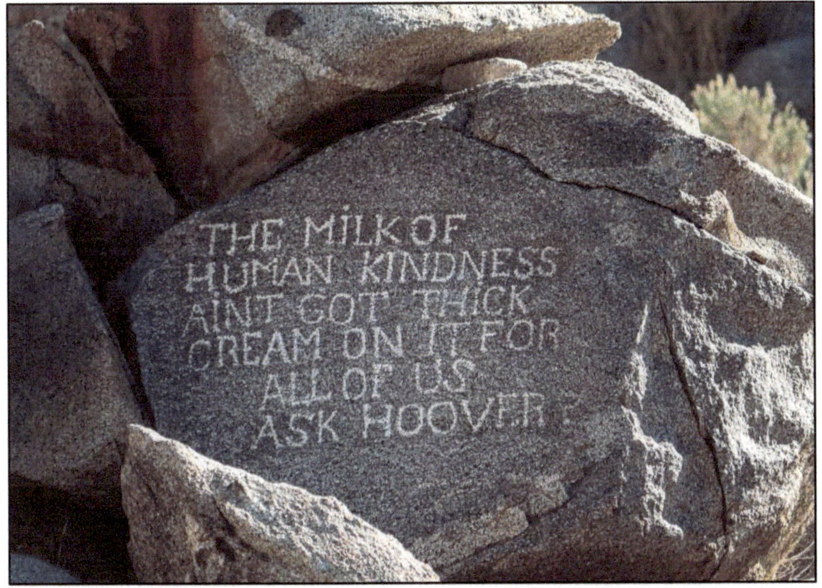

Depression-Era Poetry   400mm f/5.6 1/640s ISO400

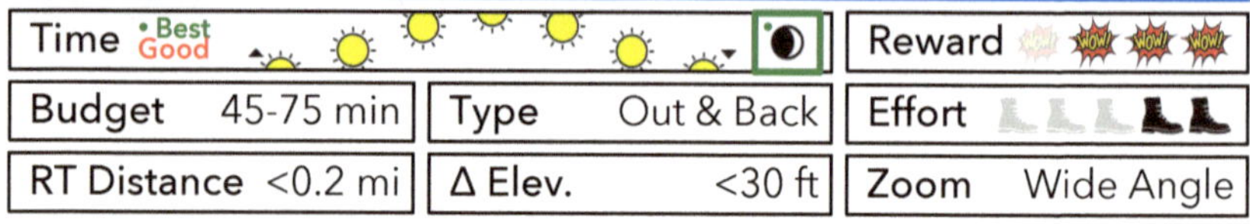

I think these are always fun – to look at, and to photograph – and I usually seek-out places in national parks where the effect translates well within a photo. My rule of thumb is that you're composing for 3 key features at minimum here – a car's head light and/or tail light "trails," the starry night sky, and then something interesting that captures "where you are." For the shot below, I selected the Quail Springs Picnic Area, from atop a large rock on the formation's northeast side, highlighting the curves along Park Boulevard.

Some other spots that also work: From across the road with Cap Rock above the passing cars. Between the Chollas along Pinto Basin Road. In proximity of the super-tall Joshua Tree (page 26), or anywhere an interesting Joshua Tree is present along the road!

OK, so now that we have a few location options at your disposal, let's tackle the technical how-to. Page 41 again covers the majority of the camera settings and setup. A lens for this work does not need to be as wide or as fast, since the lighting will be strong. (Though the trade-off is less detail in the sky, but this is not usually the primary emphasis of the photo.)

Using either a timer or a remote shutter release, listen for an approaching car, begin your exposure, and wait to see what happens! Take a look at your screen and adjust accordingly.

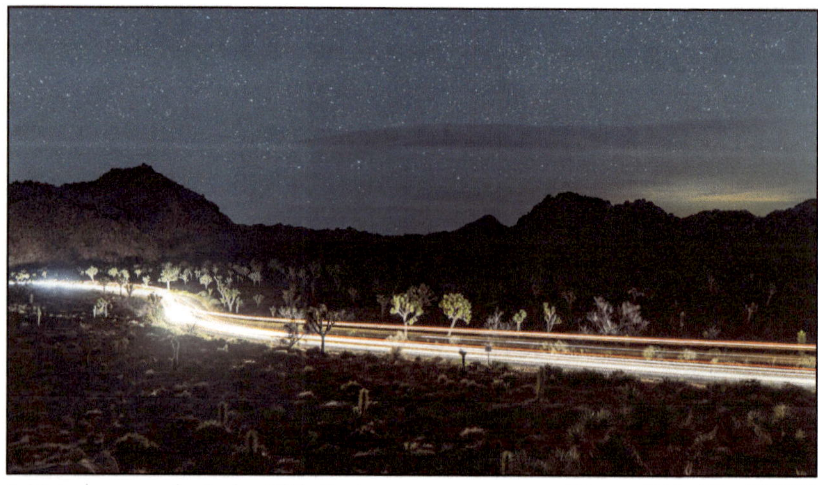

A Motorhome and a Sedan Glide Past   35mm f/3.5 30s ISO800

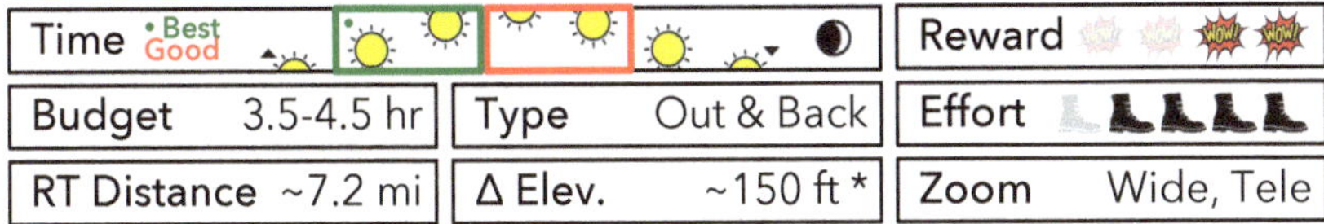

| Budget | 3.5-4.5 hr | Type | Out & Back | Effort | |
| RT Distance | ~7.2 mi | Δ Elev. | ~150 ft * | Zoom | Wide, Tele |

* Notable elevation gain and loss. See elevation profile, page 129.

This hike is as much *or more* about the journey than the destination. The "hole" is a sometimes-present water feature adjacent to this grove of Desert Willow trees. To say it differently, the trees will always be there (though only vibrant green in the spring and early summer), but the water may not be.

That said, it may be tempting to make this journey immediately after rainfall, but unfortunately the wash near the end becomes impassable in places. My recommendation would be to wait at least three days after rain to better ensure that the route is passable.

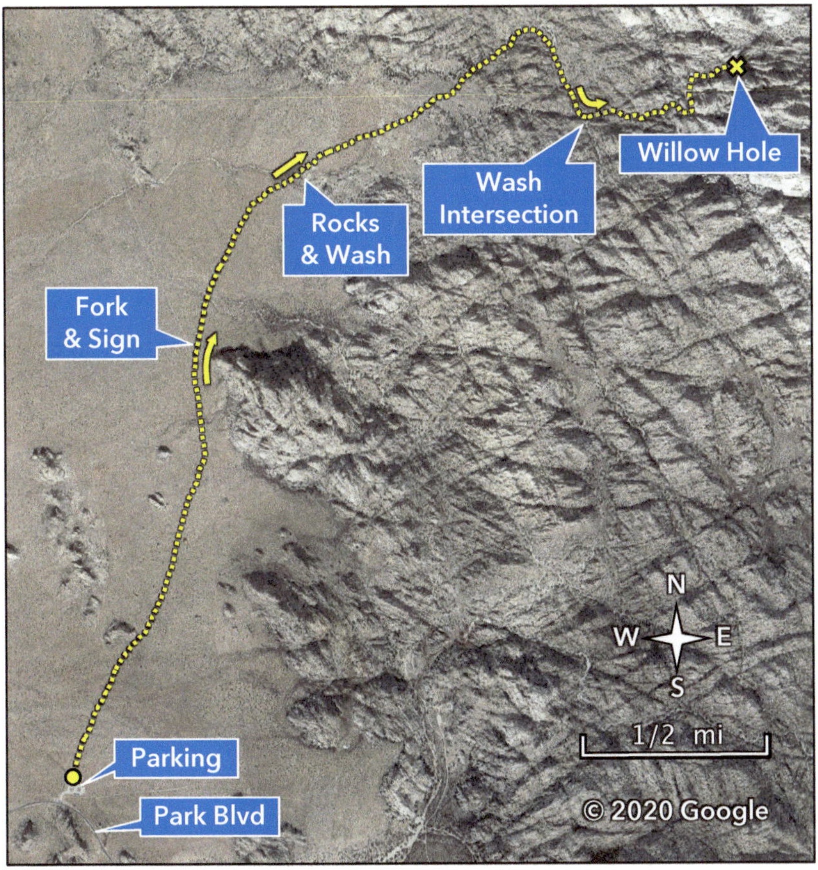

The hike is enjoyable, as the terrain and vegetation seem to change a bit every mile or less. There are many photo opportunities along the way. And if you are looking to escape weekend crowds, this is a great place to do it. Start early, arrive at Willow Hole, have a picnic lunch tucked-away in the shade among the boulders on its backside, and head back before afternoon heat really sets in.

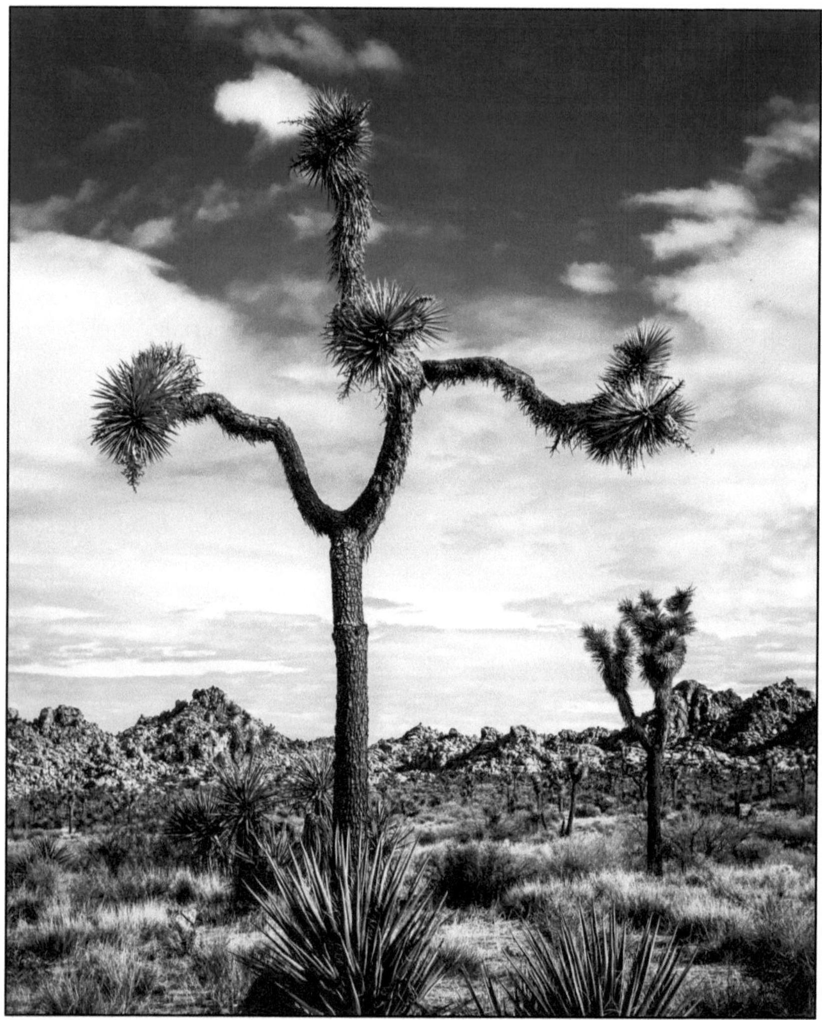

Pointing West and East   35mm f/5.6 1/500s ISO100

From the Boy Scout Trailhead (aka Keys West) parking area, head northeast along the well-marked trail. At 1.2-mile, reach a fork and a sign directing you right towards Willow Hole. At 1.9-mile, come to some barely-exposed, large rocks... Stay straight. (Do not turn right up the wash.)

72

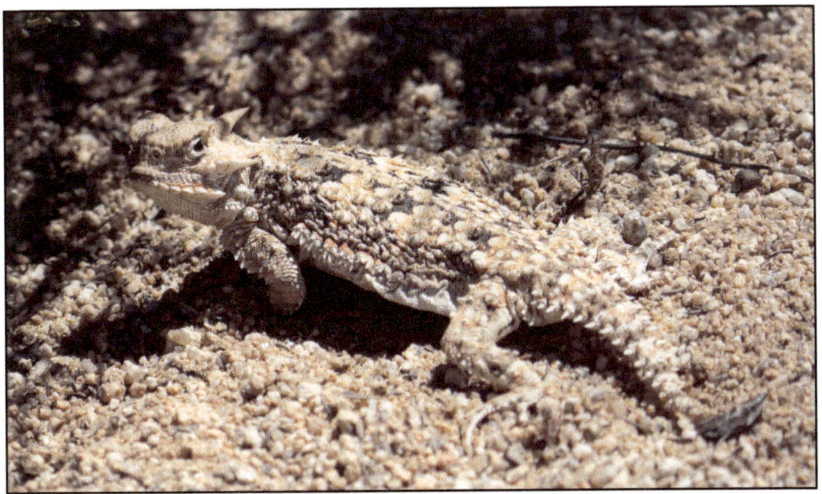

Desert Horned Lizard   600mm f/5.6 1/1250s ISO200

At 2.4-mile, the trail enters a wash. Not long after, at 2.6-mile there is a slight trail that exits the wash on the right. This is where the route changes to southerly. Re-enter the wash. At 2.9-mile two washes intersect; bear left, now heading easterly again. From here meander through rock formations to a wide, sandy opening near the end.

Watch your head – walk below and through the trees to the water hole and shaded rock formations behind. If the water is present and still, reflections of the rocks in the water can be interesting.

Explore, photograph, rest, and return!

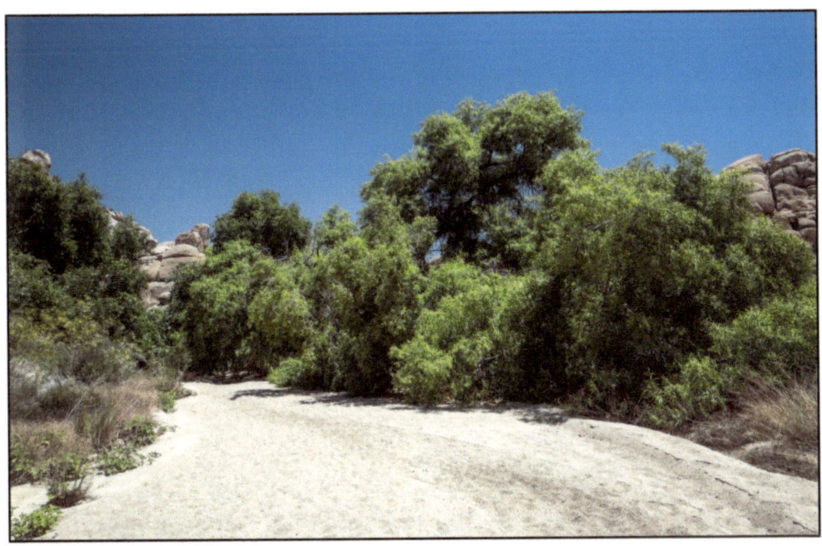

Willow Hole   24mm f/11 1/100s ISO200

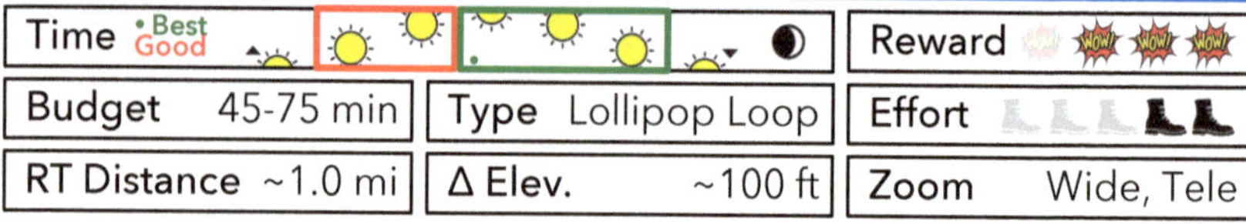

Time	Best Good		Reward
Budget	45-75 min	Type	Lollipop Loop	Effort
RT Distance	~1.0 mi	Δ Elev.	~100 ft	Zoom	Wide, Tele

Hidden Valley is a popular stop for many Joshua Tree visitors, and rightfully so. It is not so much a "valley," but it feels like one once inside because you are completely surrounded by wonderful rock formations. A favorite area for rock climbers, Hidden Valley provides a lot to see (and photograph!) along the 1-mile loop hike.

The trailhead is adjacent to the vault toilets as you drive into the parking lot. There is a readerboard also at the trailhead that provides a map and some interesting history about the valley's use as a hiding place for cattle rustlers in the late 1800's.

Begin by walking up and through an area blasted for easier access to the "valley" inside. I have walked the loop trail in both directions, but I find that more photographic subjects catch the eye when walked counterclockwise.

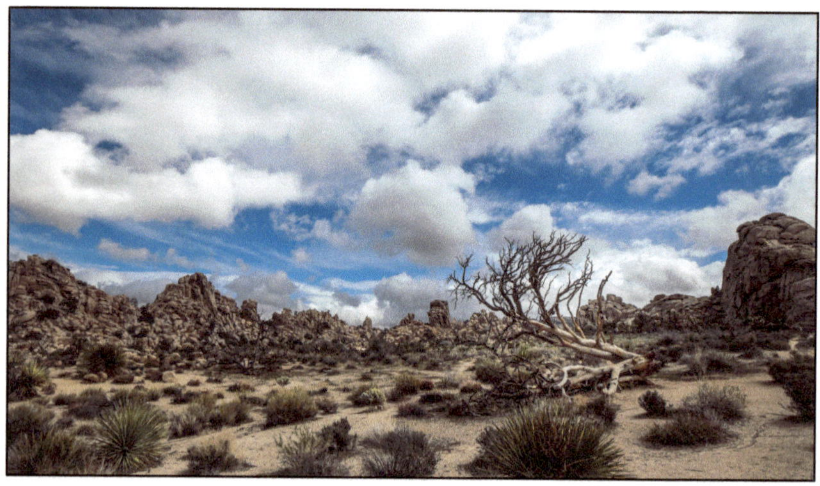

Hidden Valley 20mm f/11 1/400s ISO100

Wildflowers can be abundant here in the springtime, as moisture tends to be trapped more so than in adjacent park areas at this elevation.

Once back outside of Hidden Valley, the south end of the parking lot loop boasts excellent picnic areas. My favorites are along the short, auxiliary loop on the far southwest end. More photography opportunities are here, around and behind these rock formations.

Very many days in Joshua Tree have boring skies without clouds. I have not masked this fact with the photos in this book. Using black and white, you can redirect your viewer's eyes to your main subject. Here's an example from within the Hidden Valley Campground.

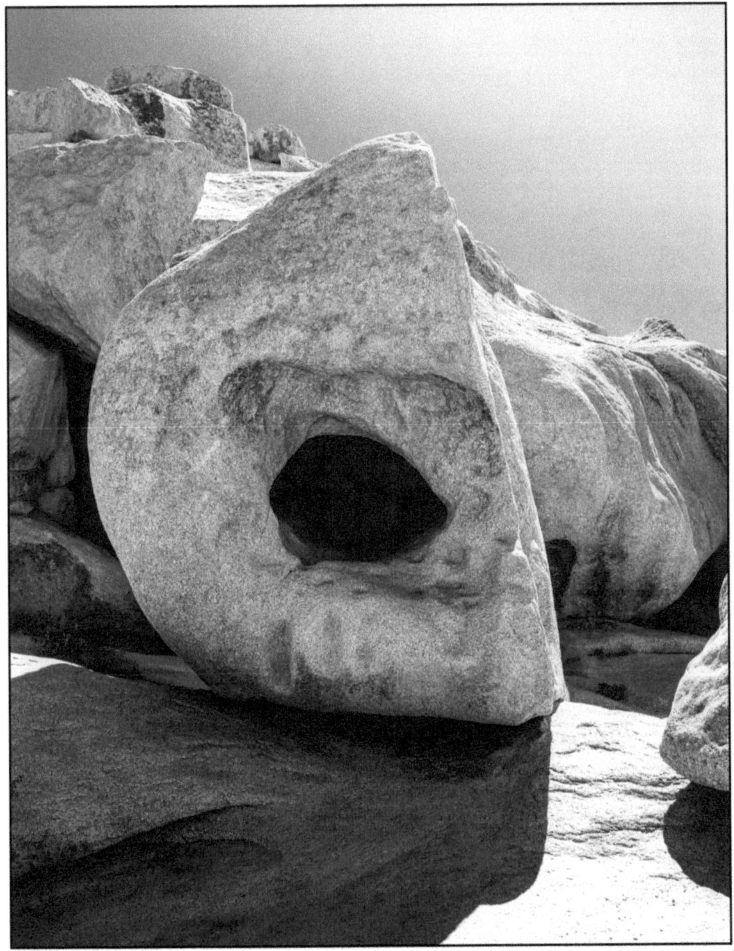

Alien Head (near Hidden Valley Campsite 11)   35mm   f/8   1/250s   ISO100

What I have found helpful (though some purists may argue that I'm bending the rules) is to grab my mirrorless digital camera with an electronic viewfinder and with the camera in monochrome mode, be able to see the composition in black and white before I take the shot. This can also be accomplished using a camera's rear screen, but sometimes glare from the sunlight challenges this method a bit.

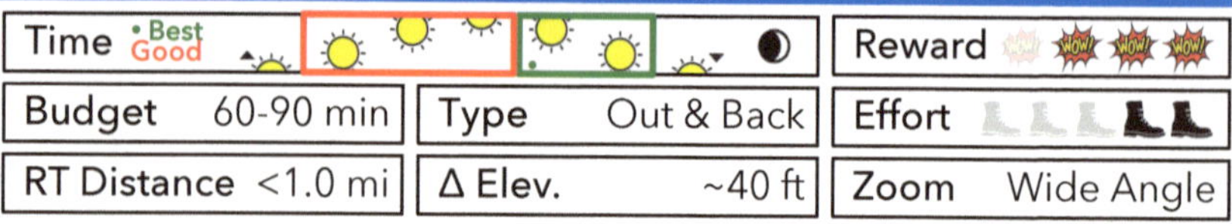

Time	Best Good							Reward	
Budget	60-90 min	Type	Out & Back	Effort					
RT Distance	<1.0 mi	Δ Elev.	~40 ft	Zoom	Wide Angle				

The "Iron Door Cave" is a little-known gem in Joshua Tree NP. What is it exactly? A man-made enclosure (the "cave") under a large boulder with an iron door at its entrance. Neither the cave nor the door are large, but once you duck through the entrance you are able to stand up inside, though there is not a lot of room to move around. What makes it interesting is its stone and mortar construction along with the aged, iron door used to enclose the space.

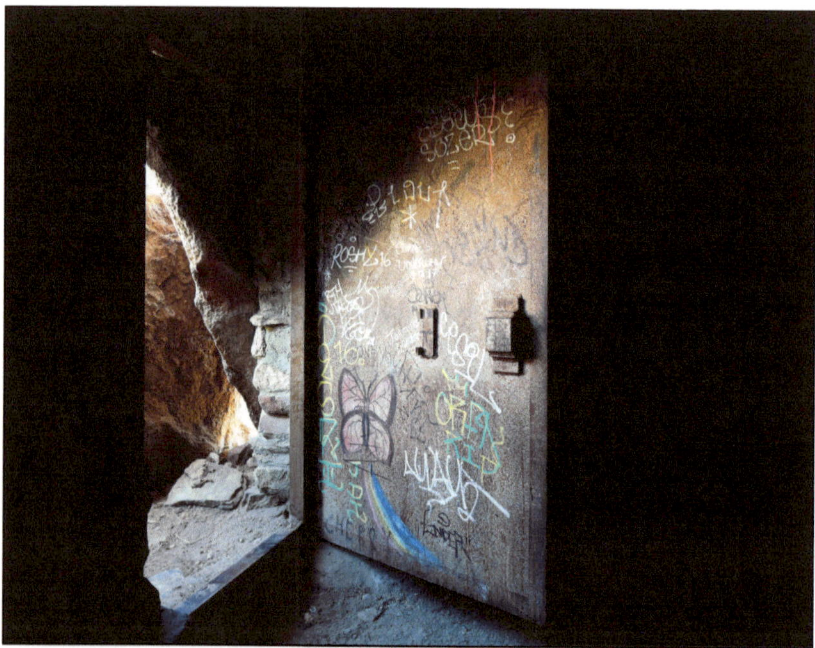

Inside the Iron Door Cave   24mm f/4 1/60s ISO800

There are two theories in circulation on the purpose of this cave, which is presumed to have been constructed in the early 1900's... Both stories agree that Bill Keys built and used the cave. The first story (the less eerie of the two) is that he used the enclosure for securely storing dynamite used for blasting in the area. The second story is that Mr. Keys would use the space to incarcerate a person or persons who dissatisfied him. How unsettling! Perhaps even, it was used for both purposes. No one may ever know for sure, but now once you enter the cave you might imagine its use in these ways.

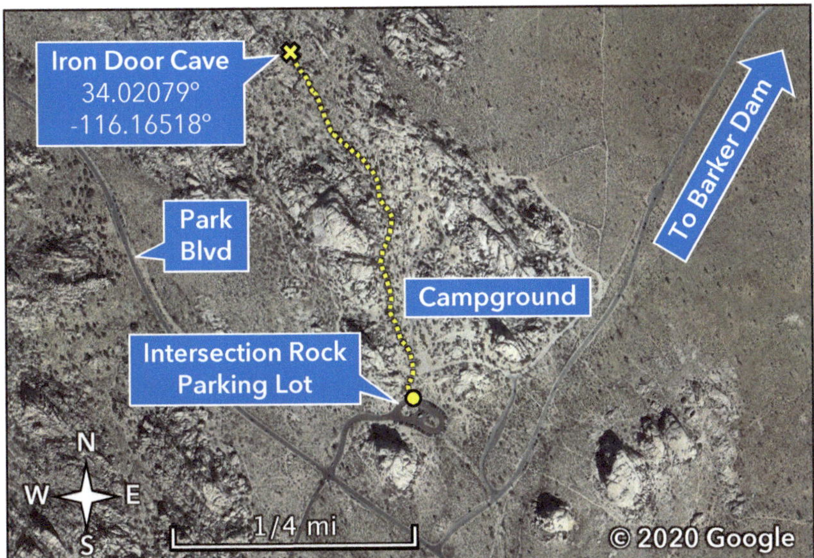

The Iron Door Cave is not far from the Hidden Valley Campground, but to find it a map is arguably inadequate. **GPS is recommended.** From near the end of the west campground loop, head northwest towards 34.02079°, -116.16518°. As you close-in on these coordinates, find the tall rock formation in front of you in the image below, and seek the identified round boulder. The door is tucked out of sight, at the bottom of this boulder.

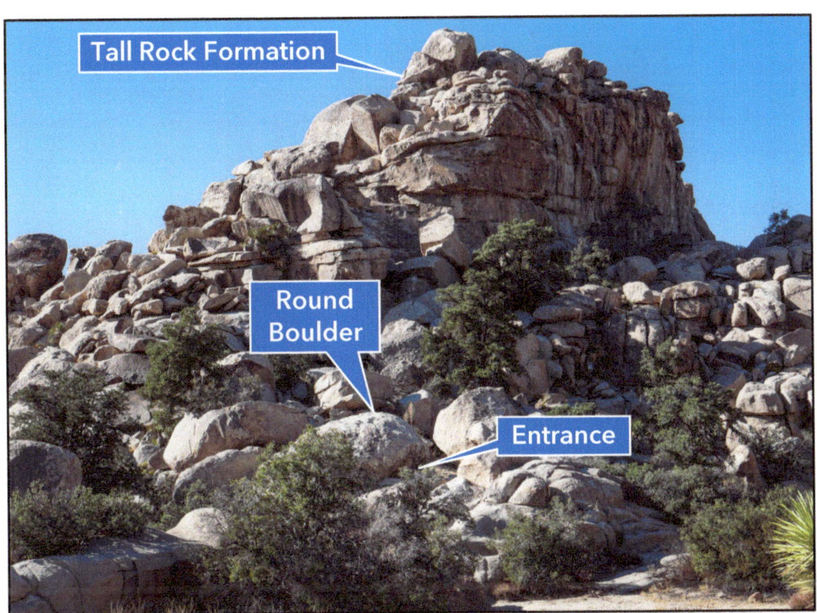

Time	Time of Day Based on Tour Time		Reward	🌟 🌟 🌟 🌟
Budget	1.5-2 hr	Type	Loop	Effort
RT Distance	<1.0 mi	Δ Elev.	~30 ft	Zoom	Norm, Tele

Bill Keys, the most legendary of all Joshua Tree's residents, arrived to the area in 1910. After having initially worked at the Desert Queen Mine, he married and raised a family on a 160-acre property he homesteaded, the heart of it today visitable and known as "Keys Ranch." As mining in the area dwindled, Keys would collect as much of the parts and machinery left behind as he could, for his own use and also for barter to other area residents. Some might say he was the first *informal* superintendent of this greater park area.

Keys Ranch access is via a National Park Service tour and requires an advance reservation.

Visit either www.nps.gov/jotr or recreation.gov for tour information and reservations. Tours are typically not provided during summer months (June-September).

Tour parties first meet at a locked gate about 1-mile away from the actual ranch area. Once checked-in by the hosting park ranger, you will caravan (drive your vehicle) to a parking area close to the ranch.

Your host park ranger and any accompanying docents will walk you to and around the ranch. The information they provide is insightful and entertaining. There is too much for me to regurgitate here and pretend to do it justice. Keys' story is a fascinating one, and his family's ranch is a **must do** if your itinerary will allow.

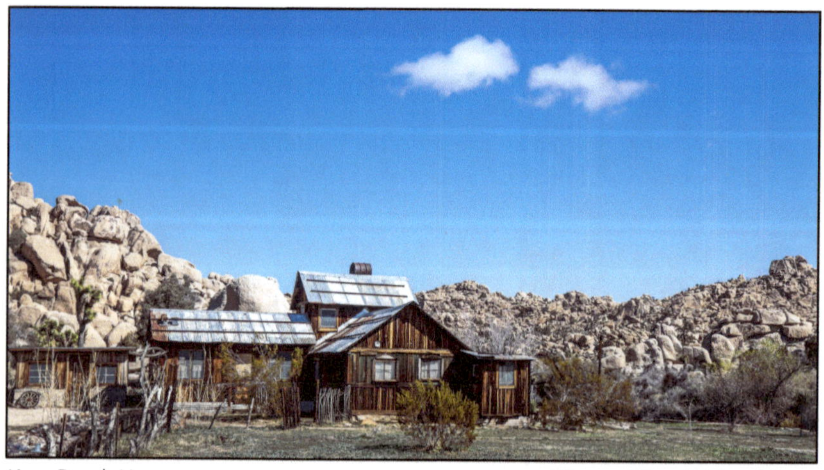

Keys Ranch House   50mm f/8 1/100s ISO100

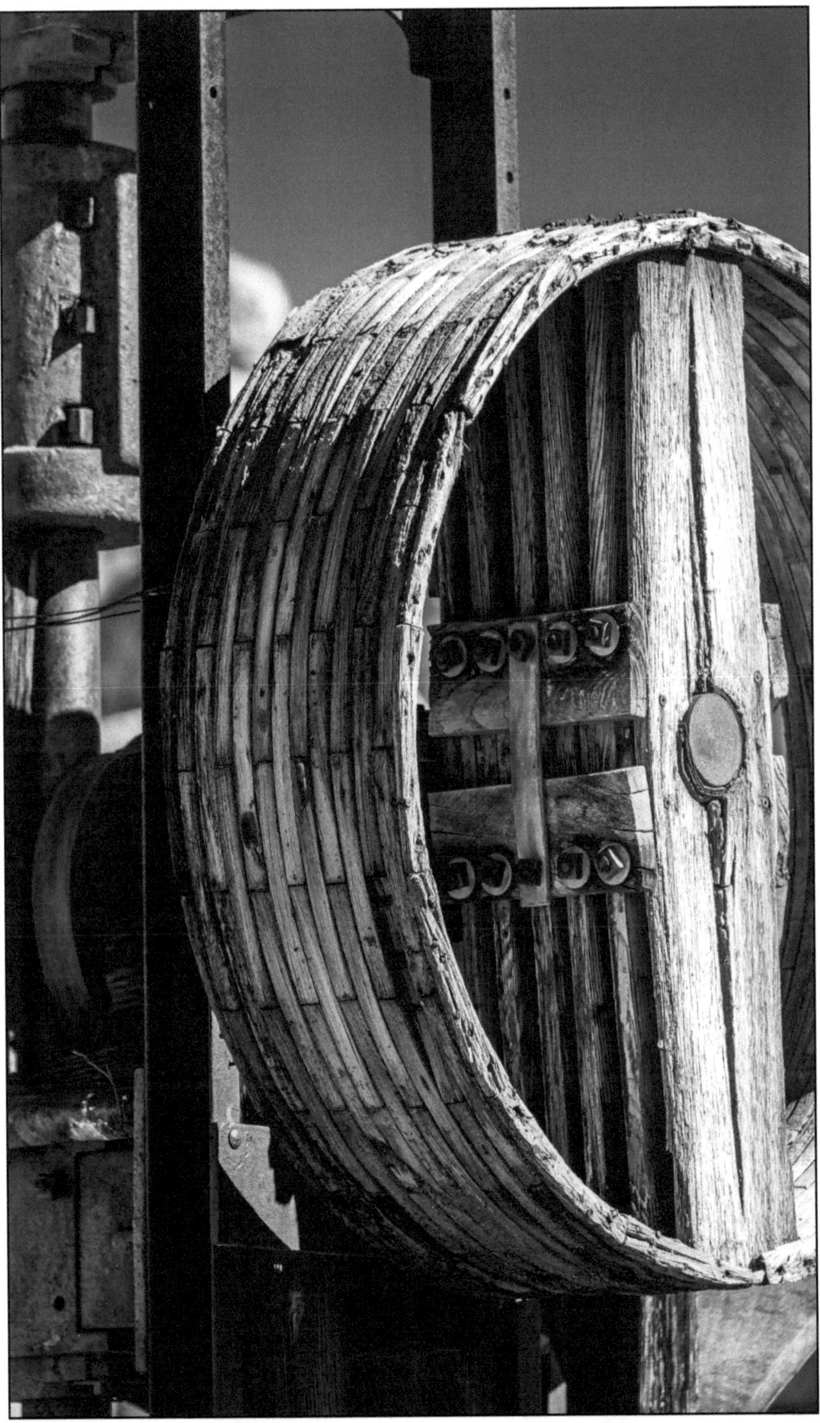

Gold Stamp Mill (at Keys Ranch)   200mm   f/5.6   1/400s   ISO200

Enjoy meandering around the property with the tour group and hearing the interesting stories about the family's life and all their relics left-behind. There is so much to photograph – you could easily create a sizeable portfolio of just Keys Ranch!

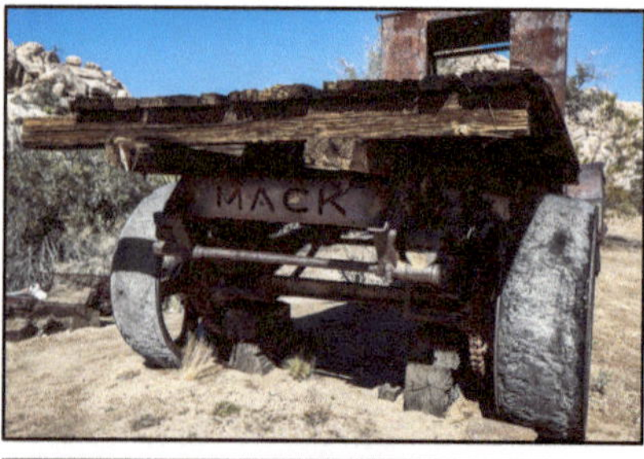
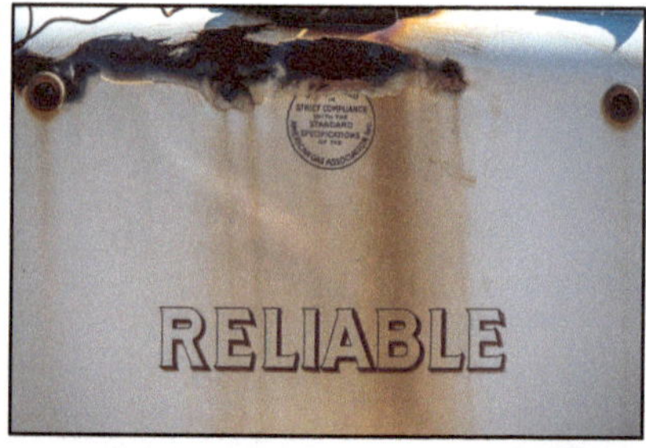

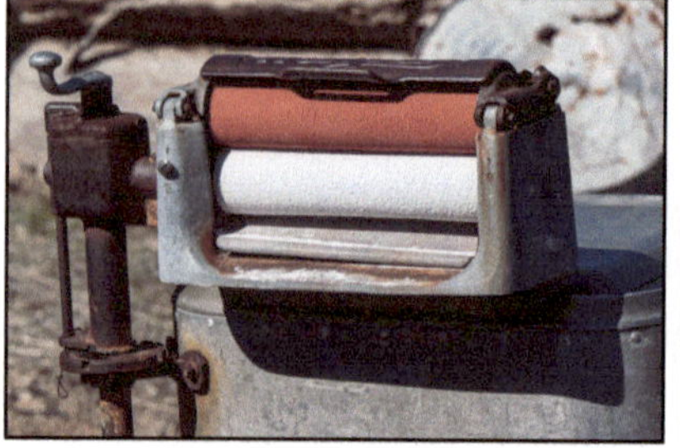
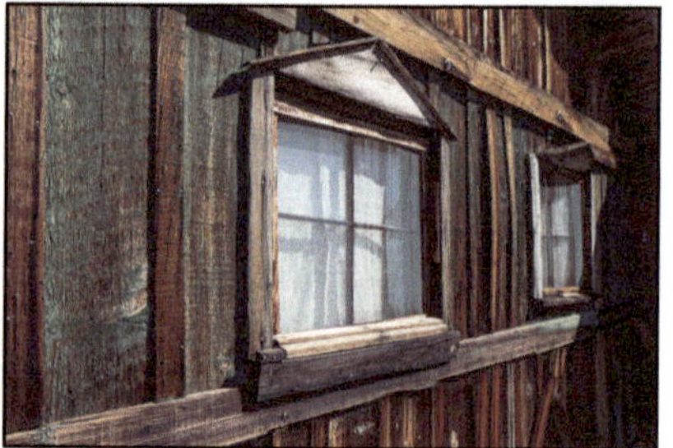

Note: tripod use is not allowed during the tour.

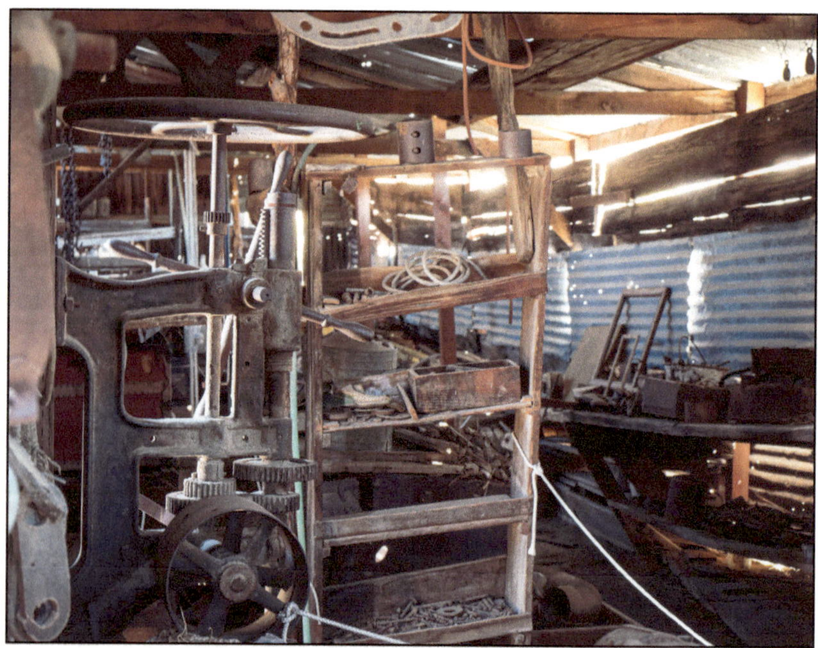

Hiding in the Shadows inside the Tool Shed   50mm f/5.6 1/10s ISO400

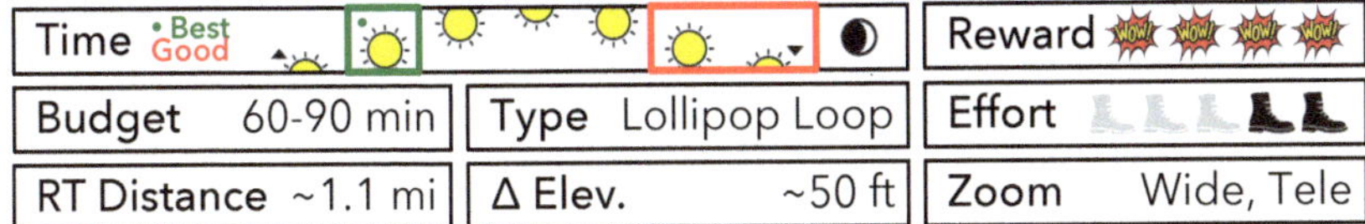

Time	Best • Good		Reward	✹✹✹✹
Budget	60-90 min	Type Lollipop Loop	Effort	🥾🥾
RT Distance ~1.1 mi		Δ Elev. ~50 ft	Zoom	Wide, Tele

Barker Dam is everyone's favorite water feature within Joshua Tree National Park. Unfortunately, many arrive and find themselves disappointed to find the water level low and/or its color to be uninteresting. Weather conditions (especially cumulative rainfall) must be favorable. April and May are perhaps the two best months for the water level to be sufficiently high. Early morning visitation is also key, for still water and vivid blue skies and its reflection on the water. Late afternoon to sunset can be productive, but it comes in at a distant second place to the early morning conditions.

I sincerely hope that you can experience Barker Dam at its best.

The good news is that the Barker Dam area does offer more than just the water itself. More on this in a moment…

The Barker Dam Nature Trail is a lollipop loop. Its beginning is clearly marked, but after a few minutes of hiking you will find yourself in a bit of a clearing with multiple trails. This is the loop's beginning and end. The signage is not very helpful. If heading first to Barker Dam (recommended), continue straight.

Walk along the well-marked trail below high rock formations. Soon you will exit into a clearing. Seek the trail; it will bend left and remain adjacent to the rock formation (at your left). If you were to stay straight, you will find yourself at one of the mouths of this ephemeral lake. If you veer to the right and cross the wash (if passable), from upon these lower rocks is a good place for afternoon-to-sunset work.

The dam is at the far left "end" of this lake area. Near the edge of the dam is a concrete inscription made by Bill Keys in 1950, when he increased its height using concrete atop the existing stone construction (circa 1902).

Be careful walking along the rocks to see this (and along all the rocks in this area). Some places are deceptively slippery at times.

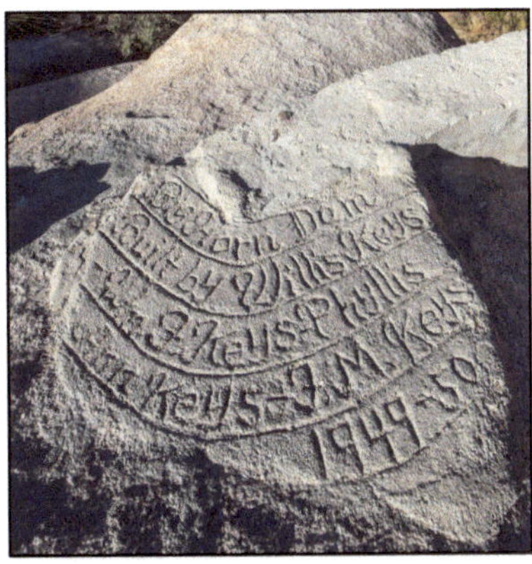

24mm f/11 1/160s ISO100

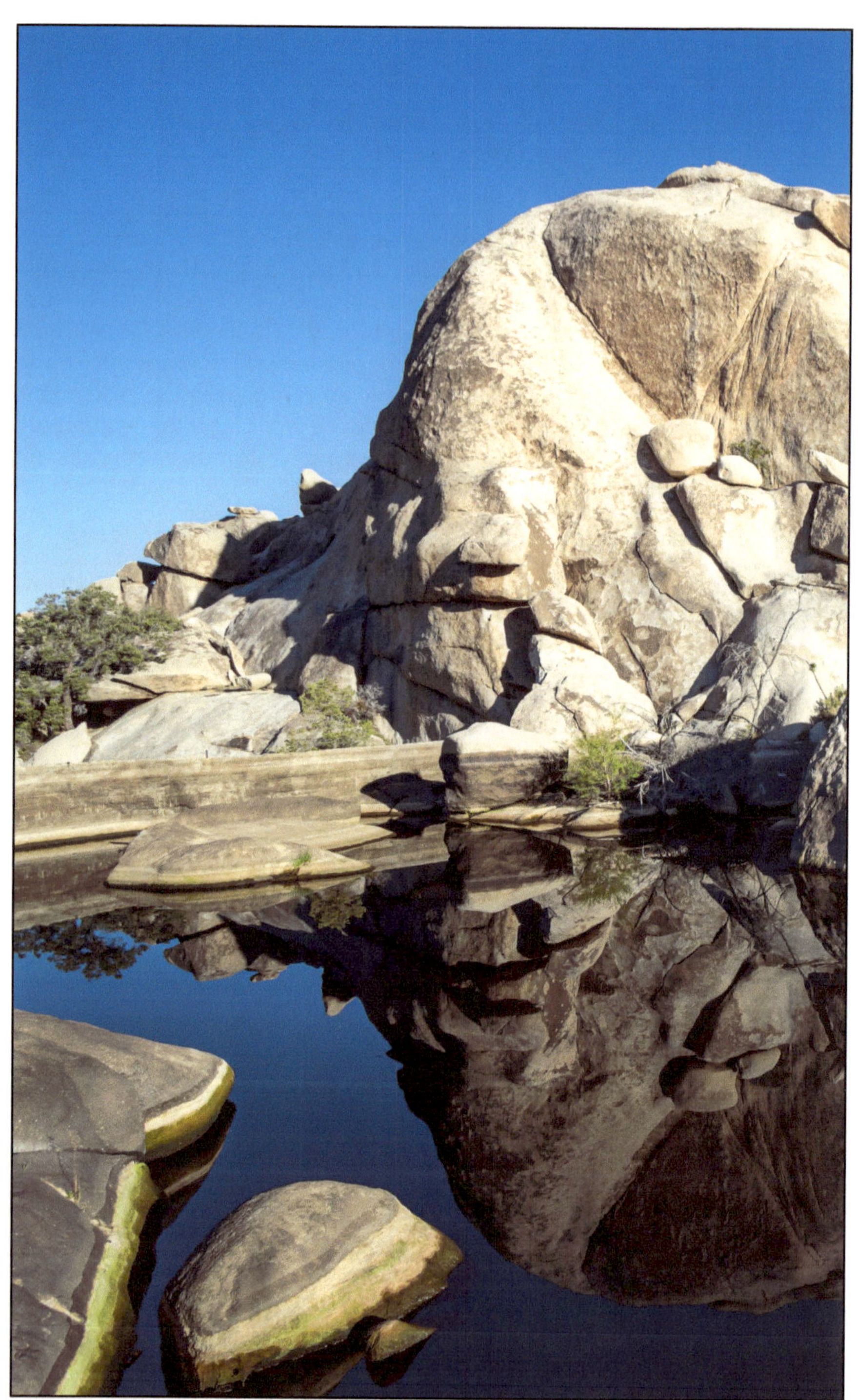

Barker Dam

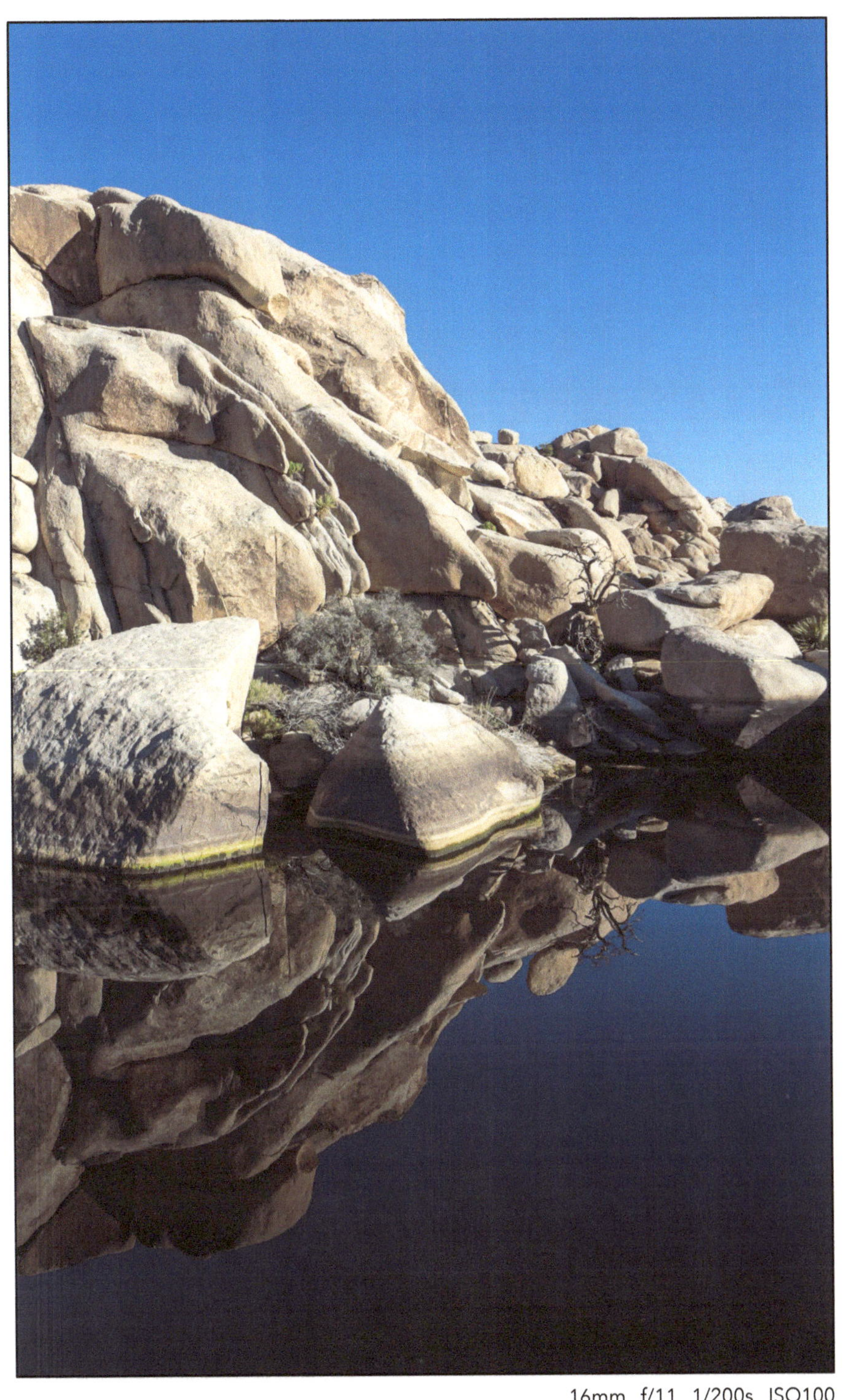

16mm f/11 1/200s ISO100

From near the dam to your left you can see a watering trough for cattle. What an interesting shape! Surely there was a reason for this.

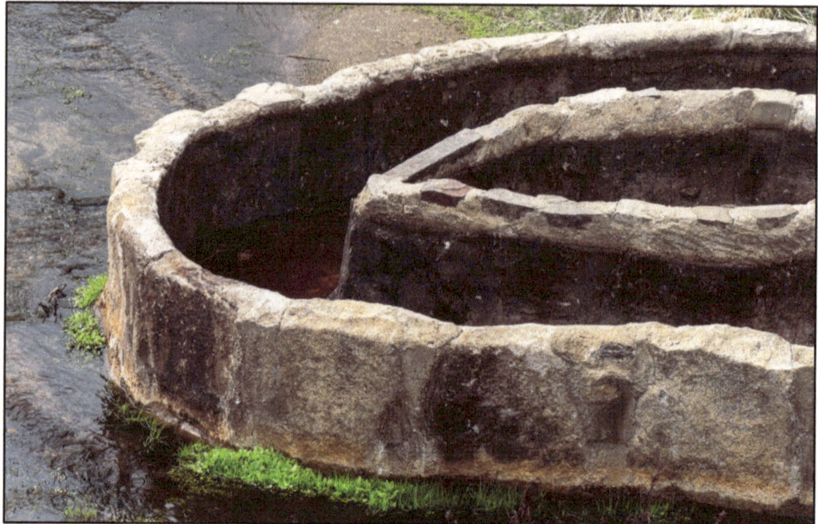

Watering Trough   200mm f/11 1/200s ISO100

Continuing on the trail, descend into an open space with many Joshua Trees - some quite large. Follow the trail a while to a well-marked formation with petroglyphs high upon the rock walls. A tele-photo is required, as climbing on the rocks is prohibited.

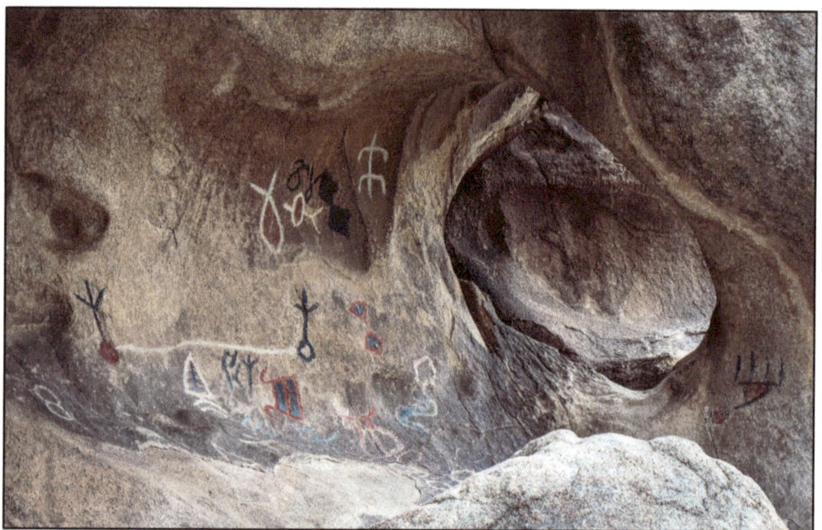

Painted Petroglyphs   100mm f/8 1/125s ISO400

Once finished at the petroglyphs site, double-back about 100 ft and follow the sign towards the parking area.

Time	Best / Good	Reward	WOW! WOW! WOW! WOW!
Budget	2-3 hr	Type	Out & Back	Effort	
RT Distance	~3.0 mi	Δ Elev.	~180 ft	Zoom	Norm, Tele

This hike is my means for deeper exploration of the Wonderland of Rocks… Rattlesnake Canyon (5), Willow Hole (10), and Barker Dam (14) wander into the "Wonderland," but only barely. Here is a way to go further.

The most "lost" I have ever been inside Joshua Tree National Park was within the Wonderland. I highly recommend GPS to track your route, so that you can more easily backtrack when the time comes. Our target destination, the Red Obelisk, essentially requires its use.

From the gravel parking lot, follow the trail to the Wonderland Ranch ruin (the structure on the cover of this book). A rusty old truck is visible – take a short detour before or after your hike for a visit.

The entrance to the wash can be a little tricky to find, due to some thick brush. It is west of the north end of the house ruin, 34.03017°, -116.13958°. Begin heading north by following the wash.

Seek subjects and compositions along the way. There are plenty. At 0.4-mile into the wash, find Shark Rock near 34.03585°, -116.14143°.

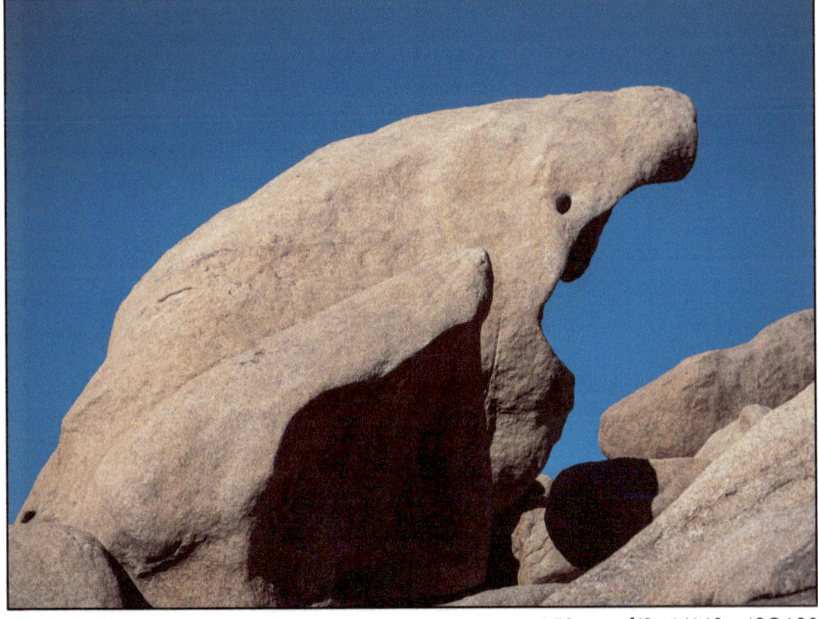

Shark Rock

150mm f/8 1/640s ISO100

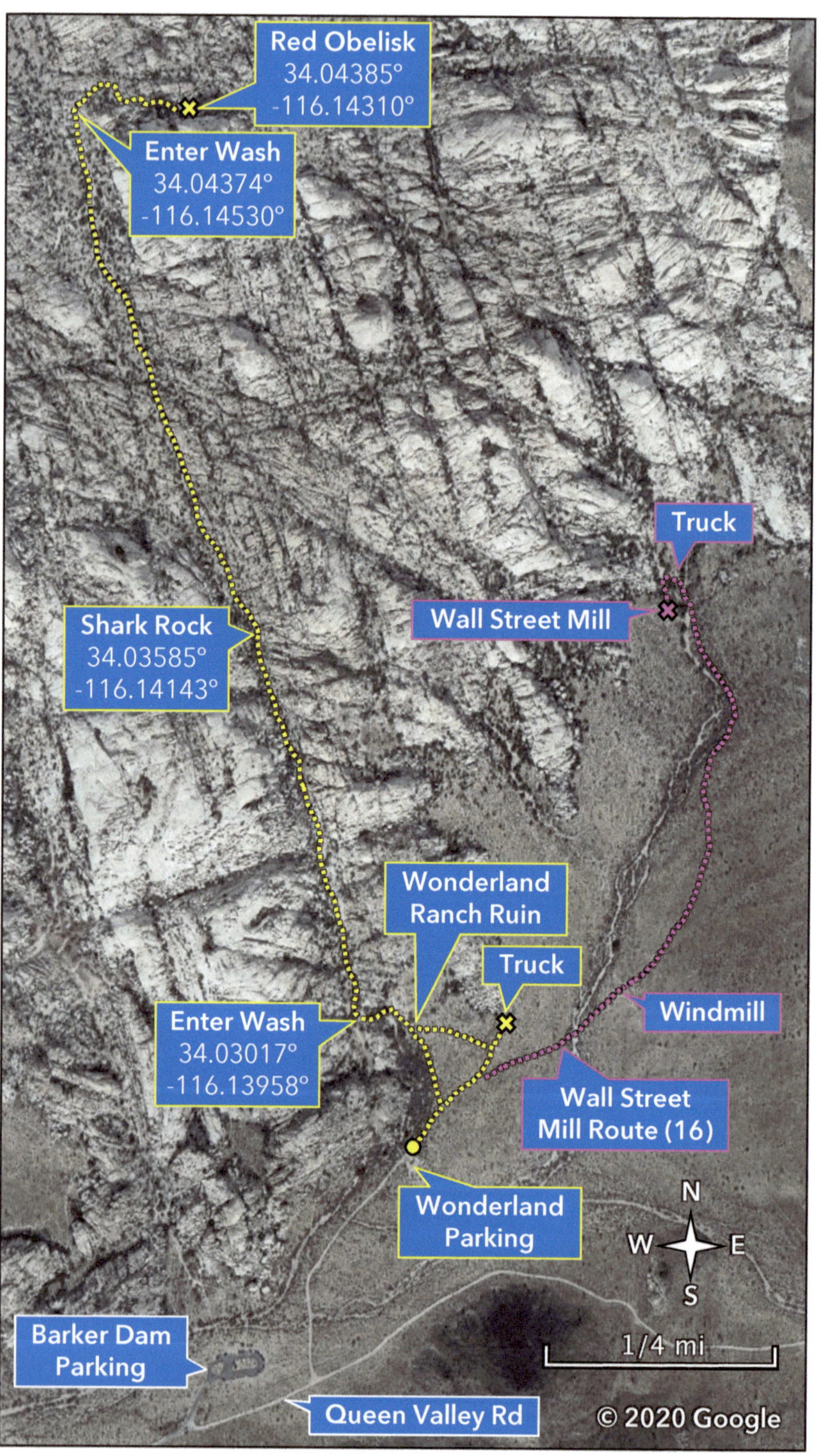

Red Obelisk
34.04385°
-116.14310°
Enter Wash
34.04374°
-116.14530°
Truck
Wall Street Mill
Shark Rock
34.03585°
-116.14143°
Wonderland
Ranch Ruin
Truck
Windmill
Enter Wash
34.03017°
-116.13958°
Wall Street
Mill Route (16)
Wonderland
Parking
N
W E
S
1/4 mi
Barker Dam
Parking
Queen Valley Rd
© 2020 Google

Shark Rock also marks the halfway point. Continue north along the wash. Finally, at 34.04374°, -116.14530° find a smaller wash that exits into the much larger Wonderland Wash. Turn right, and follow this zig-zag route to the Red Obelisk at 34.04385°, -116.14310°.

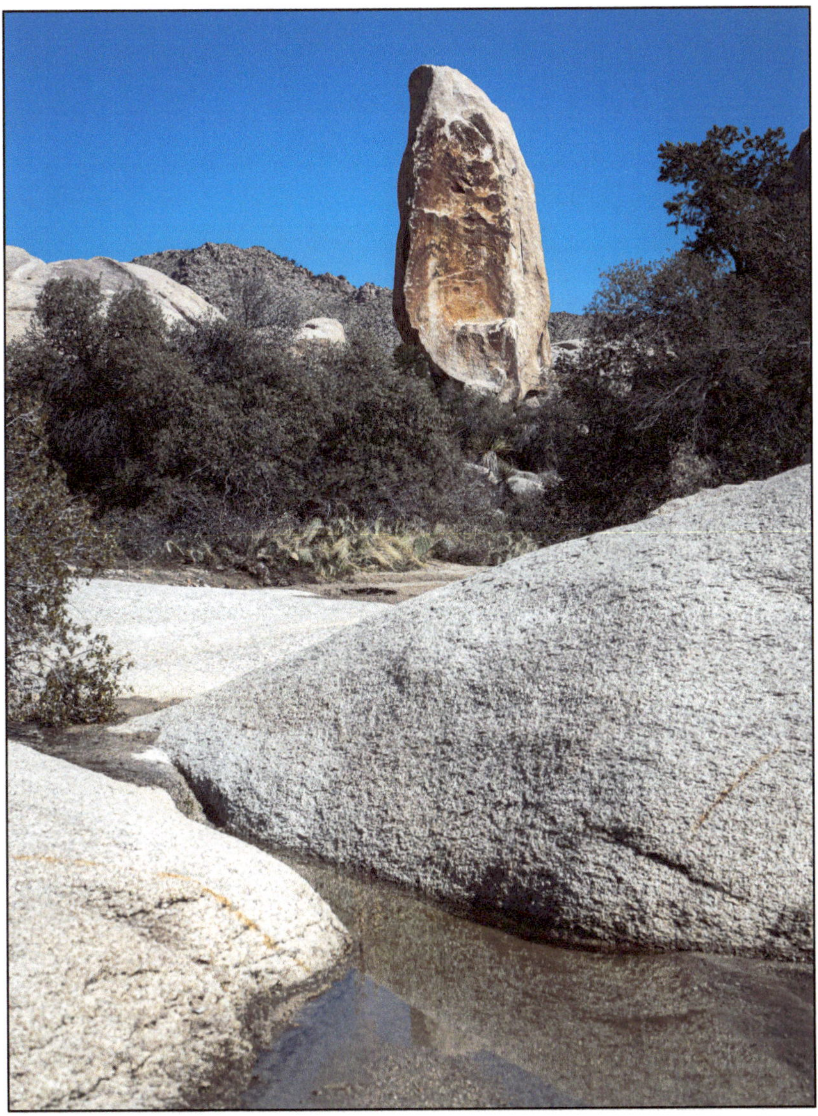

The Red Obelisk   50mm f/11 1/250s ISO100

You are deep within the Wonderland of Rocks now, but still only 1/3 of the way north to Rattlesnake Canyon (5).

Once ready, backtrack your way to the parking lot. Still keep your eye out – new compositions will "emerge" since your direction changed.

Time	Best / Good	Reward	🌟 🌟 🌟 🌟
Budget	1.5-2 hr	Type	Out & Back	Effort
RT Distance	~2.0 mi	Δ Elev.	~50 ft	Zoom	Wide Angle

This is the most photogenic "mill" site in Joshua Tree. Bonus that it is in such close proximity to Barker Dam (14), another sensational area.

Follow the parking information on page 85 and the map on page 86. Unlike Wonderland Wash, this route is much easier to follow.

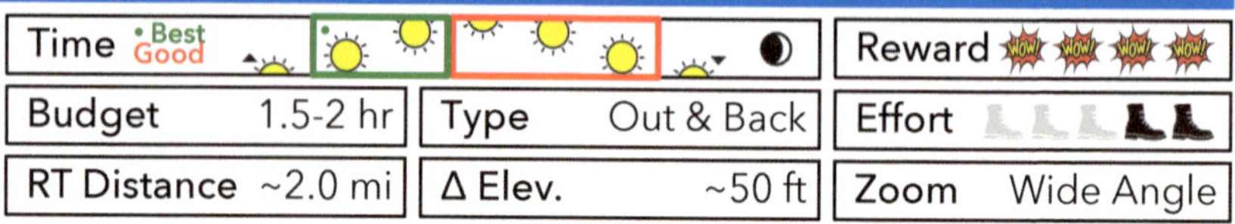

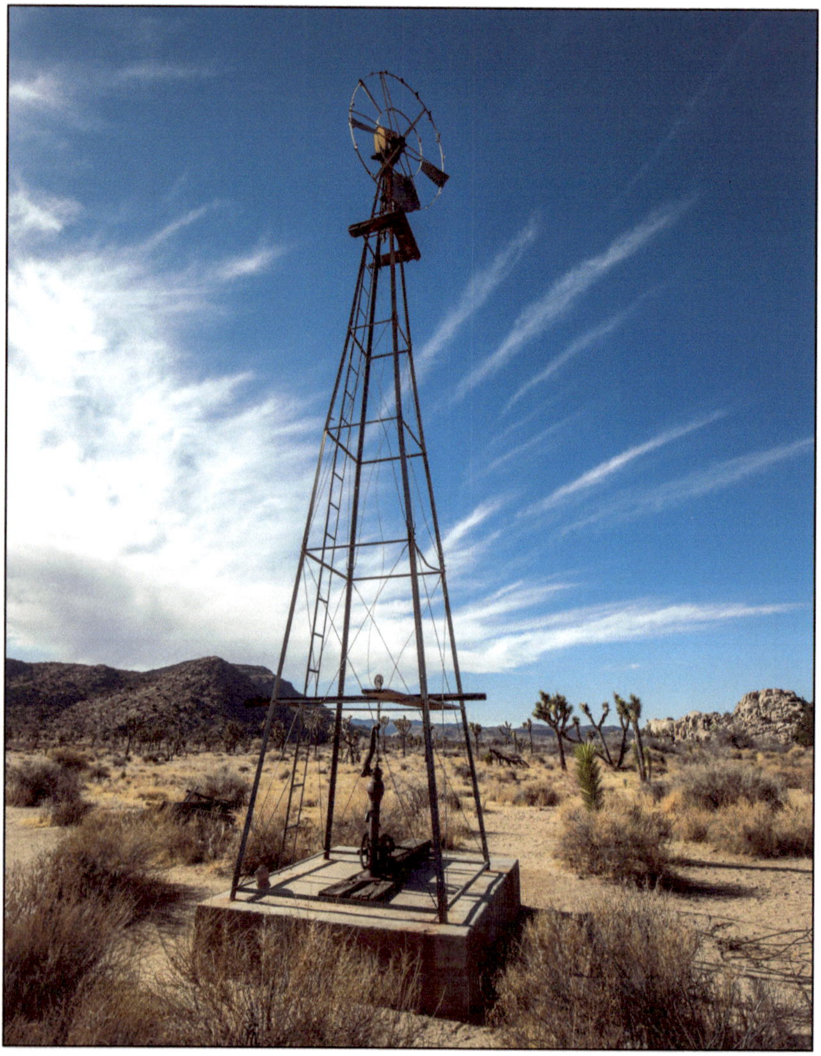

Lonely Windmill   16mm   f/11   1/250s   ISO100

The windmill is about 0.3-mile from the gravel parking lot. It makes for a useable waypoint during your exit, as it is easy between here and the mill site to mistake the wash for the trail at times.

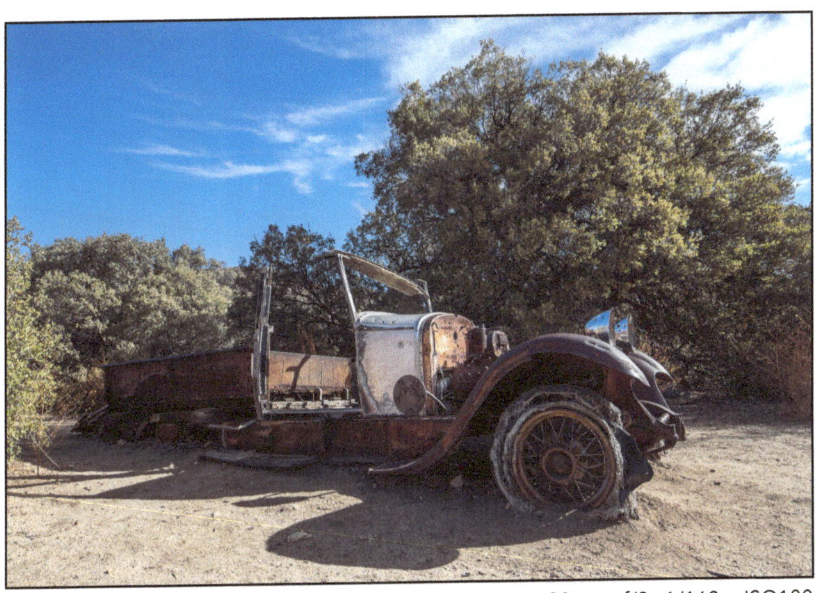

Wall Street Truck   20mm f/8 1/160s ISO100

Beyond the windmill, truck (above), and mill there is more to see. Find information on the Worth Bagley tombstone and another rusted vehicle hiding in the brush. **Do be careful – sharp metal and barbed wire are exposed in places.**

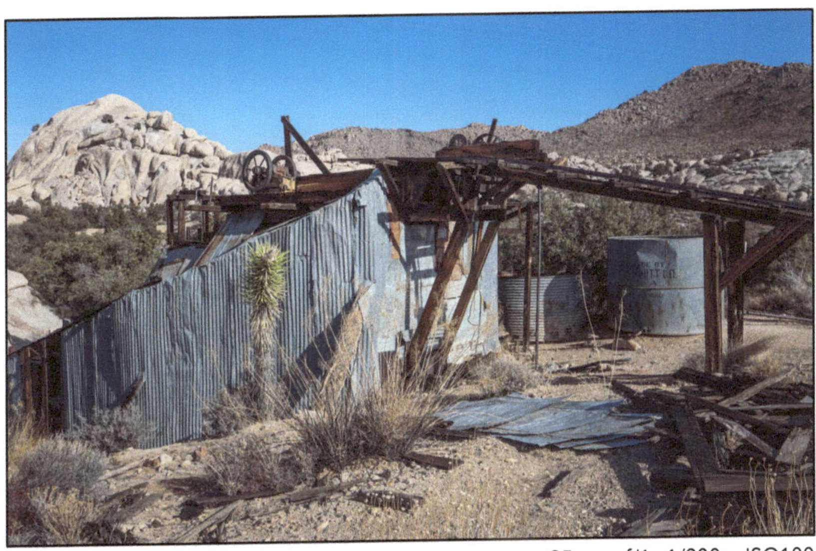

Wall Street Mill   35mm f/1 1/200s ISO100

Time	Best / Good								Reward			

Budget	15 min	Type	Roadside	Effort	
RT Distance	<900 ft	Δ Elev.	<10 ft	Zoom	Normal

Cap Rock is a waypoint within the park, at the turnoff from Park Blvd to Keys View. The feature is not sensational, but it is too easy to photograph to skip. The best perspective is from along Keys View Rd.

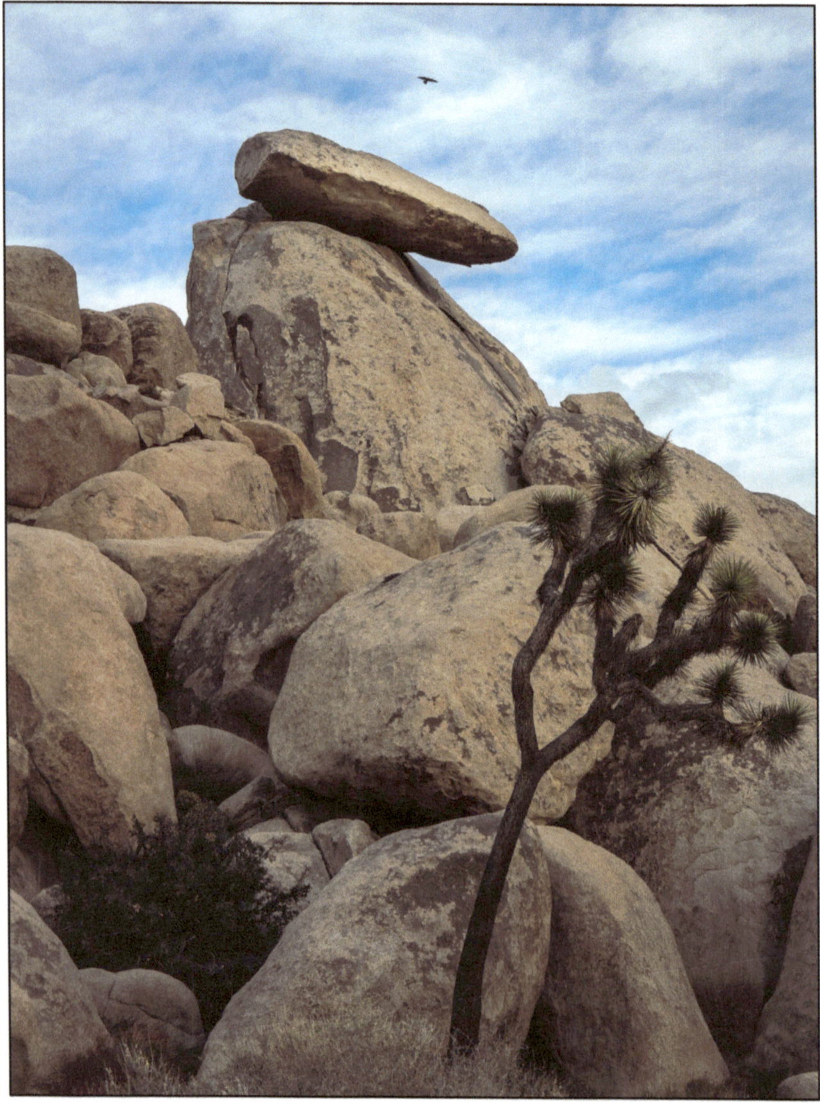

A Raven Soars above Cap Rock   50mm f/8 1/200s ISO200

Time	•Best Good							Reward	
Budget	15-30 min		Type		Roadside		Effort		
RT Distance	~0.2 mi		Δ Elev.		<10 ft		Zoom	Wide Angle	

The Johnny Lang story is one of the best (if not *the* best) among the various, charismatic pioneers of Joshua Tree. I'll provide the gist, but I encourage you to find the complete tale.

Lang left his cowboy ways from New Mexico and turned to mining, ultimately establishing Lost Horse, which became a highly profitable mine. The mine was not solely owned by Lang, and after some years his partners discovered that he was stealing some of the processed gold from the operation. He bargained a deal to sell his stake in order to avoid prosecution.

Not long after this event, the mine became unprofitable. Lang, having stayed in the area following his eviction, moved back onto the abandoned site. But by what means now was he able to support himself? From time to time, he would emerge with gold for sale!

Lang lived his final years at Lost Horse, and one day he left – to head to town for rations. He only made it about 2 miles, before the harsh winter took his life. Bill Keys found his body months later, preserved by the desert, and buried him on-site.

The tombstone reads:

JOHN LANG
DIED HERE
BURIED BY W.
F. KEYS, FRANK
KILER, JEFF
PEEDEN MAR.
25, 1925

Park at the westside, paved pullout that is 300 ft south of the turnoff to the Lost Horse Mine. Walk roadside, back north 500 ft. The tombstone is just 40 ft off the road.

Had he hidden the gold he had stolen? It is perceivable. Did he ever run out? No one knows…

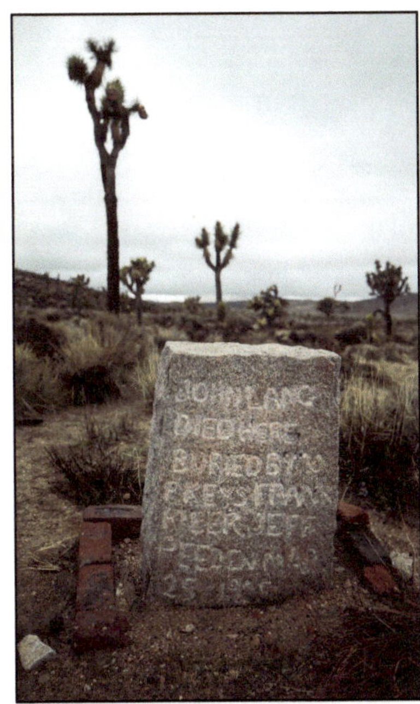

24mm f/2.8 1/500s ISO100

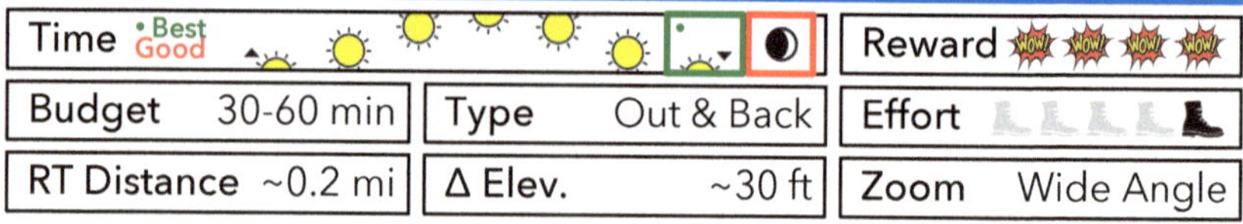

Time	Best Good									Reward	WOW! WOW! WOW! WOW!
Budget	30-60 min		Type	Out & Back		Effort	
RT Distance	~0.2 mi		Δ Elev.	~30 ft		Zoom	Wide Angle

Keys View is perhaps the one place in Joshua Tree National Park where your experience as a photographer will be the most impacted by outside forces, namely atmospheric conditions and *other visitors*.

Let's explore the view… If visiting during the daytime and the air is clear enough, you can see Palm Springs and the greater Coachella Valley all the way south to the Salton Sea. The Santa Rosa and San Jacinto Mountains climb behind the Coachella Valley, and San Gorgonio Mountain is to your right. The following is the view south, with the Salton Sea barely visible (in a deeper blue at the horizon).

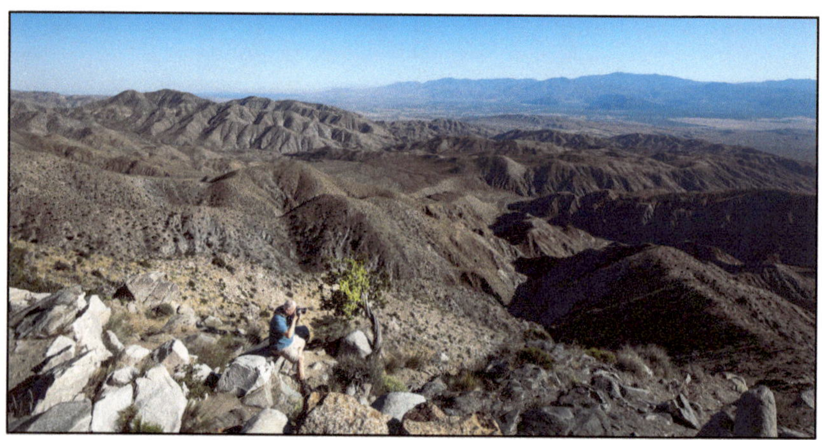

The Salton Sea and the Coachella Valley   17mm f/8 1/160s ISO50

The most exciting element of this photo is the gentleman taking a picture of the twisted tree. My point is… Typical daytime visits are OK, but do not expect remarkable photos.

Sunset, however, can be sensational. Let's now address those outside forces, one at a time.

"Atmospheric conditions" includes air quality (especially smog, and hopefully a lack thereof), clouds (we *love* clouds, as long as they're the *right* clouds), temperature, and wind. Smog, we get. It generally impedes visibility. Clouds help provide interest to a setting sun, so as long as they aren't completely blocking the setting sun. Temperature and wind – well, let's just say that it can become **bitingly cold** at this lookout in a very short amount of time. Plan and dress accordingly!

Other visitors. It can become quite crowded here for sunset, most especially on Friday and Saturday nights. As visitors continue to arrive, they vie for precious, unoccupied space. For this, I have a recommendation…

At the west end of the parking area is the paved, walking loop. Take the path on the right – the most direct route to the main viewing area. (It will be instinctual to walk this direction.) Pass a small viewing area on your right, then find the large, semi-circle viewing area ahead. This is where the crowd congregates. This is *not* where you want to be.

Continue walking a bit further and find a bench on the left. Opposite this bench are a lot of rocks (back on the right side of the path). Safely make your way down among these rocks (be careful!), relax, and watch the sun drift towards the horizon. From this vantage, the crowd at your right should remain out of the composition.

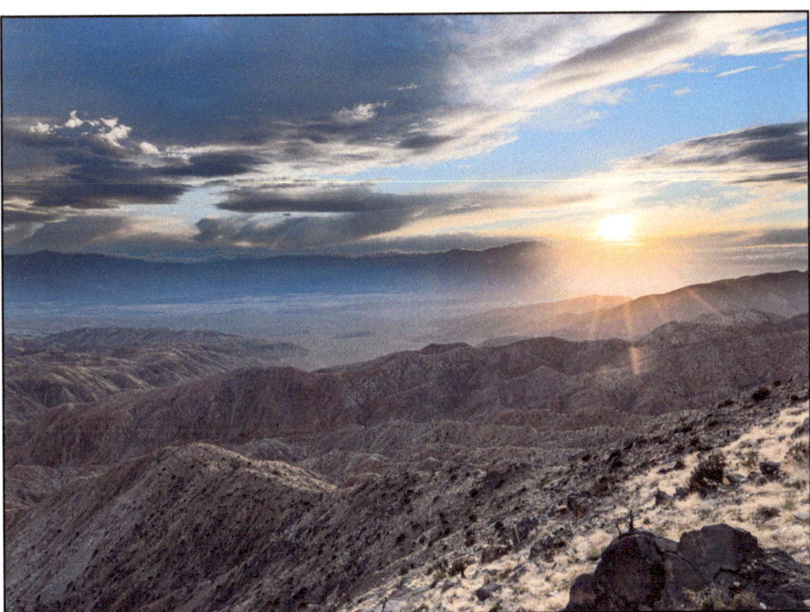

Keys View Sunset 20mm f/22 1/25s ISO100

For this shot I did use a tripod, even though I didn't have to based on shutter speed and room to move on ISO if necessary. I find in this situation the tripod allows me to set my composition, and better enjoy the "waiting" aspect. I stopped down all the way to f/22 in order to make a sunstar (the beams of light). I also set the exposure compensation to -2 stops so as to capture more color in the sky. (This does require pulling a lot of detail from the shadows in post process.)

I wish you favorable conditions, a relaxing evening, and great results!

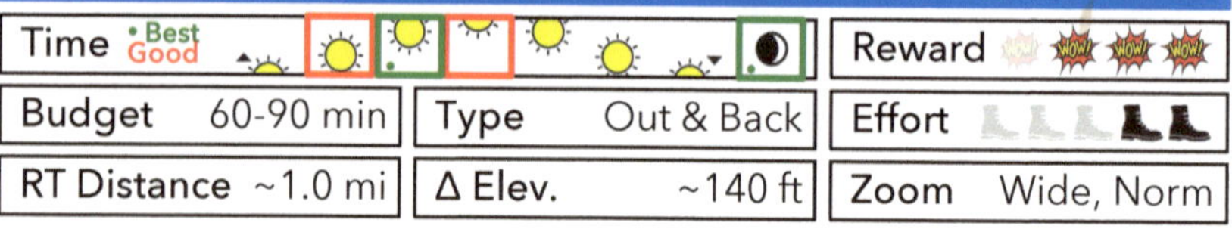

Time	Best / Good			Reward	
Budget	60-90 min	Type	Out & Back	Effort	
RT Distance	~1.0 mi	Δ Elev.	~140 ft	Zoom	Wide, Norm

Ryan Ranch is a great area to photograph and has already been highlighted twice in this book (pages 11 & 40). Its main feature is the ranch house ruin, which makes for a superb subject daytime or nighttime.

The map below highlights what I consider the "best" of the area – the ranch house ruin, a large & rusty water tank, and a small junkyard of rusty artifacts. There is though still more to find and photograph if your interest and time permits.

Like other ruin areas within the park, there are also some dangers, such as exposed barbed wire. Walk and explore cautiously. If you plan to visit at nighttime, I cannot overemphasize the benefit in visiting first during daytime to get your bearings - especially of these hazards.

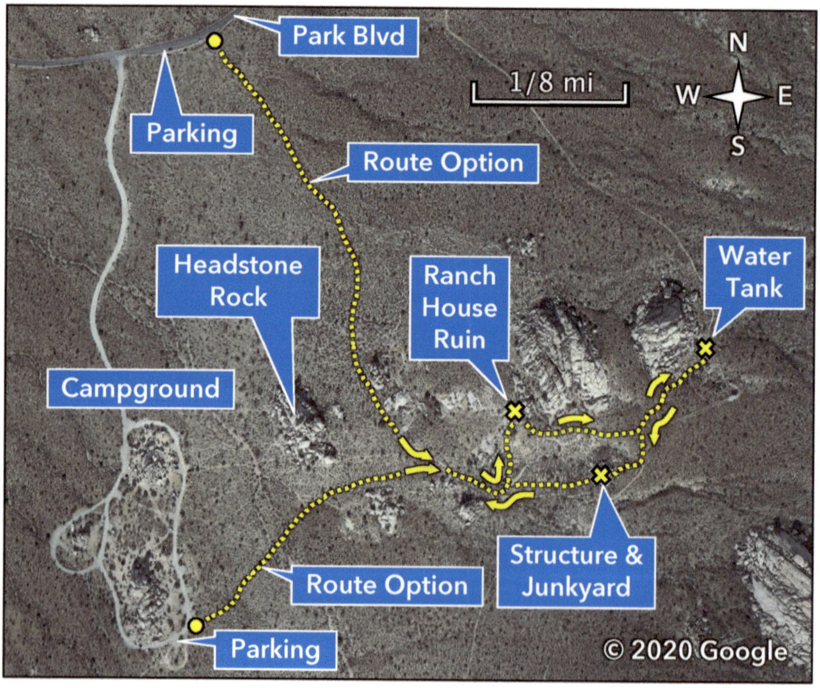

Access to this area is most direct by way of two parking areas. The first (and most direct) is from the Ryan Campground. (Though I discourage parking here outside of daytime hours, so as not to interrupt the campground with vehicle lights.) The second is from a long, paved pullout off Park Boulevard.

First up on the map is the ranch house ruin. All sides of it are photo-genic.   I typically though work here with the sun at my back. Unfortunately, there is a lot of etched graffiti, but it can be easy to camouflage with varying compositions. (Or capture any interesting details you find.)

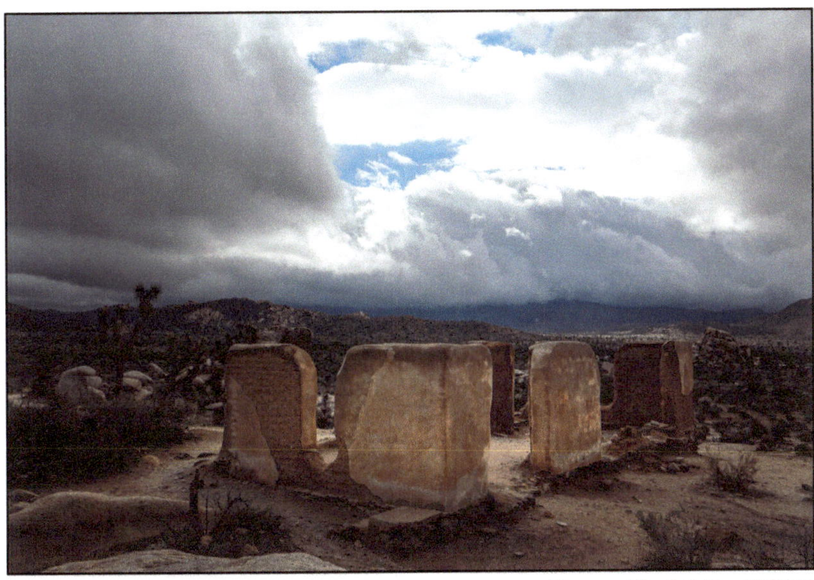

Ryan Ranch House Ruin

28mm f/8 1/640s ISO100

Once finished with this area, head in the direction of the pink, concrete block structure (which is a complete dud for photography), but then hook left around towards the second large rock formation. Find the large, rusty water tank. ...More graffiti, but it is still interesting. I think its best side is with the ladder and water gauge.

Finally, meander towards the white structure and find a handful of interesting items left behind, including the windmill turbine.

Once finished, make your way back towards where you entered, and backtrack to whichever parking area you began.

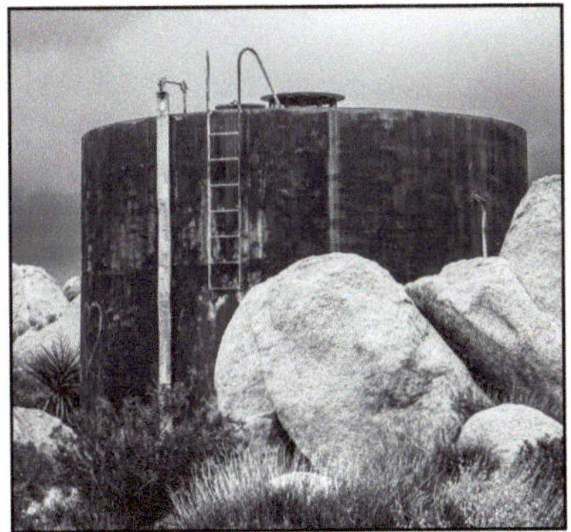

50mm f/8 1/125s ISO200

One "option" add-on is the nearby Headstone Rock. Accessing it is easy, with a slight deviation from either of the two primary routes.

OK, some of you may recognize that I have already introduced this topic. (See page 37.) This is a *variation on a theme.*

One thing is guaranteed at Joshua Tree National Park - you won't be there alone. And at sunset, others are out for the show as well. It's a wonderful time, celebrating the enjoyed activities from the day, and now welcoming the desert nighttime ahead. The human spirit is collective and great.

Perched atop rock formations, find individuals, couples, families, and friends - they make great landscape photography subjects too! As you can tell by now, I generally avoid people in my photos, but I think in this fashion, as silhouettes, they're fantastic.

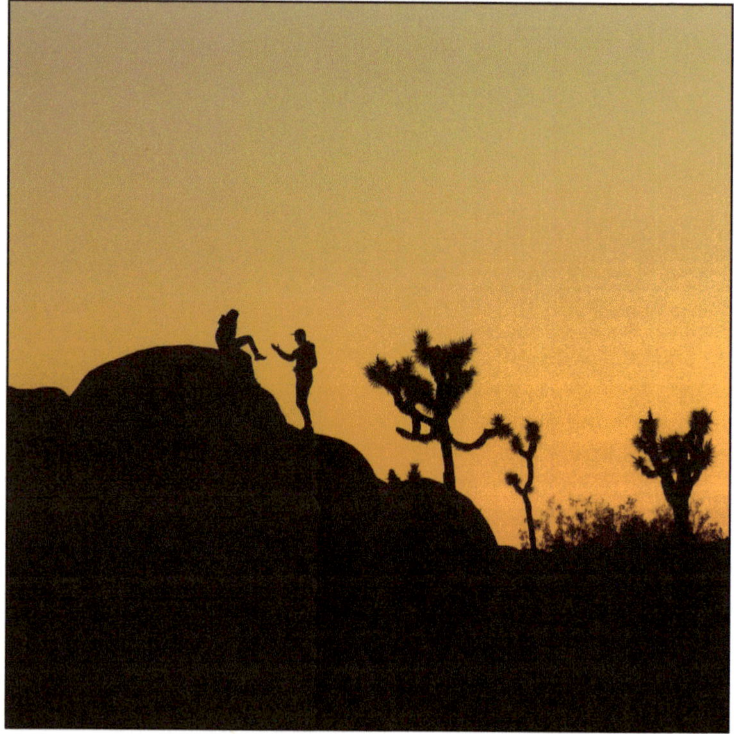

Helping Hand   300mm f/5.6 1/500s ISO200

The very best place for this is from the Jumbo Rocks Campground area. The abundance of people (many who will be staying to camp), Joshua Trees and unobstructed views of the horizon make this place perfect for capturing silhouettes - whether they be trees or fellow travelers. Longer focal lengths work best.

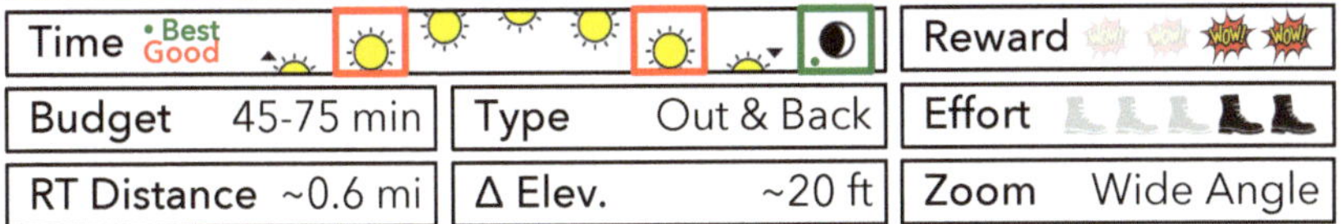

Time	Best Good					Reward		
Budget	45-75 min	Type		Out & Back		Effort		
RT Distance	~0.6 mi	Δ Elev.		~20 ft		Zoom	Wide Angle	

Wherever your photography takes you, it is always a good practice to let someone know where you're going. We know why… Dismal as it sounds, if you don't report back in, they will know where to look.

When I travel my daily prerequisite is to text or email my itinerary to my wife. I have been to the "Hall of Horrors" many times, during daytime hours *and also at nighttime*… I wonder what goes through her mind when she reads that is where I'll be going. *(Sounds scary!)*

The "hall" is a long, tall, and narrow space between two rock formations. Clearly at one time the formation split, and over time the gap grew and grew. It is wide enough for one person to easily walk through, but not a lot more.

The "horrors" are how you may feel, standing and feeling somewhat trapped, beneath a car-sized boulder held in suspension above.

Some rock scrambling is required to access the entrance, and carrying a tripod is arguably a must due to the interior's darkness. Agility and technical competency is required. Assess and decide if proceeding is safely within your abilities.

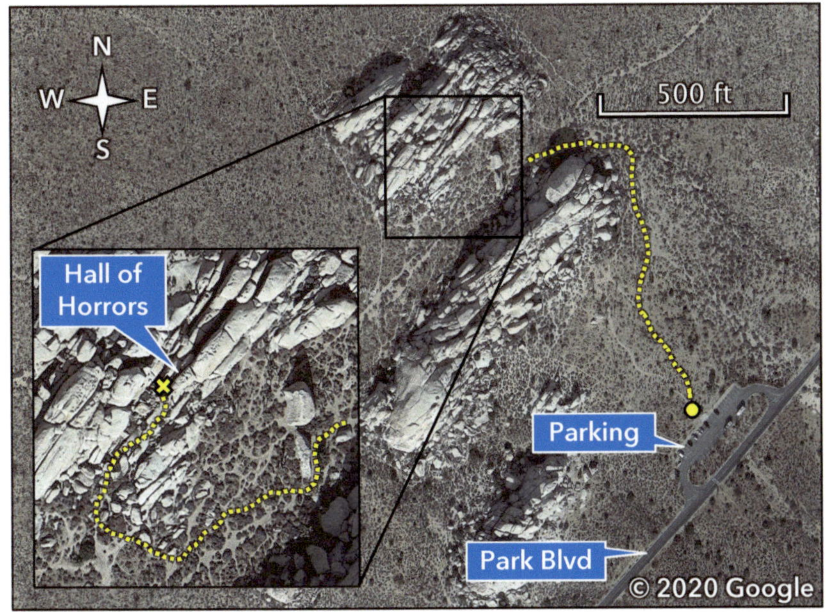

From the Hall of Horrors parking area, head along the main path towards the large rock formation. Veer to the right, to walk behind it. (This is the most direct route.) Cross an open area between these two, large rock formations towards the far end of the second formation now at your right.

Finding the route to the entrance of the hall may require some trial and error. I originally looked for it using GPS, and it didn't help much at all! So no GPS coordinates from me on this one. Study the detail view of the map on the prior page. The best way I can describe the route is to climb from the ground on top of a large rock that is more flat on top, like a table top. Cross it to another large, flat rock. Then straight ahead, to the left, and scramble up and over to the entrance.

To actually "enter" the hall, you have to descend a bit over a boulder. There is a blind "step" to help on the way down, and out (for later).

Lighting and weather play a huge role in your photography experience at the Hall of Horrors. I prefer nighttime results, as the bright light from above isn't in fierce competition with the darkness within the hall. Also, rock climbers frequent this area, and during the daytime it is uncommon to have the space to yourself. Let's explore the various shots on the next page (by the abbreviated titles)…

Rain

This is a typical daytime shot with thick cloud cover and rain. The cloud cover helps minimize the bright light above, and the long, water puddle adds interest to the bottom of the composition.

HDR

My two cameras have in-camera HDR (High Dynamic Range) capability. Many newer cameras do, and if yours doesn't there is software that can perform this task. This is a "merge" of multiple exposures, from underexposed to overexposed. If this is new to you, research the topic online… It can be useful when lighting is strong and your composition has dark elements you want to show.

B&W

This is a typical nighttime experience under clear skies. I used my headlamp to quickly illuminate the hall during the exposure and went with a black-and-white for variety.

Red

Here I am, with a red light behind me. This is an eerie photo, fitting of the site's name, that provides perspective to the hall's height by way of my size within it.

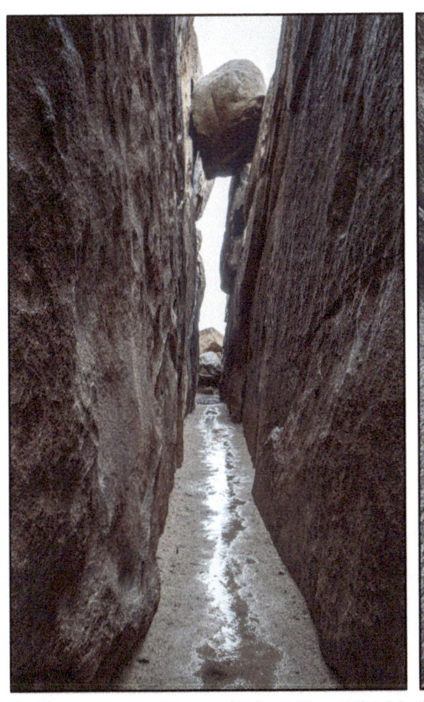
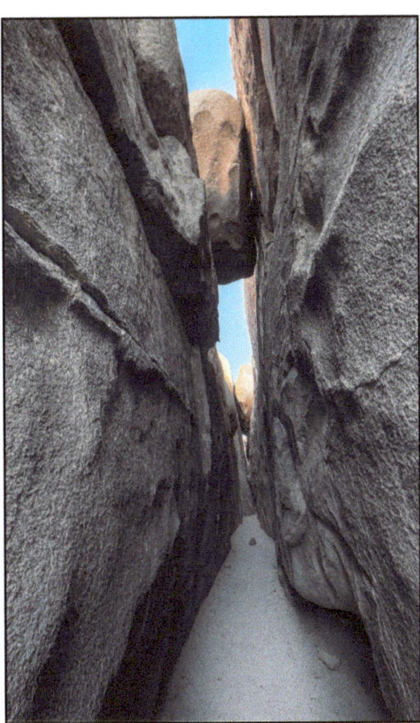

Rain   35mm f/16 1/5s ISO100   **HDR**   16mm f/8 1/5s (±) ISO100

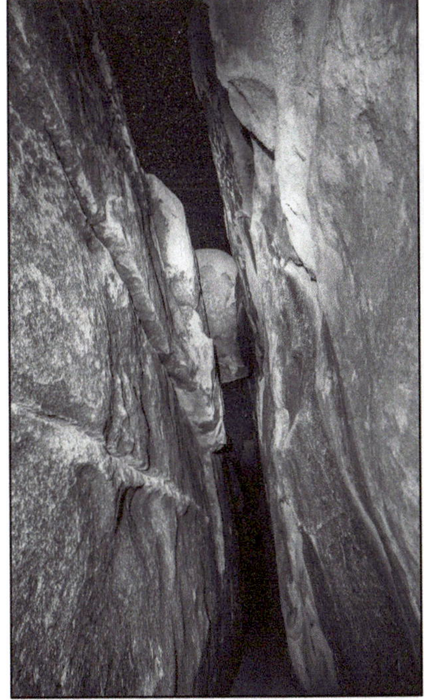
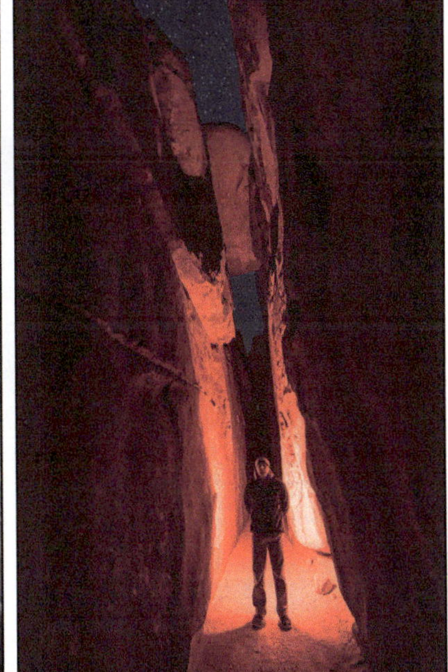

B&W   18mm f/5.6 20s ISO1600   **Red**   18mm f/5.6 30s ISO1600

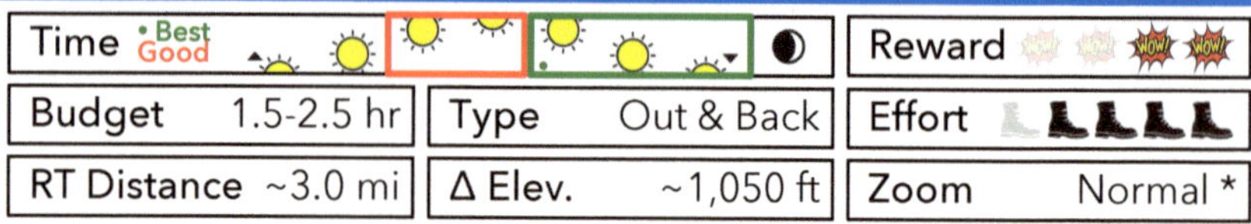

Time	•Best Good									Reward			
Budget	1.5-2.5 hr		**Type**		Out & Back		**Effort**						
RT Distance	~3.0 mi		**Δ Elev.**		~1,050 ft		**Zoom**		Normal *				

Who needs a drone when you can hike to the top of Ryan Mountain?

I consider the Ryan Mountain experience in three sections. The first section (only 1/8-mile or so) ascends through a lovely, natural desert garden. The second section provides sweeping views north towards the Hall of Horrors, Hidden Valley, and the west side of the Wonderland of Rocks. (This is my favorite section, from a photographer's perspective.) The final section is mostly a viewless final ascent to the top, where once you arrive you are granted sweeping panoramic views to your east towards Malapai Hill and west towards Ryan Ranch and San Gorgonio Mountain. *Add a telephoto lens to your kit if you want to zoom-in on these places for interest, though the photographic end result is not remarkable.

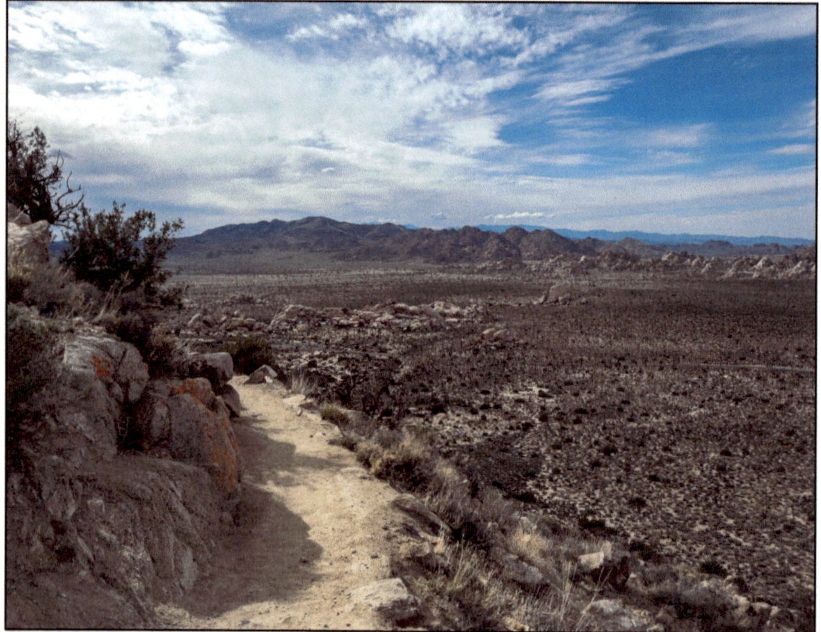

Ryan Mountain Ascent   24mm f/8 1/400s ISO100

The grade is steady, which allows for a constant pace up and down.

Near the parking area, towards the west end, is a short trail to an interesting "Indian Cave" – a large boulder with headroom underneath, clearly used for shelter by Native American inhabitants.

East Park Central

Geology Tour Road to White Tank Campground

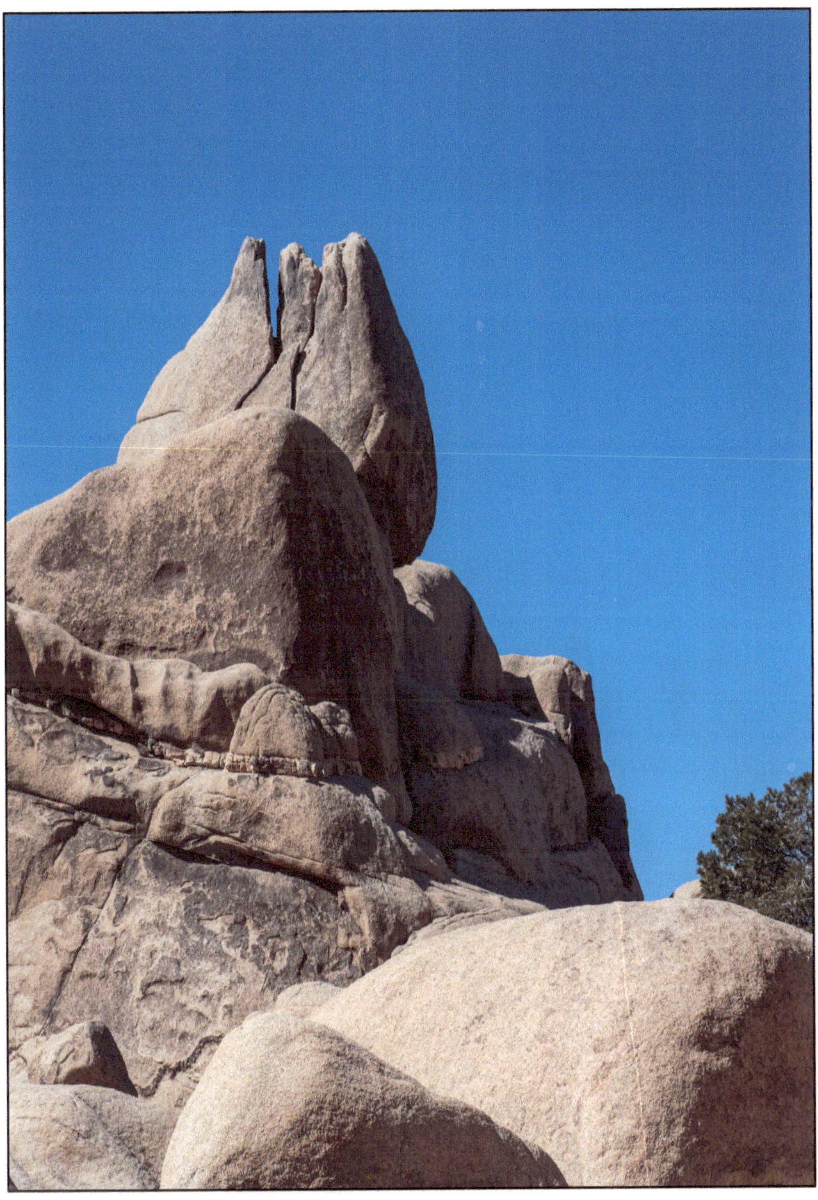

Tulip Rock along the Split Rock Loop Trail   85mm f/8 1/320s ISO100

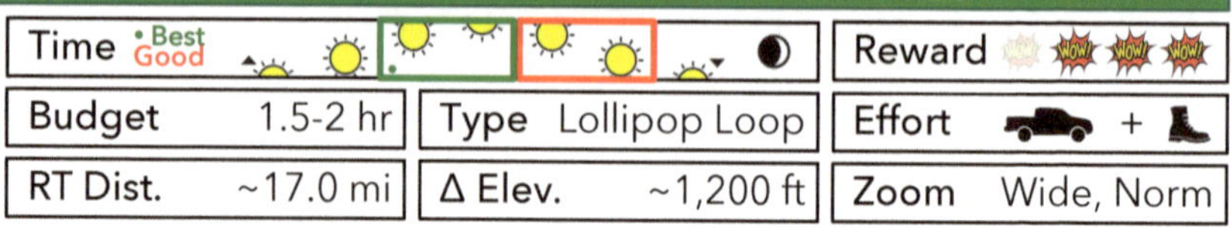

Time	Best / Good		Reward	
Budget	1.5-2 hr	Type Lollipop Loop	Effort	
RT Dist.	~17.0 mi	Δ Elev. ~1,200 ft	Zoom Wide, Norm	

Venture off-pavement through a splendid variety of unique terrain, including by Malapai Hill and across a dry lake.

This route can either be entirely behind the wheel, or if you want to stretch your legs and trek straight across the flat desert to Balanced Rock it requires ~1/2 mile (round trip) of hiking. Signage is present requiring vehicles making the complete loop to be equipped with 4WD. Much would be missed if the route was not seen in its entirety.

A brochure is made available by the National Park Service describing 16 points of interest along the drive. It is available at any of the Visitor Centers. Sometimes a steel box near the readerboard at the entrance is also filled with copies, but I would not count on it. Unfortunately, I have been unable to find a digital copy online.

By my vehicle's mileage, here are the approximate distances (in miles) from the entrance gate, for each of the points of interest:

1	2	3	4	5	6	7	8
0.2	1.1	2.7	3.0	3.5	4.0	4.5	4.9

9	10	11	12	13	14	15	16
5.2	5.5	6.0	6.7	6.8	9.4	9.5	9.6

I will cover a few in particular, even though **the entire drive is scenic.**

Balanced Rock if first-up on my list. Access is via the Point of Interest #7 (Malapai Hill) parking area. Below is a map illustrating the straightforward hike. Balanced Rock is visible from the road.

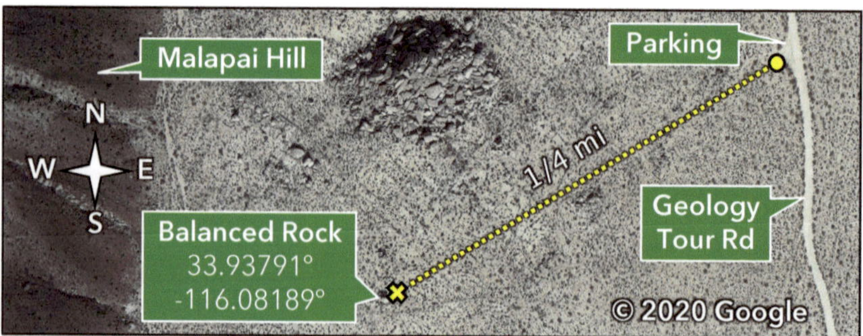

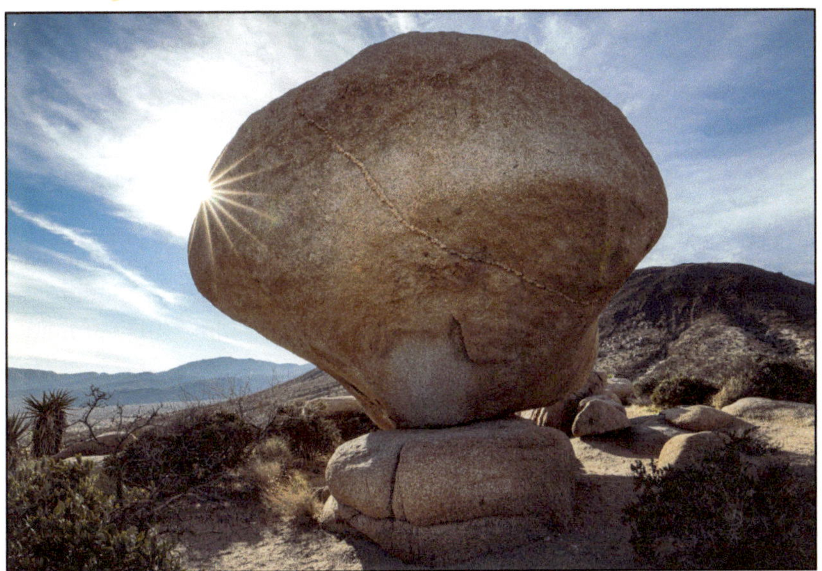

Balanced Rock   20mm f/22 1/30s ISO100

For the above, since I was shooting into the sunlight, the rock faces were dark. I pulled a lot of detail from the shadows in post-processing.

I like to hop-out at #12 and at spots between #13 & 14. The playa (dry lake) here is regularly photogenic.

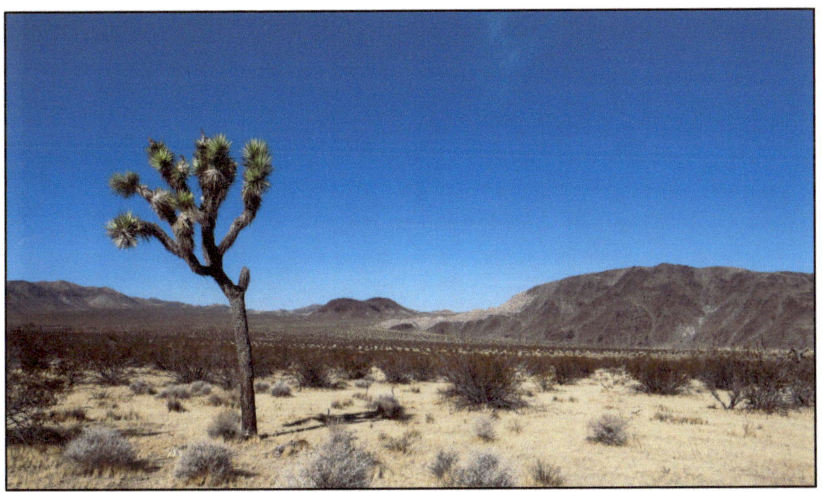

Pleasant Valley   24mm f/16 1/200s ISO100

The lichens on the Pino Gneiss at #14 can make for some good close-up photography.

Panoramic View at #16 is nice, and worth a stop, but I like the vista between #13 & 14 better. Lighting sometimes dictates which is best.

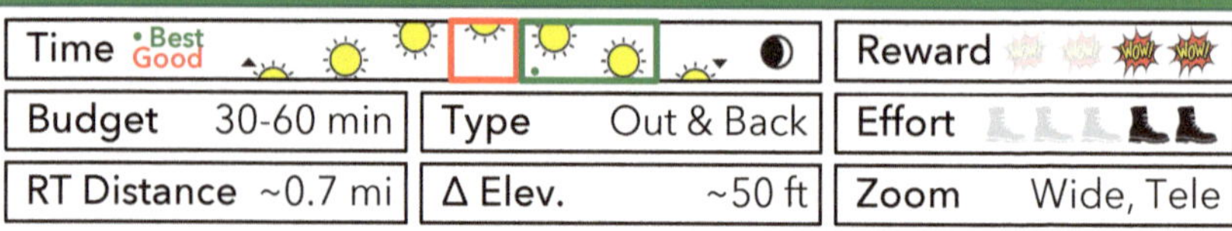

Time	Best Good		Reward	
Budget	30-60 min	Type Out & Back	Effort	
RT Distance ~0.7 mi	Δ Elev. ~50 ft	Zoom Wide, Tele		

The Desert Queen Mine was a huge operation. Remnants of it remain, and its size is distinguishable from afar. While a well-traveled route can take you to it, I have found its photogenic "potential" is minimal, so we will peer down on it from a viewpoint above. (Mining aficionados may argue otherwise!)

This short walk is easy and includes two other stops - a bunkhouse structure and a cable winch, both which supported the Desert Queen Mine. The area is dense with Parry's Nolina, which make it even more photogenic in the spring when they are flowering.

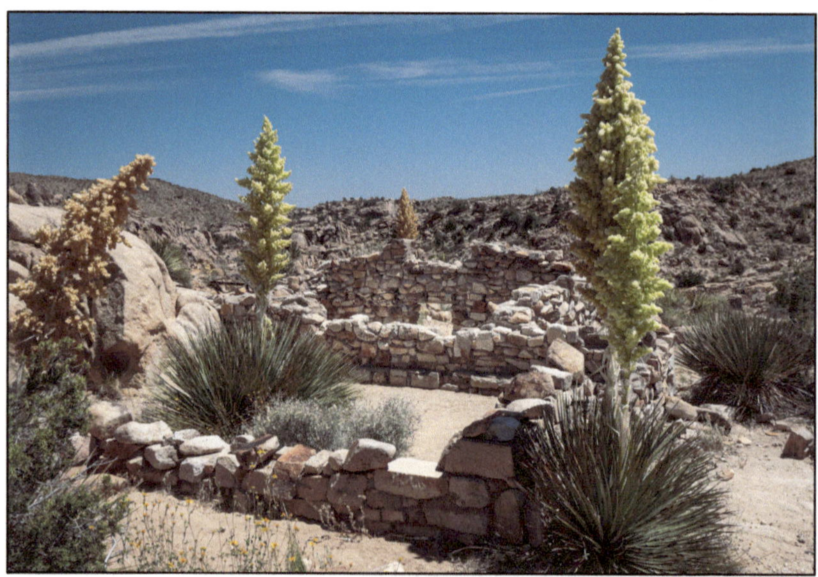

Bunkhouse Ruin   35mm   f/11   1/640s   ISO200

The hike begins from the parking area at the end of Desert Queen Mine Road, at the right of the vault toilet. The trail heads west. Walk more-or-less straight (continue west) for 0.2-mile and find at your right the bunkhouse, about 120 ft off the trail. Explore this structure, especially noting the curiously-short doorway! Once ready, backtrack to the main trail and continue west again.

After only another ~300 ft, come to the primary viewpoint. Here you can see the breadth of the Desert Queen Mine. Work with wider focal lengths, to capture it all, and with longer focal lengths to isolate interesting features. The tell-tale sign of a mine is its *tailings* (waste rock) and here the *adits* (horizontal tunnels) covered by metal panels. Look down into the wash and find equipment that lost to gravity's will.

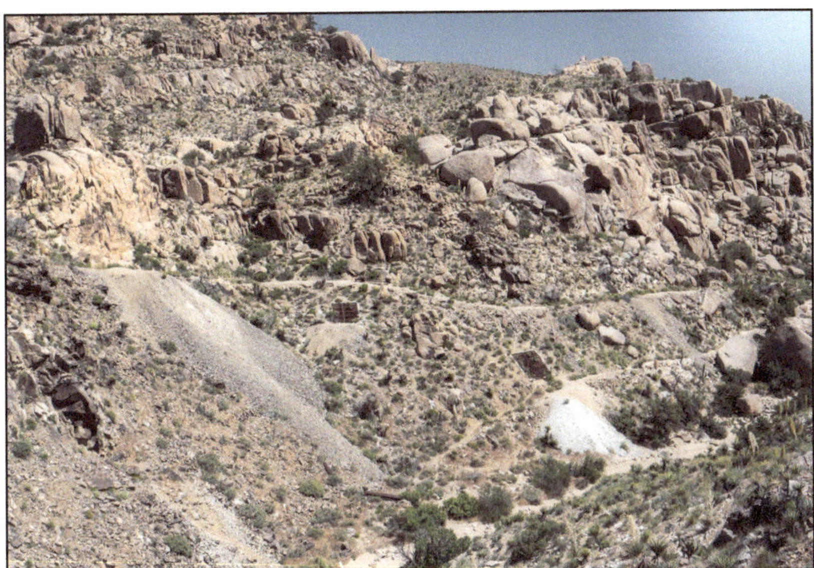

Desert Queen Adits and Tailings   35mm f/8 1/500s ISO100

From near the vista area there is a trail that heads north, gaining a bit more elevation, to a cable winch. It is another ~300 ft (long) hike.

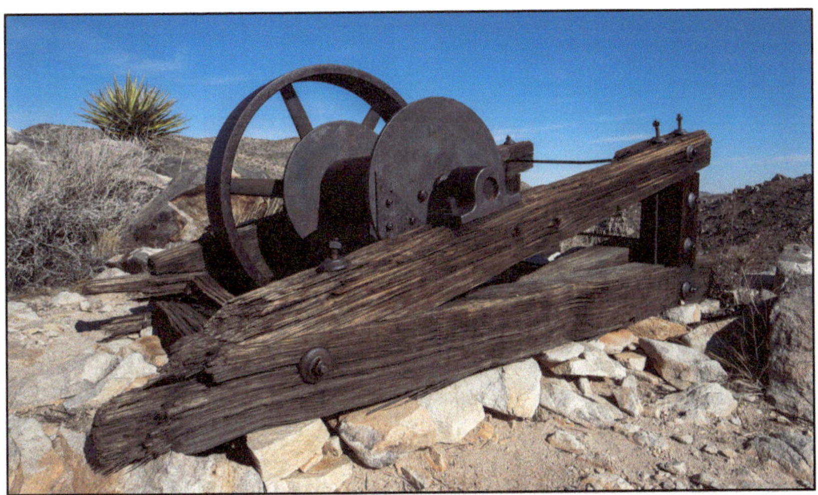

Preserved Winch and Timber   20mm f/16 1/100s ISO100

Once finished here, retrace your footsteps back to the parking area.

If instead the mine is now beckoning your visit, one of the routes to it is from the bunkhouse. The path is well-beaten and easy to follow.

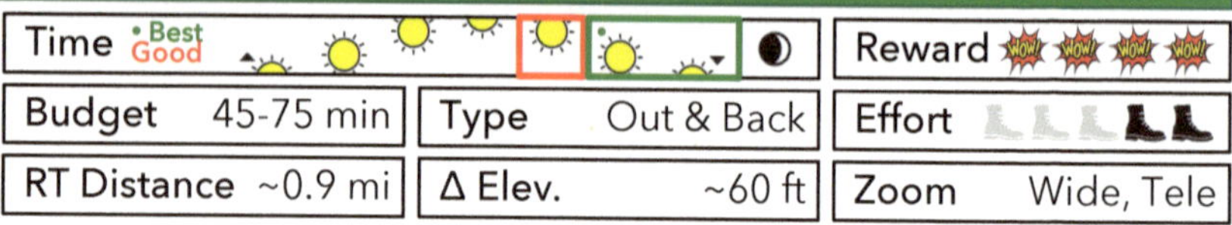

Time	Best Good								Reward
Budget	45-75 min	Type	Out & Back	Effort					
RT Distance	~0.9 mi	Δ Elev.	~60 ft	Zoom	Wide, Tele				

"Jumbo Rocks" is a fun name, even if doesn't distinguish this area from many others in the national park. Jumbo rocks are everywhere!

There are two *exceptional* rock formations here at the Jumbo Rocks Campground... Penguin Rock and Atlas. Park in one of the few available spaces at the campground entrance or along Park Blvd. Study the readerboard map on your way in and begin your walk.

Penguin Rock (opposite) is found directly behind campsite 19. Please be courteous when this area's campsites are occupied... It is easy to hike onto the rocks, above, and around to Penguin Rock from the main campground road so as not to interrupt anyone there.

For this composition, you will work from very low to the ground. **Penguin Rock is actually quite larger than this tree! It is a textbook example of perspective.** Late afternoon softly lights the rock and tree.

Atlas is found further down the main campground road, off the entrance to Skull Rock Trail. Go up the steps, then bend right to a broad stone platform.

Alternatively, Atlas can be photographed from the campground's amphitheater with a longer focal length.

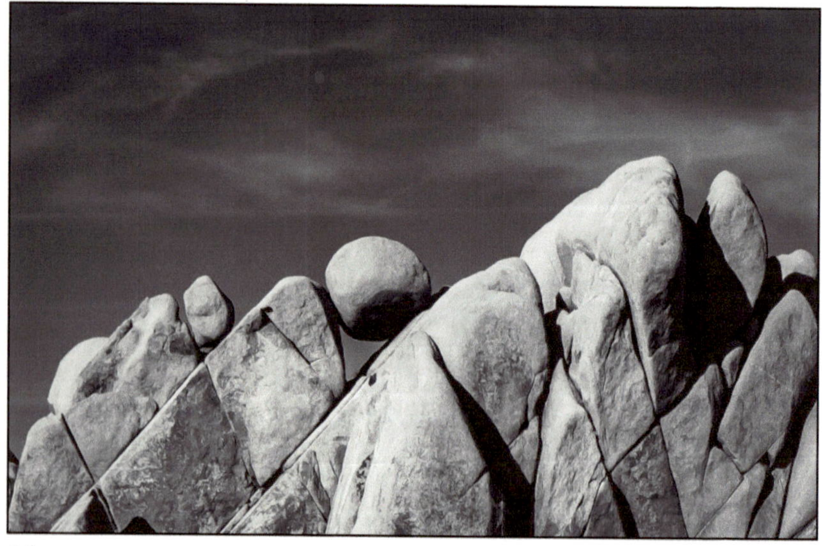

Atlas

135mm f/5.6 1/640s ISO200

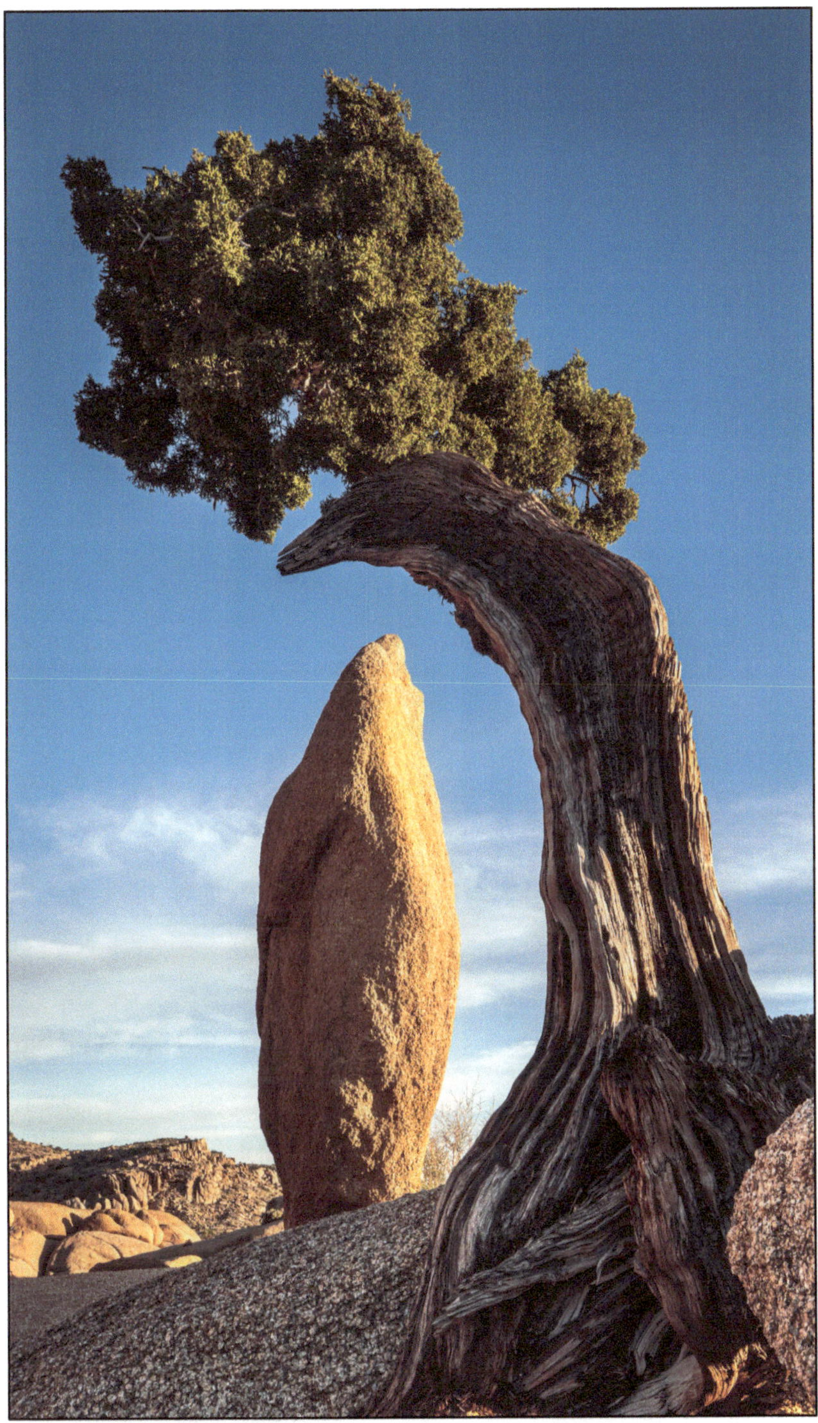

Juniper & Penguin Rock

28mm f/22 1/50s ISO400

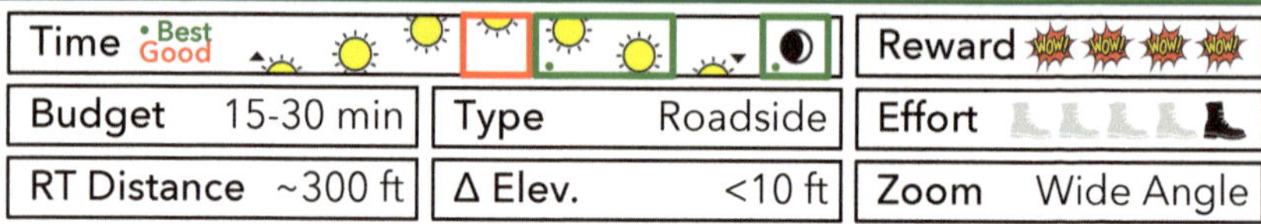

Time	•Best Good		Reward	WOW! WOW! WOW! WOW!
Budget	15-30 min	Type	Roadside	Effort
RT Distance	~300 ft	Δ Elev.	<10 ft	Zoom Wide Angle

Everyone stops at Skull Rock. It's roadside and perhaps the most interestingly-shaped rock in the entire park.

At right is what most people capture. The bravest visitors climb into the eye sockets, but I strongly recommend against it. I have witnessed falls.

If by luck (or brilliant planning) you visit during foggy weather, I think this is when Skull Rock is at its best. It adds an other-worldly mystery to the picture's mood.

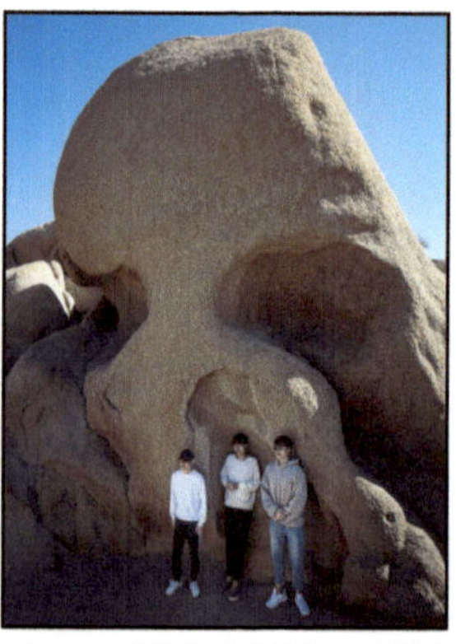

18mm   f/5.6   1/200s   ISO50

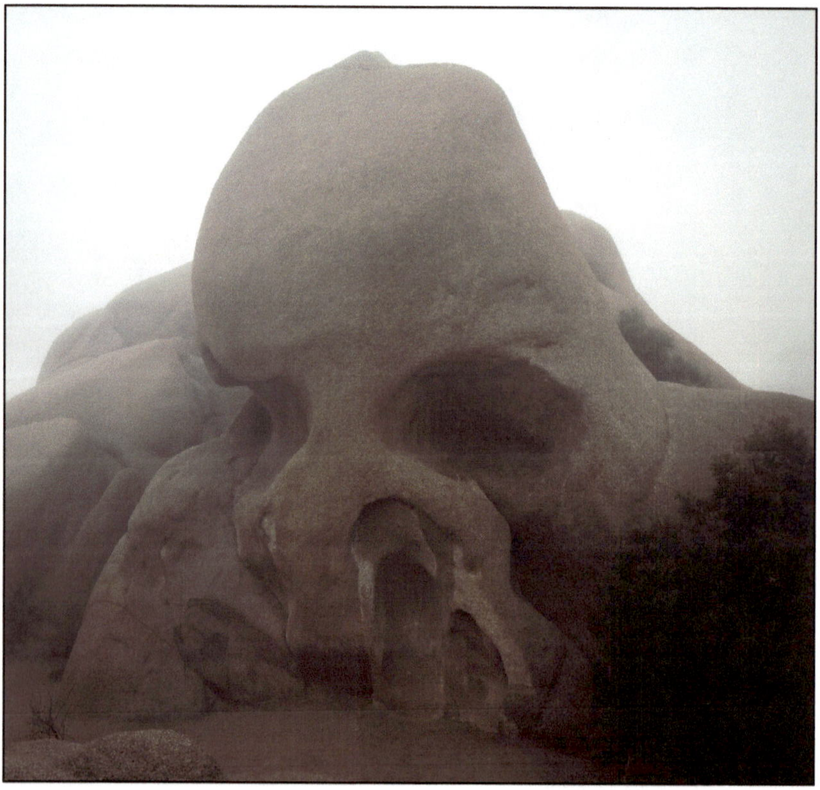

Shrouded in Fog   20mm   f/5.6   1/500s   ISO400

Though, nighttime experimentation with light is fun too. Below I used an off-camera flash with a snoot (a tube to help "focus" the light within a smaller area) and different color gels (colored plastic films) to color the two eye sockets.

There is an easy-to-climb and not-too-high rock formation in front to shoot from up on. During the day it is relatively safe, but at night it can be tricky. Watch your step.

Quality photos are easy to produce here – however you go about it!

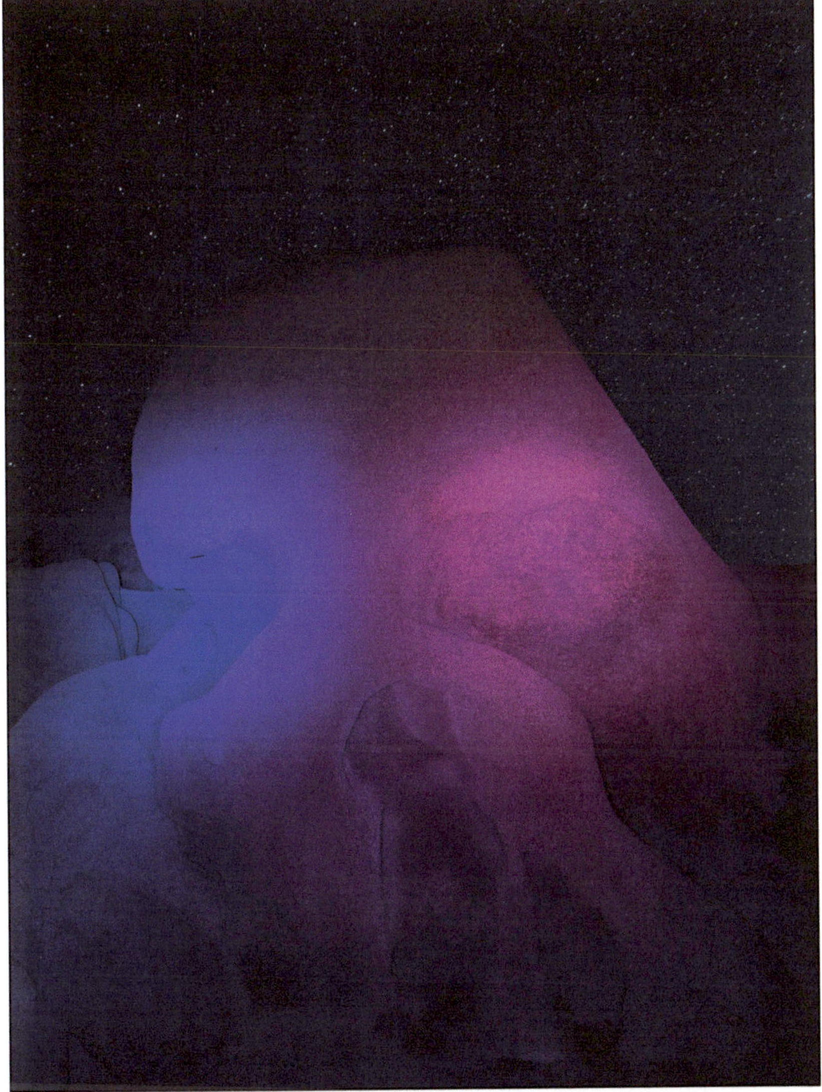

Crazy Cranium   18mm f/5.6 30s ISO1600

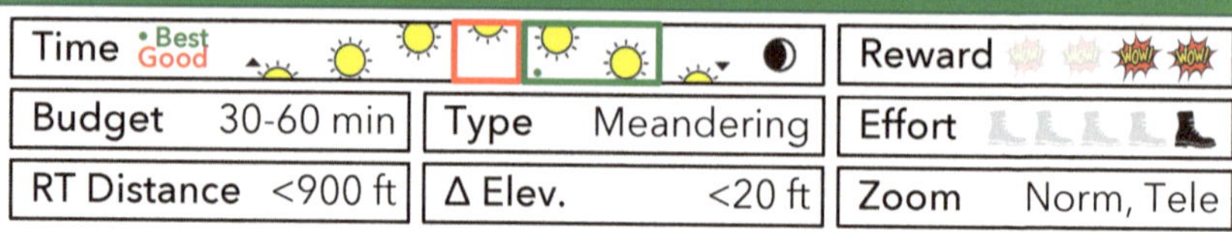

Time	Best / Good		Reward			
Budget	30-60 min	Type	Meandering	Effort		
RT Distance	<900 ft	Δ Elev.	<20 ft	Zoom	Norm, Tele	

Live Oak, Skull Rock's quiet next-door neighbor, is perhaps the most overlooked, easy-to-visit site along Park Boulevard. Above I have 30-60 minutes to really explore, but if you have 15 minutes to give and are OK working quickly, give it your attention. It's deserving.

Not but about 0.1-mile after pulling off of Park Boulevard, curve right towards the west picnic area. From here while eating a sack lunch one day in March I took the photo on page 27. I believe the clouds really make that shot. (They usually do.) If you are looking for a relaxing spot for lunch or a snack, this is a good area.

Back on the unpaved road heading west, begin to notice the sensational ribbons appearing to run through the monzogranite rock formations. These are called dikes, and they were formed by magma filling existing voids within the surrounding formation. They are abundant in this area, and make for an outstanding subject, exemplifying texture. Experiment with wide shots and also close-up. (Ah-oh, this is where time can begin to melt away at Live Oak!)

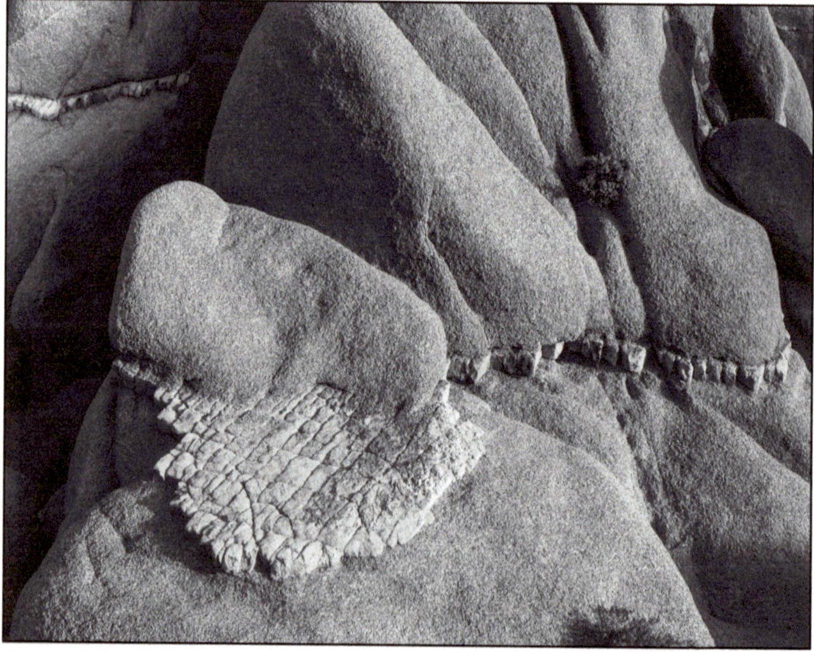

Quartz-Rich Dikes   50mm f/5.6 1/320s ISO200

The road is not long and ends with a small circle used for parking and to turn around. The Live Oak tree is just beyond this area, slightly downhill into the desert wash. It is impressive in size, given these harsh desert conditions.

What is a Live Oak? An oak tree, with *evergreen* leaves. The Live Oak tree's leaves remain green throughout the fall and winter, and only drops leaves in the spring to make room for new growth. This cycle in the spring, however, is relatively quick.

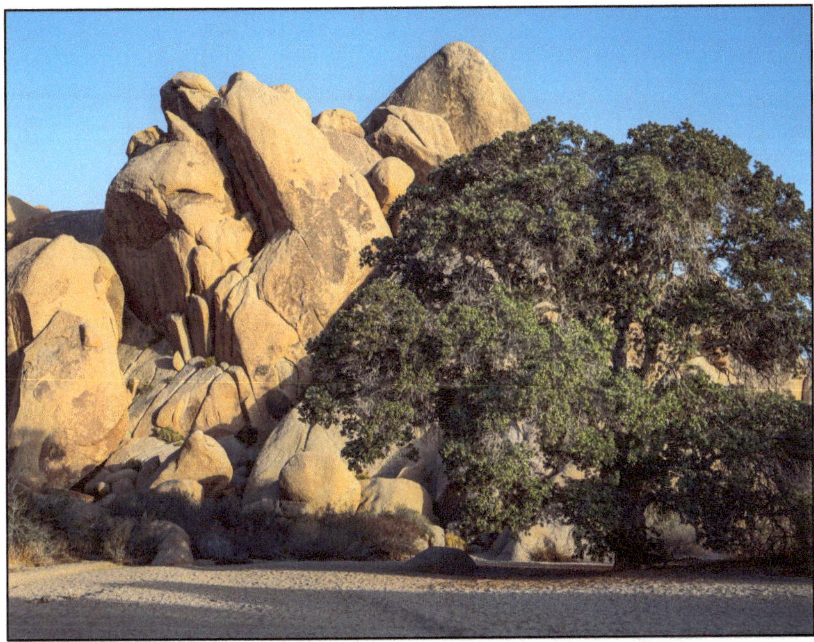

The Live Oak Tree   35mm f/8 1/320s ISO400

The acorns attract birds, and if some are present double-back to your car and grab the telephoto. At right is a Woodhouse's Scrub-Jay. One day I enjoyed watching this one having a great time with the abundant acorns in the shade.

Just past the Live Oak down the wash is a weathered rock with a naturally-eroded window. With some clever positioning, it can make a good "picture frame" for a headshot portrait of your travel companion.

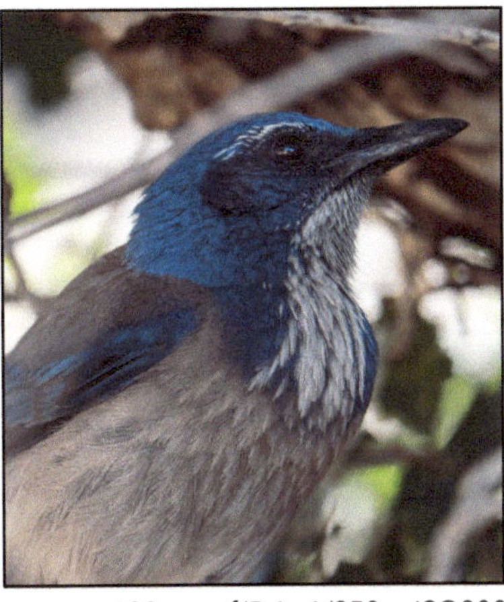

600mm f/5.6 1/250s ISO800

111

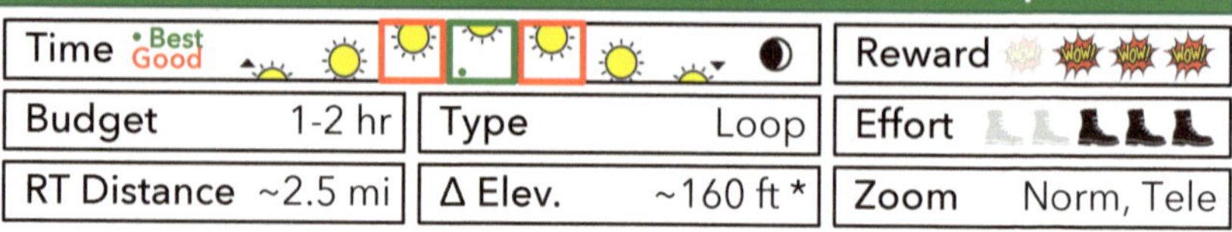

Time	Best Good	☀ ☀ ☀ ☀ ☀ ☀ ◖	Reward	🌸 💥 💥 💥
Budget	1-2 hr	Type	Loop	Effort	👢 👢 👢👢👢
RT Distance	~2.5 mi	Δ Elev.	~160 ft *	Zoom	Norm, Tele

* Regular elevation gain and loss. See elevation profile, page 129.

"Split Rock" is a rock (though it may be different rock), and it is also a loop trail. Not to worry; I'll speak to each of these.

Opposite the entrance to Live Oak is another entrance – this one to Split Rock. The drive in is about 0.5-mile. This area can become crowded, so some patience may be required. The good news is that a lot of people come only briefly, then depart.

This is another good place for a picnic lunch, with multiple tables.

The title details reflect the Split Rock Loop Trail. I highly recommend it. **This is one of the places where midday photography produces great results.** The trail reminds me of a children's roller coaster at your hometown carnival. It gently ascends and descends over most of its route. It's not "easy," but it's also not invigorating. For a midday hike, it's *just right*.

What I believe to be *the* Split Rock is at the trail entrance, when walking the route counterclockwise. The best view is from the side of the rock opposite the parking area. Inspect the cave below.

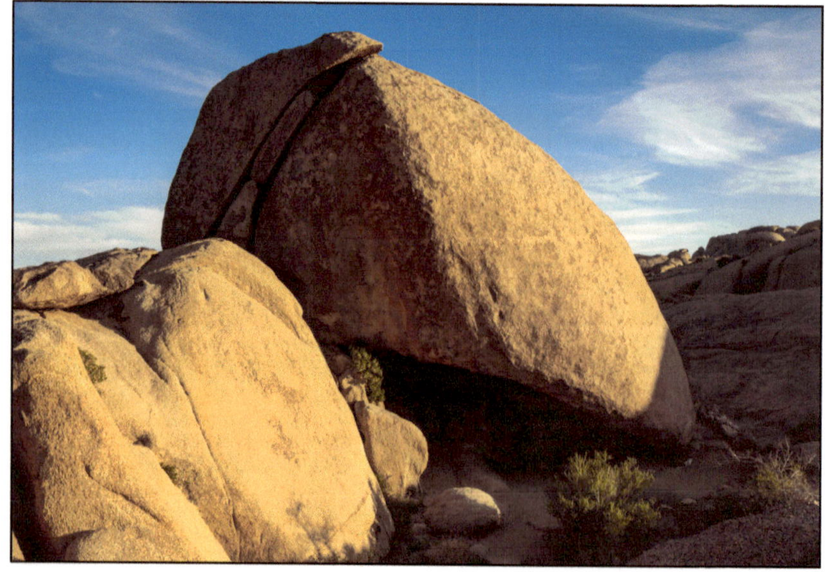

Split Rock

35mm f/8 1/200s ISO200

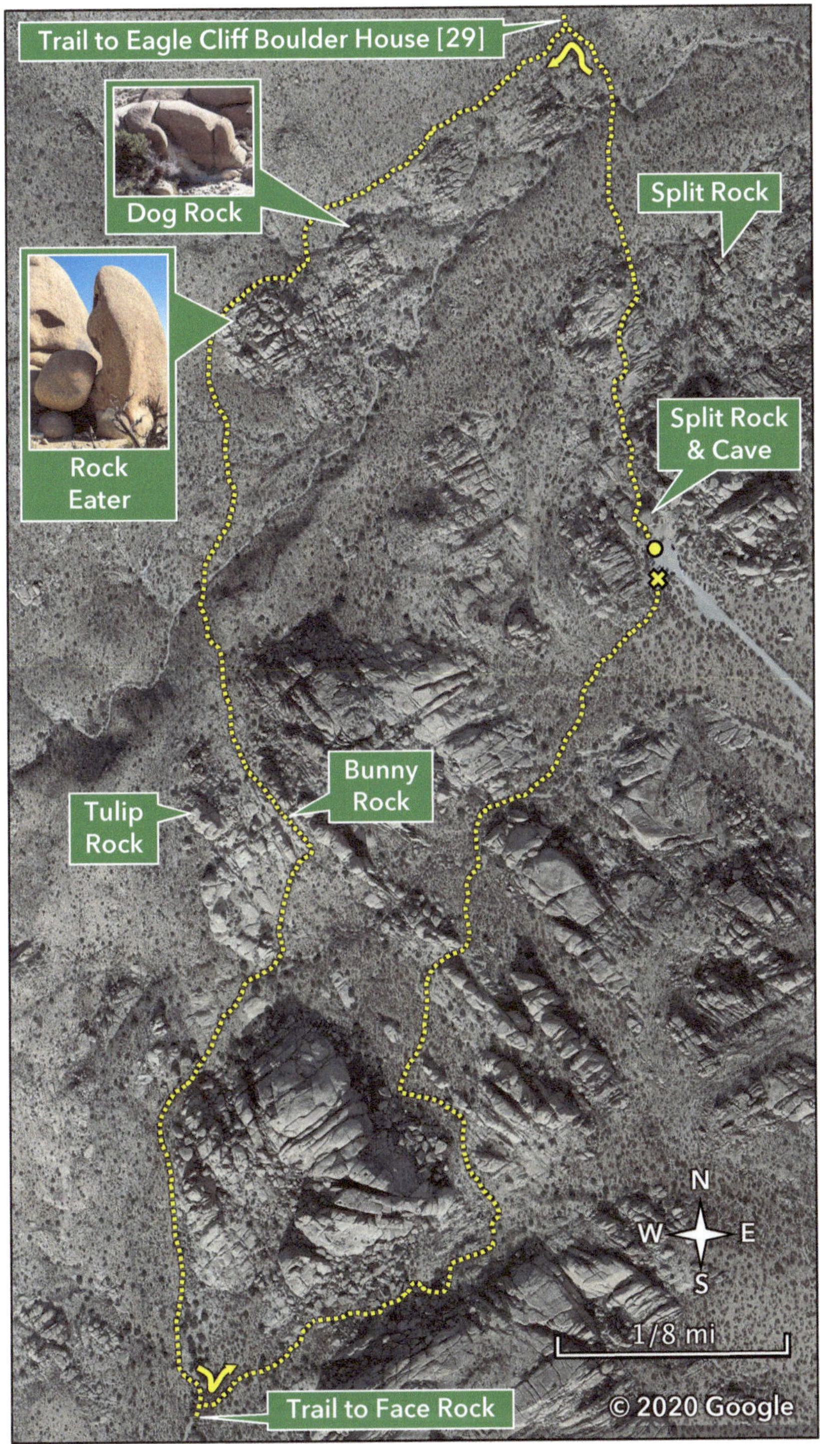

Trail to Eagle Cliff Boulder House [29]
Dog Rock
Rock Eater
Split Rock
Split Rock & Cave
Tulip Rock
Bunny Rock
N
W E
S
1/8 mi
Trail to Face Rock
© 2020 Google

But we also have *this* Split Rock, which you will easily spot just minutes into the hike…

There are very many split rocks in this area, so perhaps they all qualify!

At the most northern point of this route is a subtle intersection. This less-beaten path is for the hike to the Eagle Cliff Boulder House (29).

Now heading southwest, come upon more rock formations at your left. Here are additional, fun-shaped rocks. I have placed two that have caught my eye on the

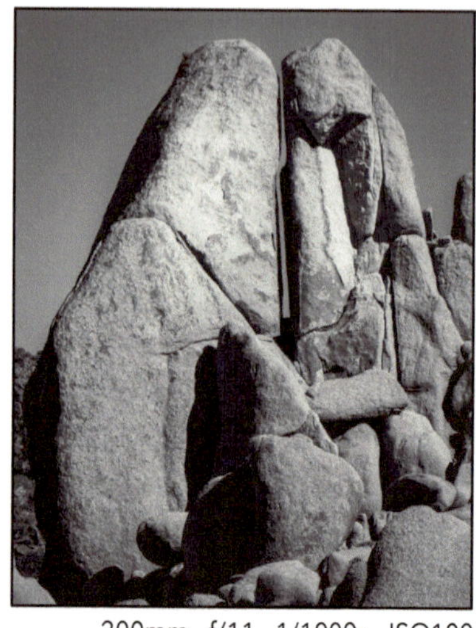

200mm f/11 1/1000s ISO100

map for you to try and spot as well. "Rock Eater" and "Bunny Rock" are my favorites. Tulip Rock is shown on page 101.

There is another trail intersection, to Face Rock Trail (and beyond). Gauge your time and daily itinerary – consider adding, if interested. Face Rock is a popular shape. A telephoto is required for it.

Finally, finish at the south side of the parking area where you began.

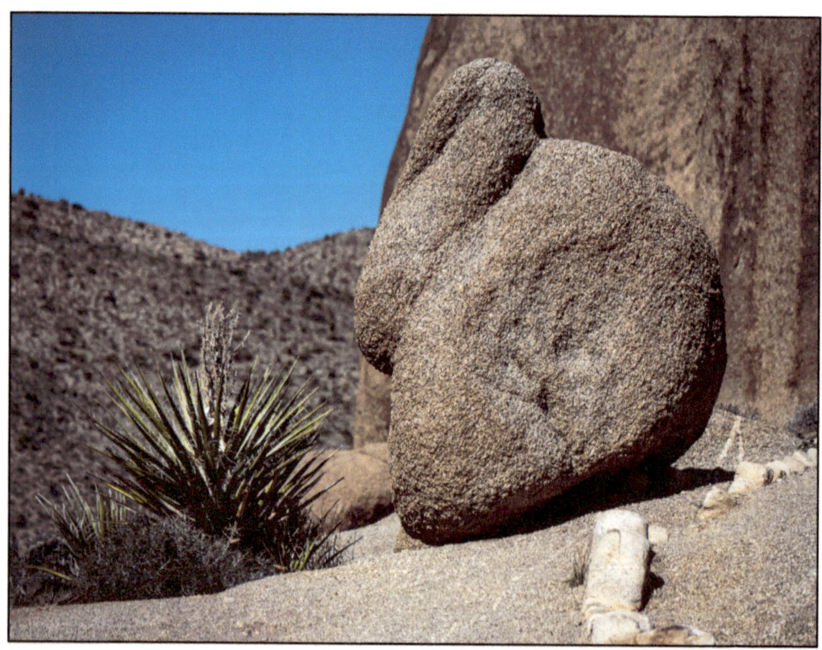

Bunny Rock

135mm f/5.6 1/2000s ISO100

Time	Budget	2-3 hr	Reward

Budget	2-3 hr	Type	Out & Back	Effort

RT Distance	~2.4 mi	Δ Elev.	~600 ft	Zoom	Wide Angle

The Eagle Cliff Boulder House is an *extremely well-preserved* miner's shelter built under large rocks. It is, without question, one of the best sites to visit within Joshua Tree National Park.

The Boulder House is a uniquely-precious site, as it is unguarded and allows visitors intimate access. It is as it is, and if disturbed could never be resuscitated to its present glory. Please demonstrate utmost respect and leave it unaltered, for fellow visitors to enjoy it in its preserved state. *Touch nothing but the ground you walk on.*

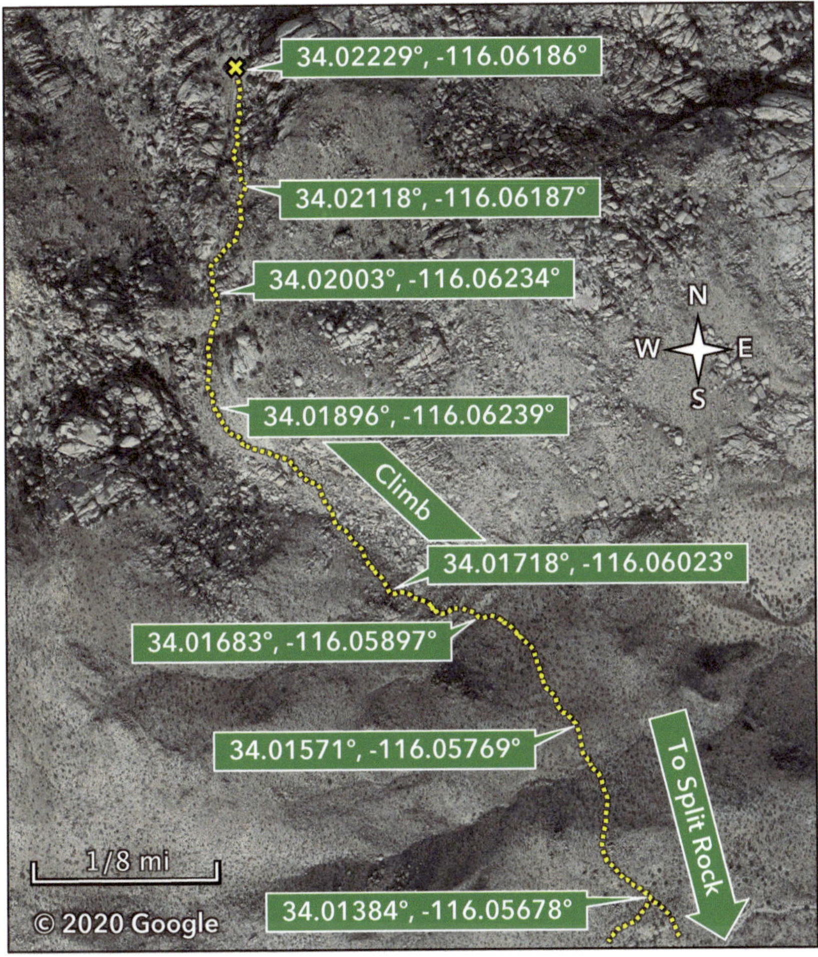

The National Park Service does not have a map in circulation for this hike, and it would be impractical for me to provide turn-by-turn directions, so for this route **GPS is required**. You will be hiking along a faint trail from waypoint to waypoint, using the map on the prior page. **Only those competent with GPS should proceed.**

The hike begins at the Split Rock Loop trailhead. Follow the route on page 113 to the first waypoint.

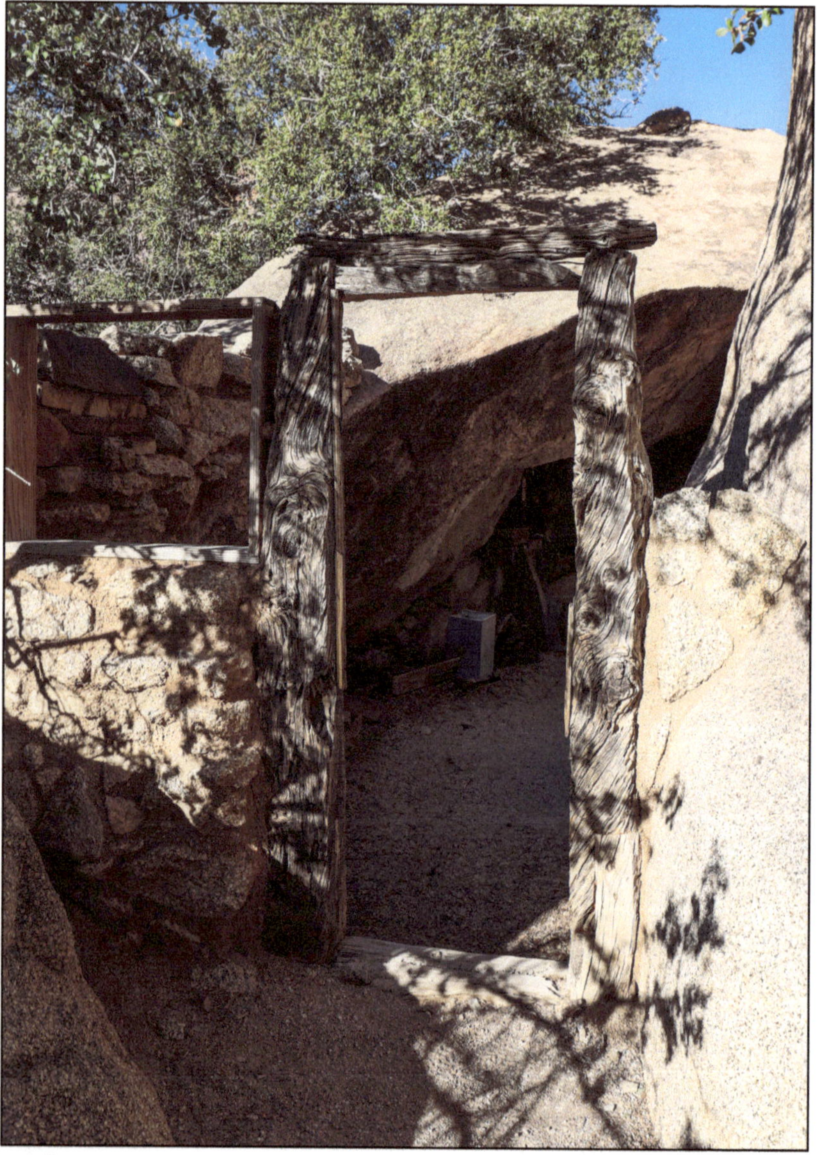

Dwelling Entrance

28mm f/8 1/320s ISO200

The entrance is camouflaged a bit. Some exploration is required.

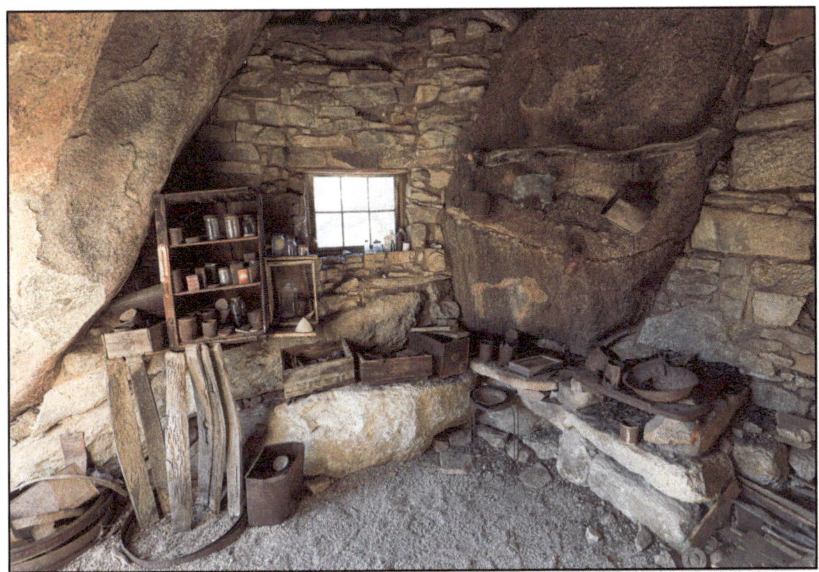

Dwelling Interior & Artifacts   16mm f/5.6 1/30s ISO800

Capture an abundance of detailed photos. Then, if you have not already done so, find the fantastic stonework outside…

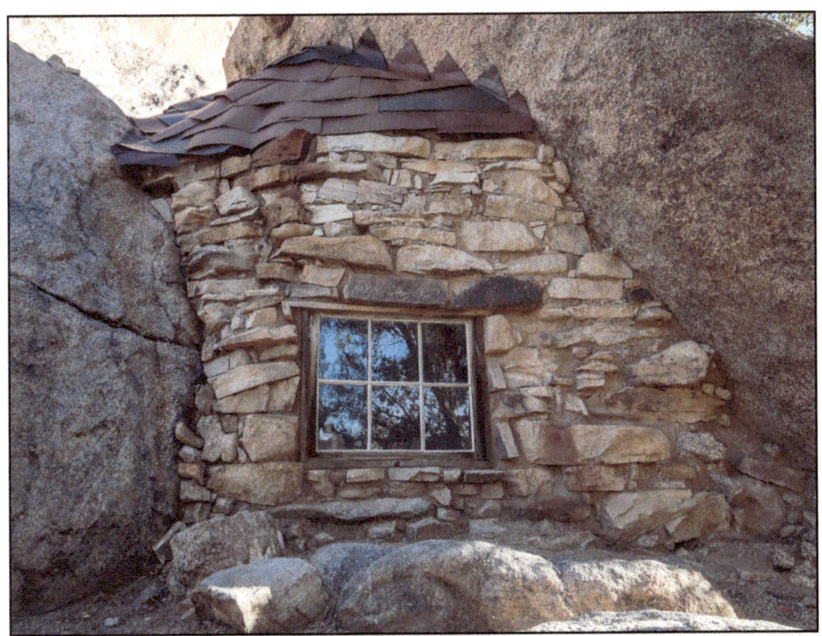

Stonework and Glass   24mm f/8 1/50s ISO200

Once finished, bid farewell, and head on back to Split Rock.

Time	Best / Good	☀	Reward	WOW! WOW! WOW! WOW!
Budget	45-75 min	**Type** Out & Back	**Effort**	👢👢
RT Distance ~0.8 mi		**Δ Elev.** ~30 ft	**Zoom**	Wide Angle

Here is an extraordinary, natural arch that is accessible by a short and easy hike. Perhaps the only real challenge is getting a parking spot. Just four parking spaces are available in the White Tank Campground, adjacent to where the Arch Rock Nature Trail begins.

The walk to Arch Rock is well-marked and enjoyable. Once at Arch Rock, rock scrambling is required to position yourself under it.

Arch Rock runs north-south, and its "best" face is its west one. Afternoon light provides ideal backlighting. Try many different focal lengths and compositions. You can really have some fun here and produce a broad variety of results from just this one formation.

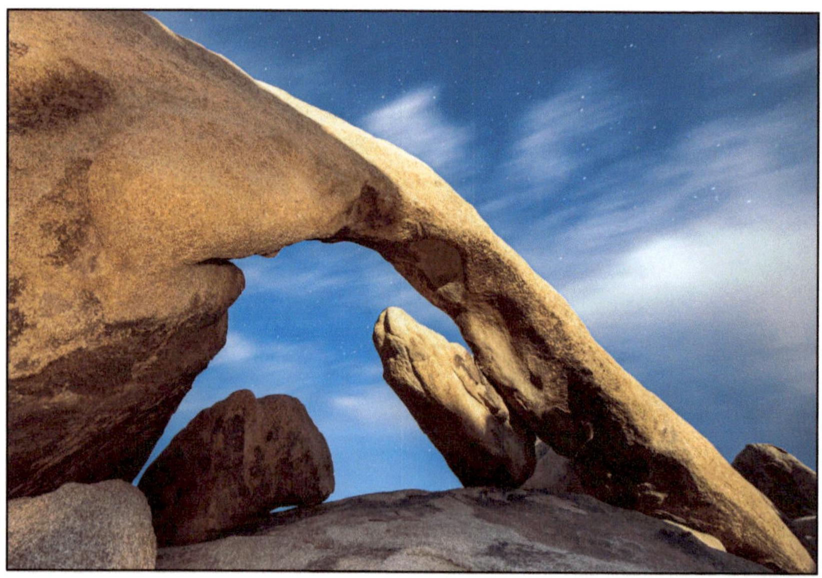

Arch Rock at Pre-Dawn under Moonlight   16mm   f/4   30s   ISO400

Heart Rock is on further, beyond the end of the formal trail, about 0.2-mile northeast. It's not a "must do," but if in the area and interested in exercising your GPS skills, it can be found at 33.98817°, -116.01341°. If you have recorded your entire route (from the beginning), you will find there is a more direct, westerly route back, from Heart Rock to the campground.   35mm

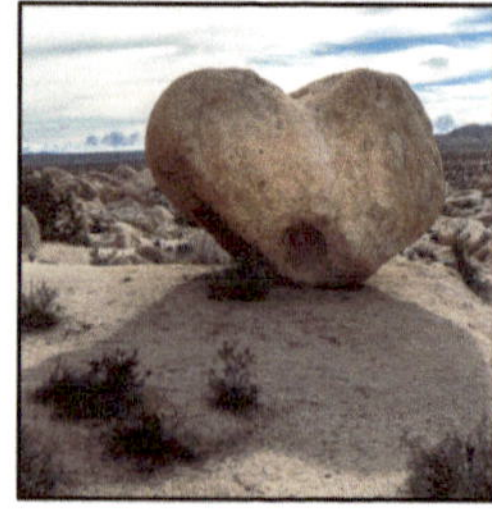

Pinto Basin Road

Cholla Cactus Garden to Cottonwood Spring

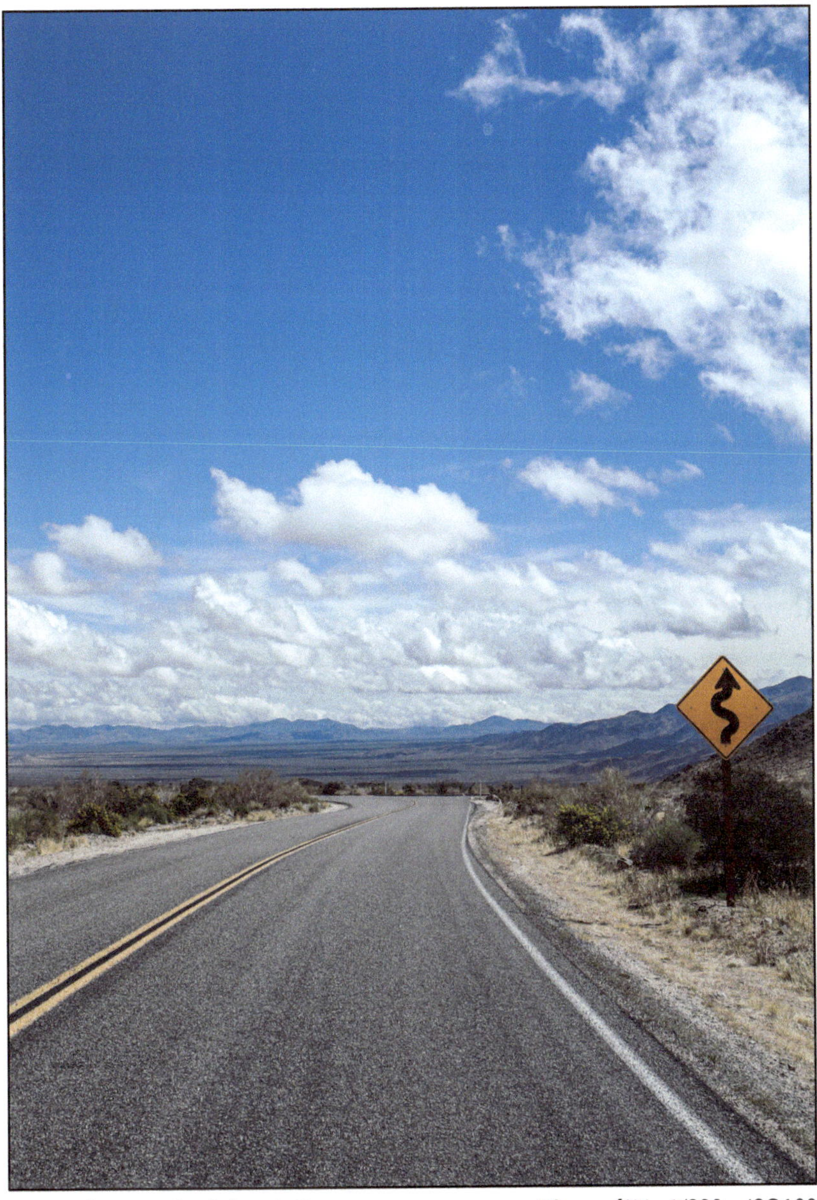

Descending into the Colorado Desert

50mm f/11 1/320s ISO100

Time	Best / Good							Reward	WOW! WOW! WOW! WOW!
Budget	30-45 min				**Type**	Loop		**Effort**	
RT Distance ~0.3 mi					**Δ Elev.**	~10 ft		**Zoom**	Norm, Tele

The most challenging photography within Joshua Tree National Park is at the Cholla Cactus Garden.

Though, depending on your taste, it may also be the most rewarding.

There, now that we have that out of the way, let's talk about what it takes to be successful here.

First, forget about typical daytime lighting. I mean it. Just forget about it. It's kind of a boring scene. (Being truthful here.)

Cholla photography is all about that first or last light of the day radiating *through* the cactus, directly towards your camera. So, two options are present – sunrise and sunset. The results, however, are quite different.

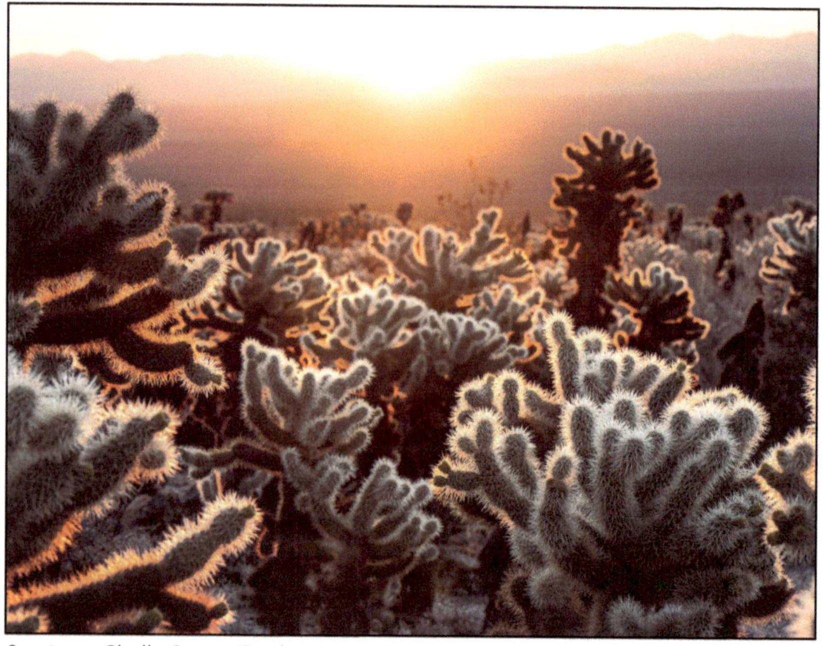

Sunrise at Cholla Cactus Garden   150mm f/11 1/25s ISO200

Exciting as this may be, before we talk sunrise and sunset I need to convey to you the **inherent danger** within this area. These cactus are not called "Jumping Chollas" for nothing. **You *really* must be careful not to brush up against these cacti.** Their barbs will impale your skin, even through thicker clothing. Once settled, the barb's shape resists removal. It is an entirely painful experience. Please – be mindful of your body's position at all times while here. **Do not touch the Cholla!**

Pinto Basin Road runs east-west through this area, and the generously-sized parking area for Cholla Cactus Garden is on the south side of the road. The formal walking trail is a ¼-mile loop. From the parking lot, as you face the two, fenced trail entrances in front of you, the one on the right provides quickest access to some of the best places to set up for sunrise and sunset. The trail zig-zags a lot after this entrance for about 500 ft, before it changes direction and goes over a small, wooden bridge. My advice is to work between the entrance and this bridge.

If you are a first-time visitor to Cholla Cactus Garden, you may be surprised to see that the cacti have a lot more space between them than regularly seen in photos. Also there are some unsightly plants in the mix. Seek compositions where the Cholla are dense in your framing and the other plants are out of sight.

Sunrise

The result at sunrise is my favorite of the two, though I know that some prefer sunset. The sunrise "effort" is challenging – waking & driving-in early (summer months *very* early), scouting your position/composition & setting up in dawn light, *guessing* where exactly the sun will crest the horizon, and finally only then to have at most 5 minutes of working time before the morning light becomes too bright. But it's all worth it.

Along this section of the trail I have prescribed, after walking-in from the parking lot you will be framing to your left (facing east). Scout a place where you can fill the bottom ~2/3 of the frame with cacti using a telephoto focal length between 100-200mm. The longer focal length helps compress the cacti within the frame. (This helps make them appear closer together.)

A tripod is necessary. Set up, and await the sunrise. As usual with sunrise and sunset, I recommend to adjust your exposure compensation to -2 stops. Be ready for its entrance, and throughout its swift rise continue to take photos, sometimes adjusting your focal length and framing for various results.

It happens quickly! I suppose some luck is involved… Hence my advice to take many photos!

Sunset

If you read through the above Sunrise section, breath a sigh of relief! You have a lot more time to work during sunset. *Vhew.*

Again along the same section of trail, now you will be framing to your right (facing west). Here, the Hexie Mountains will be close in your background. Scout a place as before, but now both normal and telephoto focal lengths can work equally well. The reason for this is now you are framing the cacti *uphill*. They tend to more naturally cluster within the composition.

Set up your tripod, and experiment with different focal lengths and framing. Because sunset proceeds more slowly (with abundant color), you have more time to try a variety of things – even relocating to an adjacent spot…

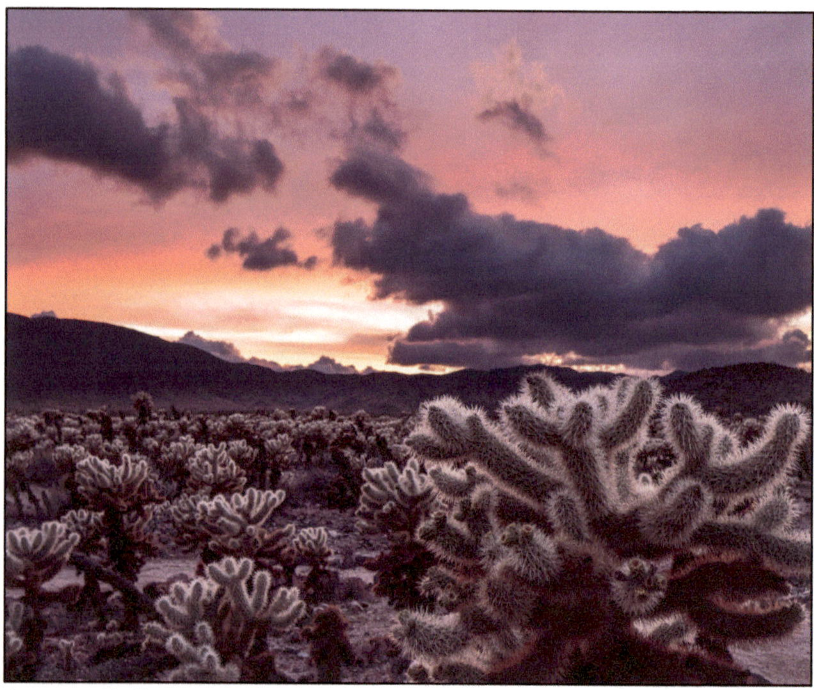

Sunset at Cholla Cactus Garden   40mm f/3.5 1/25s ISO200

The benefit to sunrise – more "illumination" of the Cholla needles.

The benefits to sunset – more time to work, and typically more colorful skies. Perhaps a third – more flexibility to work with normal focal lengths.

Photography at Cholla Cactus Garden is invigorating, and the results extraordinary. For me, it took multiple visits to finally understand the site's inherent limitations and then recipes for success. I hope that you can find success on your first visit, whether it be during sunrise or sunset.

Time	Best / Good	☼	Reward	🌸 🌸 🌸 💥
Budget	15-30 min	Type	Meandering	Effort
RT Distance	<0.2 mi	Δ Elev.	<10 ft	Zoom	Normal

Ocotillo is a plant and not a cactus.

The Ocotillo Patch along Pinto Basin Road is well-marked, and this congregation of them is obvious. There is a parking area on the right side of the road if you are driving south.

Fortunately, or perhaps unfortunately (depending on your timing), they are photogenic with bright green stems and vibrant red flowers following rainfall. This occurs most frequently in the springtime.

This area is easy to explore on foot, with minimal effort. Each Ocotillo has its own personality. I recommend photographing one as a whole (from a short distance away) and also closely. Experiment with a variety of camera angles.

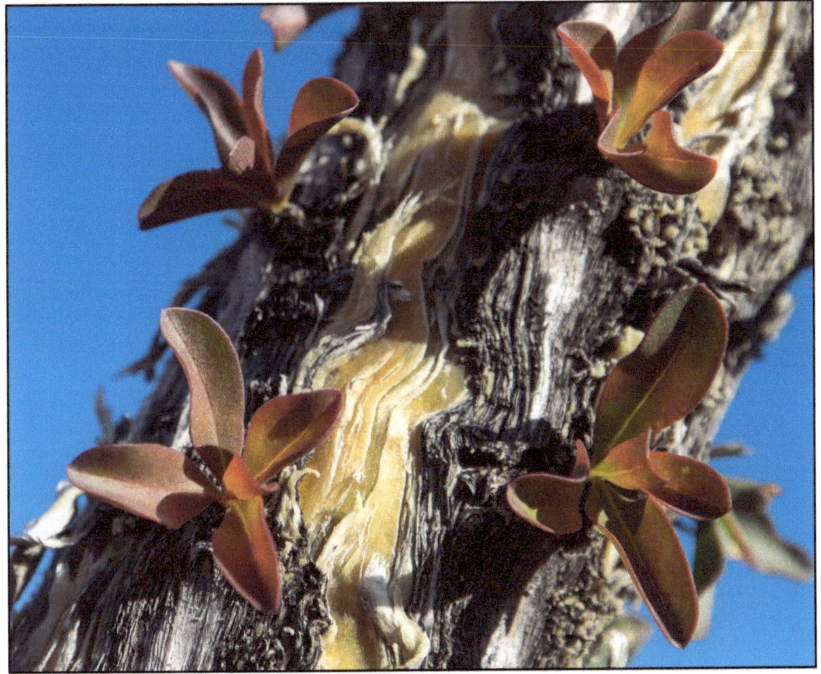

Ocotillo Stem   35mm f/5.6 1/500s ISO100

If you find yourself visiting this area "off season" (when they are not as vibrant from a distance), still do inspect them close up. They have a stem structure and texture that is still quite interesting year-round.

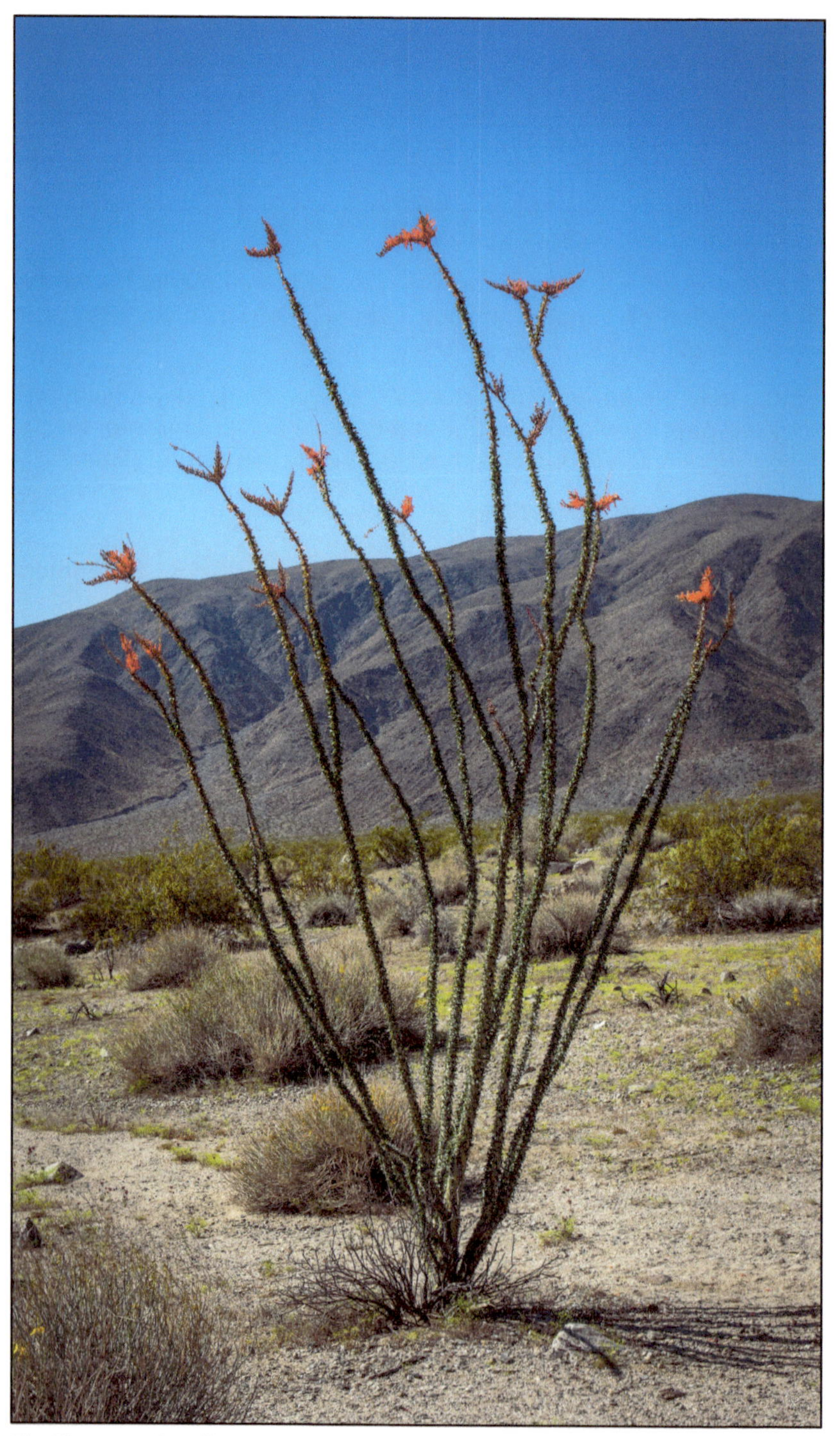

The Flowering Ocotillo

40mm f/8 1/320s ISO100

| Time | Budget | 30-45 min | Type | Meandering | Effort |
| RT Distance | <0.5 mi | Δ Elev. | <20 ft | Zoom | Wide Angle |

The stretch of Pinto Basin Road between the Ocotillo Patch and Cottonwood Spring can at times feel like a means to an end. (Or more politely, to your next destination.) It's desolate. There is of course beauty in this, but at times it feels lost.

One shrub, the "Smoke Tree," captured my attention early on this drive north and south. It caught my attention before I knew what it was, sort of all up and down Pinto Basin Road (specifically the Colorado Desert side). After some trips, I noticed their multitude at Smoke Tree Wash. Of course, I quickly put one and one together.

The Smoke Tree, under overhead light, seems to illuminate in a platinum radiance. My best results with them have been with active, cloud-filled skies, and typically shooting with a polarizing filter to really help these subtlety-complimentary colors "pop."

Smoke Tree Wash is well-marked both northbound and southbound along Pinto Basin Road. Find the one paved parking area on the east side and pull in there. Take a walk around… Find compositions that suit your taste. Generally, frame wide and from ground level, to accentuate their shape and also capture the brilliant blue sky above.

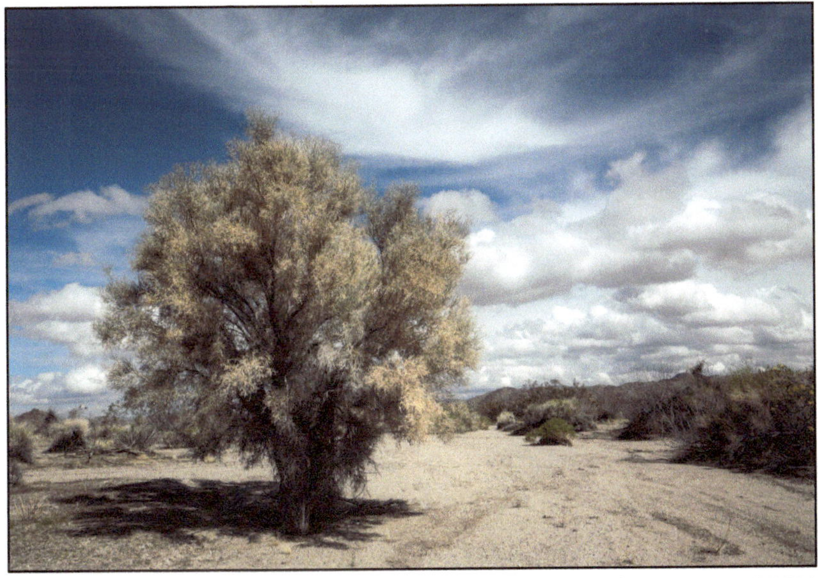

The Smoke Tree   24mm f/11 1/250s ISO200

Time	Best Good		Reward	
Budget	15-30 min	Type	Out & Back	Effort
RT Distance	~0.1 mi	Δ Elev.	~30 ft	Zoom	Normal

Of the *dense* desert oases in Joshua Tree, Cottonwood Spring is the easiest to access. (Oasis of Mara is also easy, but it lacks the dense cluster of trees found here.) These trees are a mere ~300 ft from the large parking lot. In fact, in my opinion one of the two better compositions is taken from the parking lot (below).

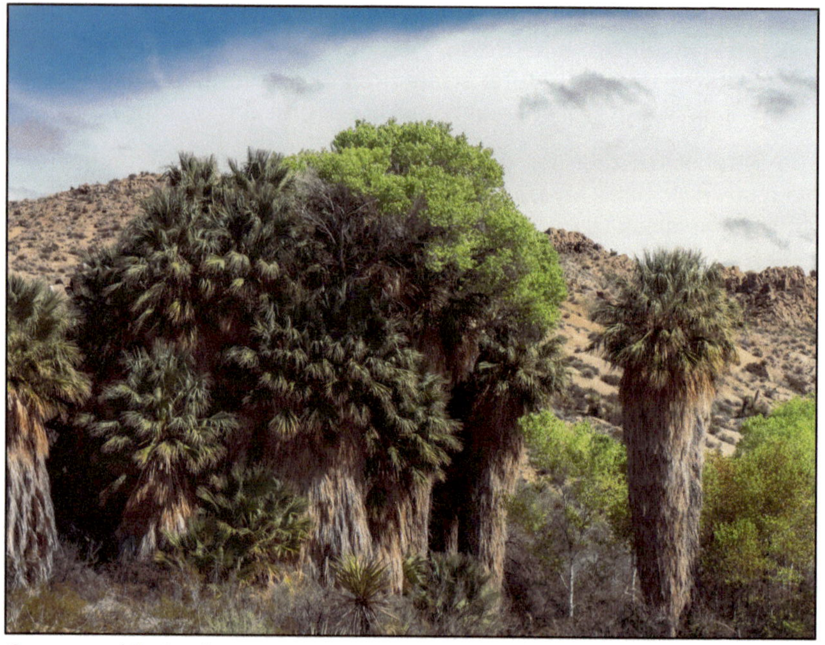

Cottonwood Spring Oasis   70mm f/8 1/320s ISO200

Another great composition is taken from directly below the trees, looking high up, in portrait orientation. Here you can capture the height of the trees and details of the varying leaves.

Unfortunately, the desert wash around Cottonwood Spring is now permanently closed due to toxic chemicals and metals from the area's mining era. Signage and ropes prevent entry today.

Just beyond the oasis are multiple bedrock mortars (holes) used for grinding seeds into flour by Cahuilla Native Americans.

...In winter the Cottonwoods will be void of leaves, but the trees' structure is a photogenic, bright silver color under midday light.

Time	Best / Good							Reward	WOW! WOW! WOW! WOW!
Budget	3.5-4.5 hr			Type		Out & Back		Effort	𝕃𝕃𝕃𝕃
RT Distance	~7.5 mi			Δ Elev.		~500 ft		Zoom	Wide, Tele

"Which is better - Fortynine Palms or Lost Palms Oasis?" is often asked. They're similar but still too dissimilar to compare simply, and I think this is why the answer is elusive.

Lost Palms Oasis tends to have much less traffic (most especially midweek), and the potential solitude is reason enough for some people to choose it as a favorite. The hike is quite a bit longer but only steep near the end, as you descend from a ridge down into the trees. The trees at both sites are wonderful, and whereas Lost Palms typically does not have standing water as an additional subject to capture, the colonnade of trees is longer - allowing more exploration.

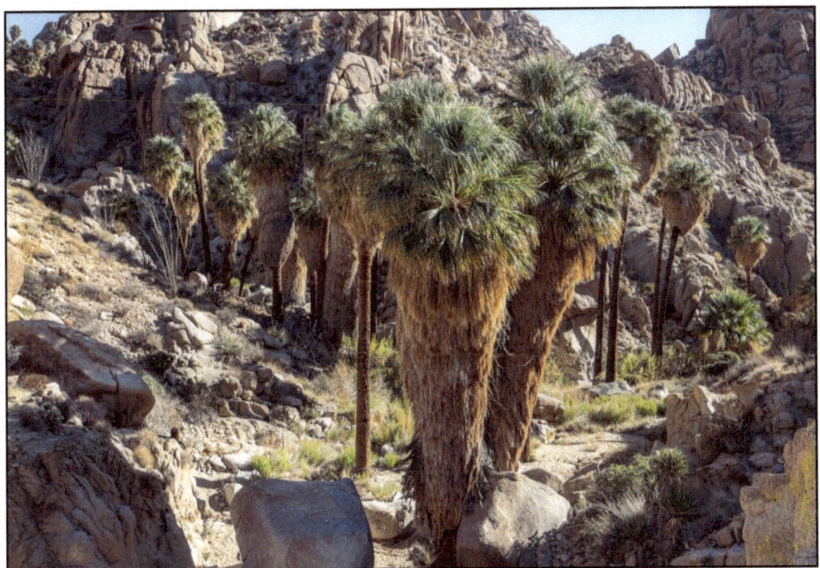

Lost Palms Oasis   35mm f/8 1/125s ISO100

The route is mostly straightforward. Its primary direction (heading) remains constant. Be on the lookout for subtle changes when reaching desert washes - sometimes you walk briefly through a wash; other times you cross. Near the end the trail drops down left through rocks, all the way to the oasis. If you find that you continue to walk along an exposed ridge and see the trees to your left but cannot figure out how to get to them, then you missed the turnoff into the rocky descent.

Trail runners rejoice! This is a popular route for many because of its "just right" distance and grade. Pack a light camera and check it out.

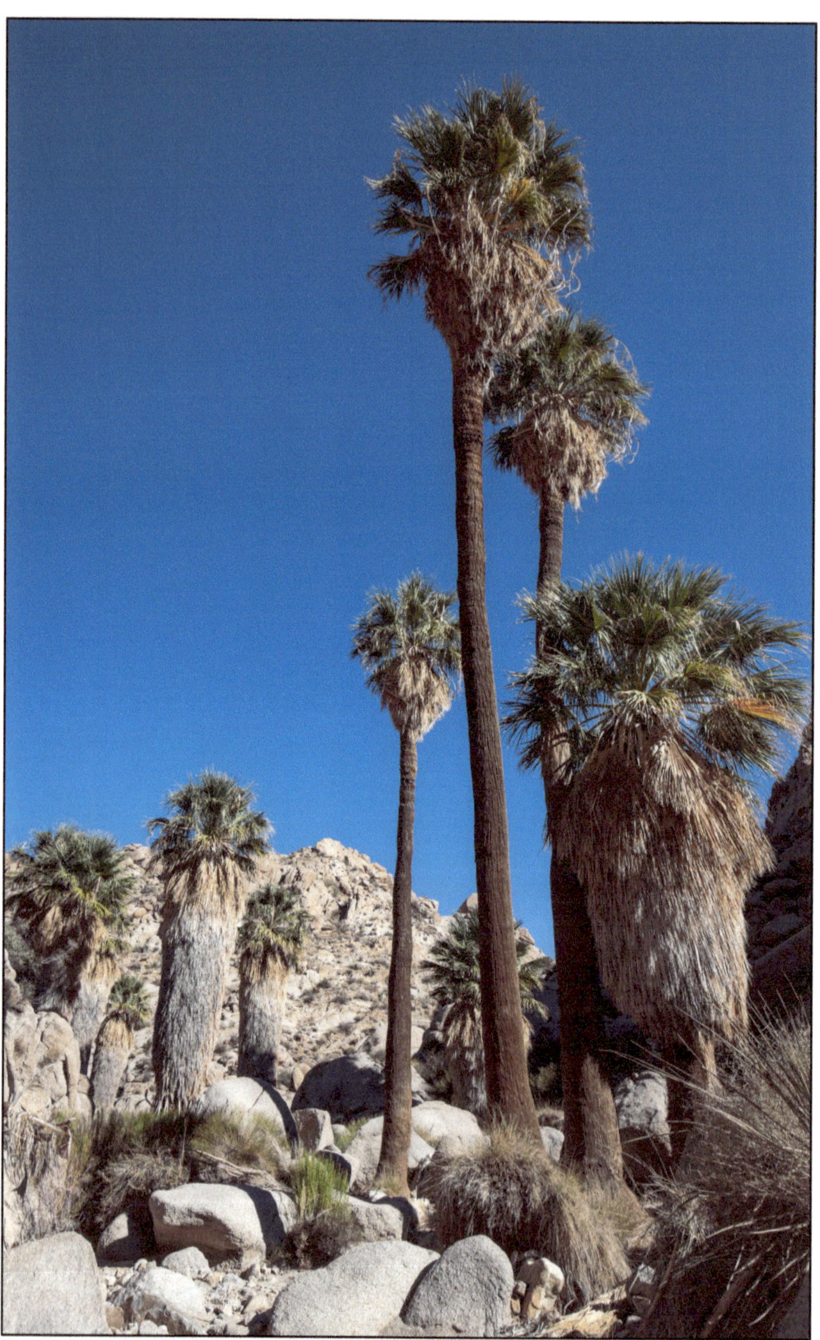

Lost Palms Variety in Height & Ornament   20mm f/8 1/500s ISO100

Appendix - Select Elevation Profiles

For three sites within this book, the "Δ Elev" doesn't sufficiently represent the route's grade. The following elevation profiles better complete the story on for these three:

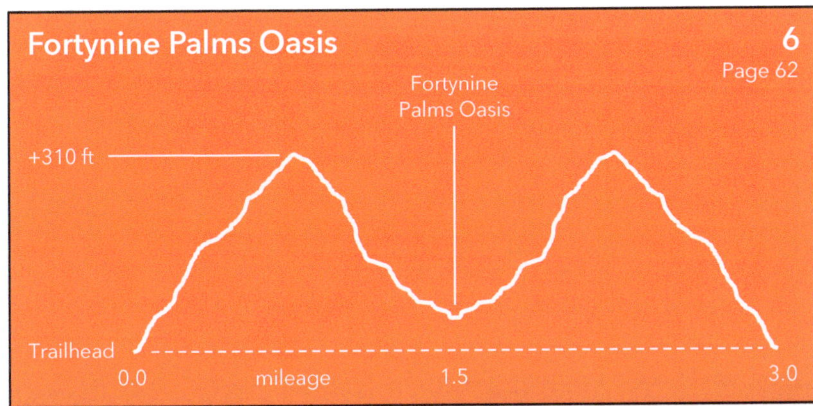

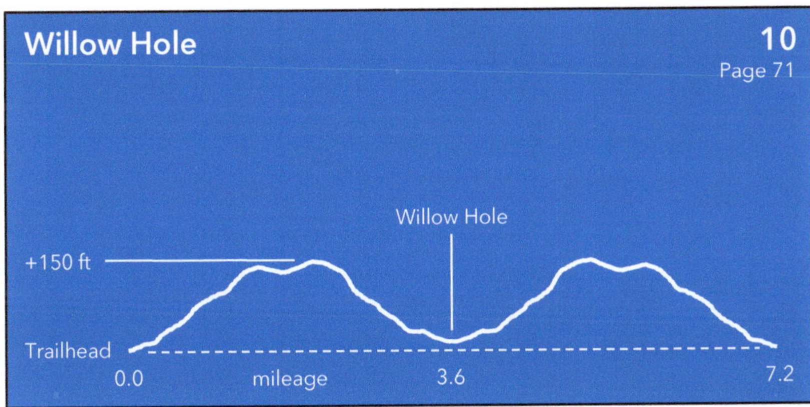

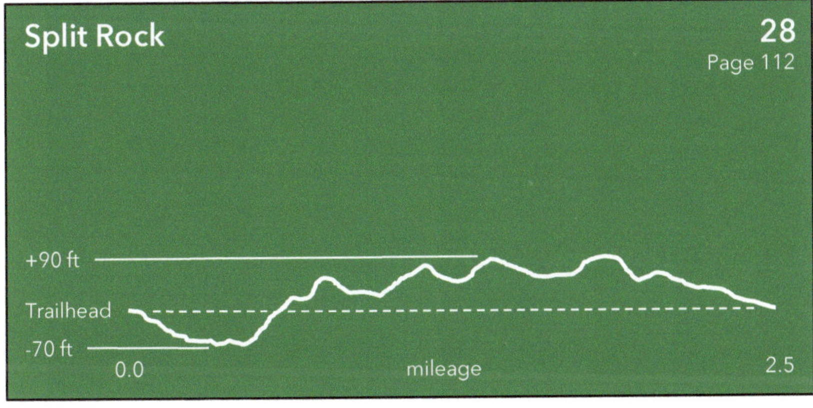

No.	Page	Site	Time	
			Best	Good
1	46	High View	SR	-AM & SS
2	48	Black Rock Area on Horse	-AM thru MID	-
3	53	Covington Flat Roads to Eureka Peak	MID thru -PM	-AM thru AM+
4	56	Pioneertown	-AM	Nighttime
5	58	Rattlesnake Canyon	-AM thru MID	-PM thru PM+
6	62	Fortynine Palms Oasis	SR thru -AM	AM+ thru MID
7	66	Painting with Light	Nighttime	-
8	68	Samuelson's Rocks	-PM thru PM+	-AM thru MID
9	70	Nighttime Car Light Trails	Nighttime	-
10	71	Willow Hole	-AM thru AM+	MID thru -PM
11	74	Hidden Valley	MID thru PM+	-AM thru AM+
12	76	Iron Door Cave	-PM thru PM+	-AM thru MID
13	78	Keys Ranch	Tour Time	-
14	81	Barker Dam	-AM	PM+ thru SS
15	85	Wonderland Wash	MID thru -PM	-AM thru AM+
16	88	Wall Street Mill	-AM thru AM+	MID thru PM+
17	90	Cap Rock	PM+	MID thru -PM
18	91	Johnny Lang Tombstone	-AM thru AM+	MID thru -PM
19	92	Keys View	SS	Nighttime
20	94	Ryan Ranch	AM+ & NT	-AM & MID
21	97	Hall of Horrors	Nighttime	-AM & PM+
22	100	Ryan Mountain	-PM thru SS	AM+ thru MID
23	102	Geology Tour Road	AM+ thru MID	-PM thru PM+
24	104	Desert Queen Vista	-PM thru PM+	MID
25	106	Jumbo Rocks	PM+ thru SS	-PM
26	108	Skull Rock	-PM thru PM+ & NT	MID
27	110	Live Oak	-PM thru PM+	MID
28	112	Split Rock	MID	AM+ & -PM
29	115	Eagle Cliff Boulder House	-AM thru AM+	MID thru -PM
30	118	Arch & Heart Rocks	-PM & NT	MID & PM+
31	120	Cholla Cactus Garden	SR & SS	-
32	123	Ocotillo Patch	AM+ & -PM	MID
33	125	Smoke Tree Wash	AM+ & -PM	MID
34	126	Cottonwood Spring	-AM thru AM+ & -PM	MID
35	127	Lost Palms Oasis	-AM thru AM+	MID thru -PM

Reward (Wow's)	Budget	Type	Effort (Boots)	RT Distance	Δ Elevation	Zoom
1	1-1.5 hr	Loop	2	~1.3 mi	~400 ft	Norm, Tele
4	2-6 hr	Varies	Yeehaw!	5-15 mi	200-1,500 ft	Normal
2	2-2.5 hr	Out & Back	4WD + 1	~18 mi	~1,700 ft	Wide, Tele
3	30-60 min	Meandering	0	<0.3 mi	<10 ft	Norm, Tele
4	2-3 hr	Out & Back	5	~1.2 mi	~270 ft	Wide, Tele
4	2-3 hr	Out & Back	4	~3.0 mi	See pg. 129	Wide, Tele
3	30-60 min	Roadside	0	<500 ft	<10 ft	Wide Angle
3	1.5-2 hr	Out & Back	3	~3.0 mi	~150 ft	Wide, Tele
3	45-75 min	Out & Back	2	<0.2 mi	<30 ft	Wide Angle
2	3.5-4.5 hr	Out & Back	4	~7.2 mi	See pg. 129	Wide, Tele
3	45-75 min	Lollipop Loop	2	~1.0 mi	~100 ft	Wide, Tele
3	60-90 min	Out & Back	2	<1.0 mi	~40 ft	Wide Angle
4	1.5-2 hr	Loop	0	<1.0 mi	~30 ft	Norm, Tele
4	60-90 min	Lollipop Loop	2	~1.1 mi	~50 ft	Wide, Tele
3	2-3 hr	Out & Back	3	~3.0 mi	~180 ft	Norm, Tele
4	1.5-2 hr	Out & Back	2	~2.0 mi	~50 ft	Wide Angle
1	15 min	Roadside	0	<900 ft	<10 ft	Normal
2	15-30 min	Roadside	0	~0.2 mi	<10 ft	Wide Angle
4	30-60 min	Out & Back	1	~0.2 mi	~30 ft	Wide Angle
3	60-90 min	Out & Back	2	~1.0 mi	~140 ft	Wide, Norm
2	45-75 min	Out & Back	2	~0.6 mi	~20 ft	Wide Angle
2	1.5-2.5 hr	Out & Back	4	~3.0 mi	~1,050 ft	Normal
3	1.5-2 hr	Lollipop Loop	4WD + 1	~17.0 mi	~1,200 ft	Wide, Norm
2	30-60 min	Out & Back	2	~0.7 mi	~50 ft	Wide, Tele
4	45-75 min	Out & Back	2	~0.9 mi	~60 ft	Wide, Tele
4	15-30 min	Roadside	1	~300 ft	<10 ft	Wide Angle
2	30-60 min	Meandering	1	<900 ft	<20 ft	Norm, Tele
3	1-2 hr	Loop	3	~2.5 mi	See pg. 129	Norm, Tele
4	2-3 hr	Out & Back	4	~2.4 mi	~600 ft	Wide Angle
4	45-75 min	Out & Back	2	~0.8 mi	~30 ft	Wide Angle
4	30-45 min	Loop	0	~0.3 mi	~10 ft	Norm, Tele
1	15-30 min	Meandering	0	<0.2 mi	<10 ft	Normal
2	30-45 min	Meandering	0	<0.5 mi	<20 ft	Wide Angle
2	15-30 min	Out & Back	0	~0.1 mi	~30 ft	Normal
4	3.5-4.5 hr	Out & Back	4	~7.5 mi	~500 ft	Wide, Tele

About the Author

Anthony Jones, who friends and family call "AJ," lives in the Seattle, Washington area with his wife and their two daughters.

In April 2011 he visited Joshua Tree National Park, laying the foundation for what would become regular photography pilgrimages to many other U.S. National Parks.

AJ enjoys the planning and logistics aspect of a trip as much as the trip itself, and in so he realized a shortage of available books focused on the photographer's specific needs while visiting national parks. Thus, his idea to write a series of these types of books was born…

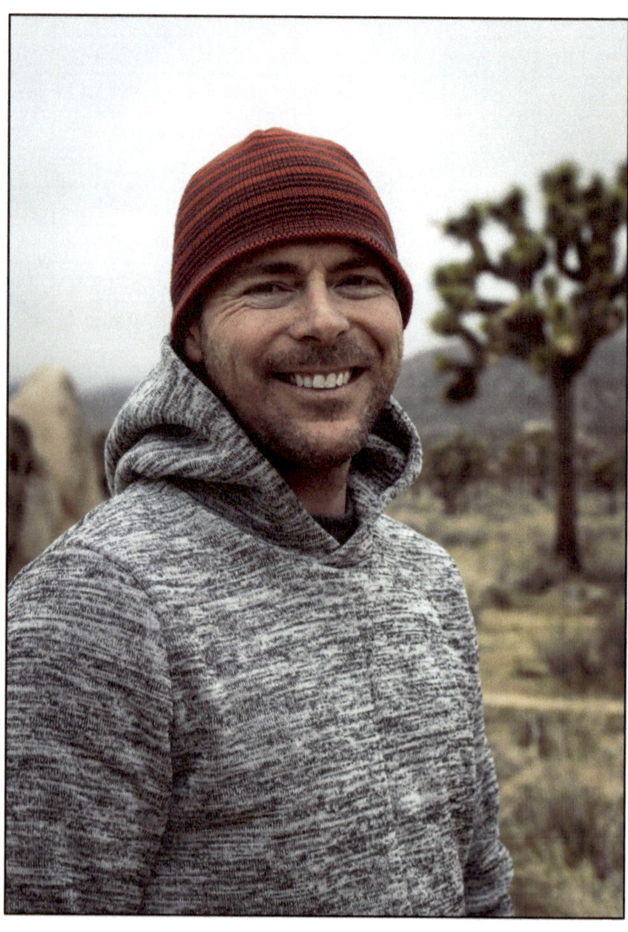